PRACTICE - ASSESS - DIAGNOSE

180 Days of MATH for Fourth Grade

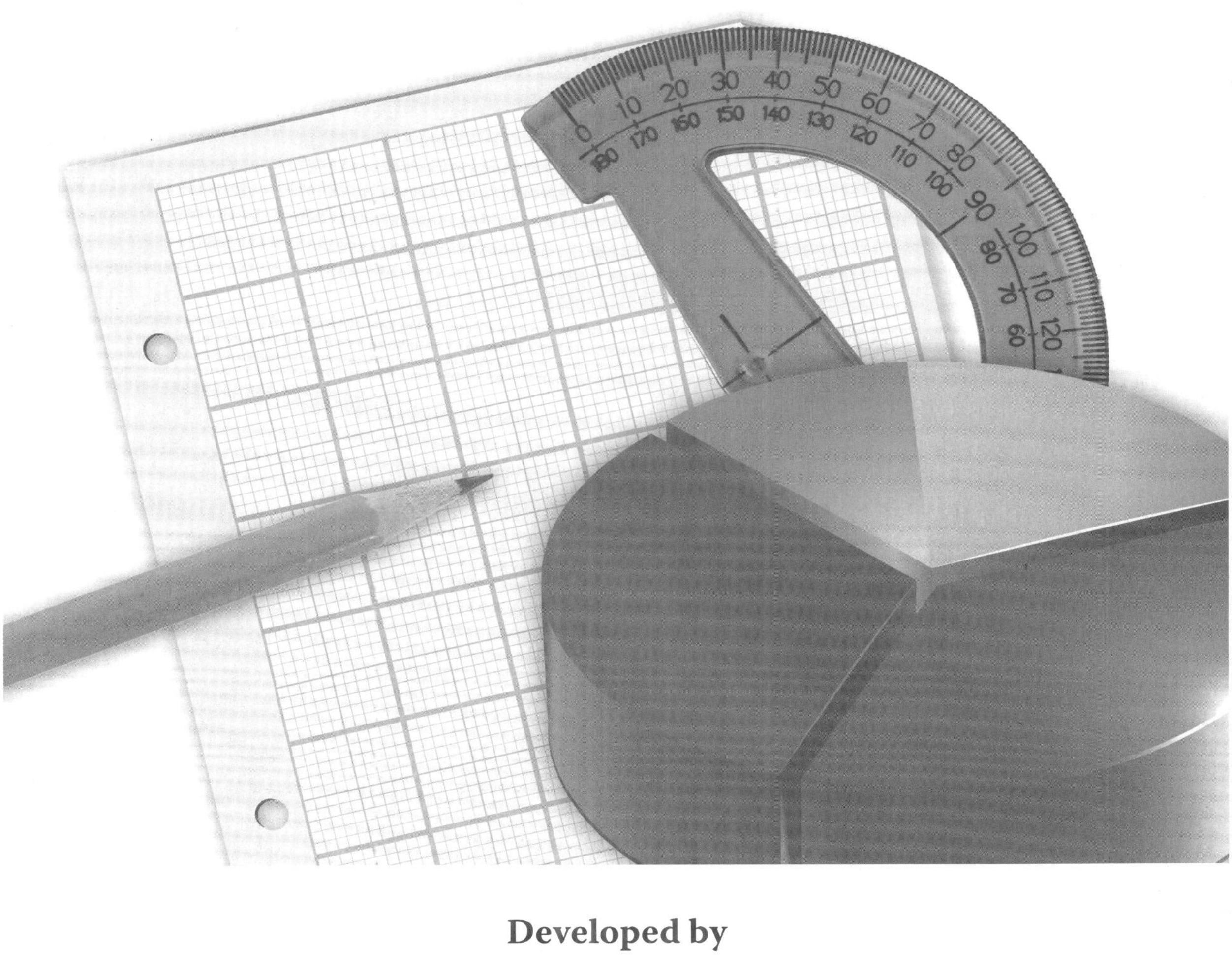

Developed by
Jodene Smith

Shell Education

Publishing Credits

Dona Herweck Rice, *Editor-in-Chief*; Lee Aucoin, *Creative Director;*
Don Tran, *Print Production Manager;* Timothy J. Bradley, *Illustration Manager;*
Chris McIntyre, M.A.Ed., *Editorial Director*; Sara Johnson, M.S.Ed., *Senior Editor*;
Aubrie Nielsen, M.S.Ed., *Associate Education Editor*; Juan Chavolla, *Cover/Interior Layout Designer;*
Robin Erickson, *Production Artist*; Corinne Burton, M.A.Ed., *Publisher*

Shell Education
5482 Argosy Avenue
Huntington Beach, CA 92649-1030
www.tcmpub.com/shell-education

ISBN 978-1-4258-0807-5

Printed by: 51497
Printed in: China

TABLE OF CONTENTS

INTRODUCTION AND RESEARCH

The Need for Practice

In order to be successful in today's mathematics classroom, students must deeply understand both concepts and procedures so that they can discuss and demonstrate their understanding. Demonstrating understanding is a process that must be continually practiced in order for students to be successful. According to Marzano (2010, 83), "practice has always been, and will always be, a necessary ingredient to learning procedural knowledge at a level at which students execute it independently." Practice is especially important to help students apply their concrete, conceptual understanding to a particular procedural skill.

Understanding Assessment

In addition to providing opportunities for frequent practice, teachers must be able to assess students' understanding of mathematical procedures, terms, concepts, and reasoning (Kilpatrick, Swafford, and Findell 2001). This is important so that teachers can adequately address students' misconceptions, build on their current understanding, and challenge them appropriately.

Assessment is a long-term process that often involves careful analysis of student responses from a lesson discussion, project, practice sheet, or test. When analyzing the data, it is important for teachers to reflect on how their teaching practices may have influenced students' responses and to identify those areas where additional instruction may be required. In short, the data gathered from assessments should be used to inform instruction: slow down, speed up, or reteach. This type of assessment is called *formative assessment* and is used to provide a seamless connection between instruction and assessment (McIntosh 1997).

HOW TO USE THIS BOOK

180 Days of Math for Fourth Grade offers teachers and parents a full page of mathematics practice activities for each day of the school year.

Easy to Use and Standards-Based

These activities reinforce grade-level skills across a variety of mathematical concepts. The questions are provided as a full practice page, making them easy to prepare and implement as part of a classroom morning routine, at the beginning of each mathematics lesson, or as homework.

Every fourth-grade practice page provides 10 questions, each tied to a specific mathematical concept. Students are provided the opportunity for regular practice in each mathematical concept, allowing them to build confidence through these quick, standards-based activities.

Question	Mathematics Concept	NCTM Standard
1	**Addition or Subtraction**	Understands meanings of operations such as addition and subtraction and how they relate to one another
2	**Multiplication or Fractions, Decimals, Percents**	Understands various meanings of multiplication; Recognizes and generates equivalent forms of fractions, decimals, and percents
3 4	**Division**	Understands various meanings of division; Understands meanings of operations and how they relate to one another; Computes fluently and makes reasonable estimates
5	**Place Value or Number Sense**	Understands representations of numbers, relationships among numbers, and number systems; Understands place-value structure of the base-ten number system
6	**Algebra and Algebraic Thinking**	Understands patterns, relations, and functions; Represents and analyzes patterns and functions, using words, tables, and graphs
7 8	**Measurement**	Applies appropriate techniques and formulas to determine measurements; Understands measurable attributes of objects and the units, systems, and processes of measurement
9	**Geometry or Data Analysis**	Uses visualization and spacial reasoning to solve problems; Analyzes properties of two- and three-dimensional geometric shapes
10	**Word/Logic Problem or Mathematical Reasoning**	Solves problems that arise in mathematics and in other contexts

Standards are listed with the permission of the National Council of Teachers of Mathematics (NCTM). NCTM does not endorse the content or validity of these alignments.

HOW TO USE THIS BOOK *(cont.)*

Using the Practice Pages

As outlined on page 4, every question is aligned to a mathematics concept and standard.

Practice pages provide instruction and assessment opportunities for each day of the school year.

Each question ties student practice to a specific mathematics concept.

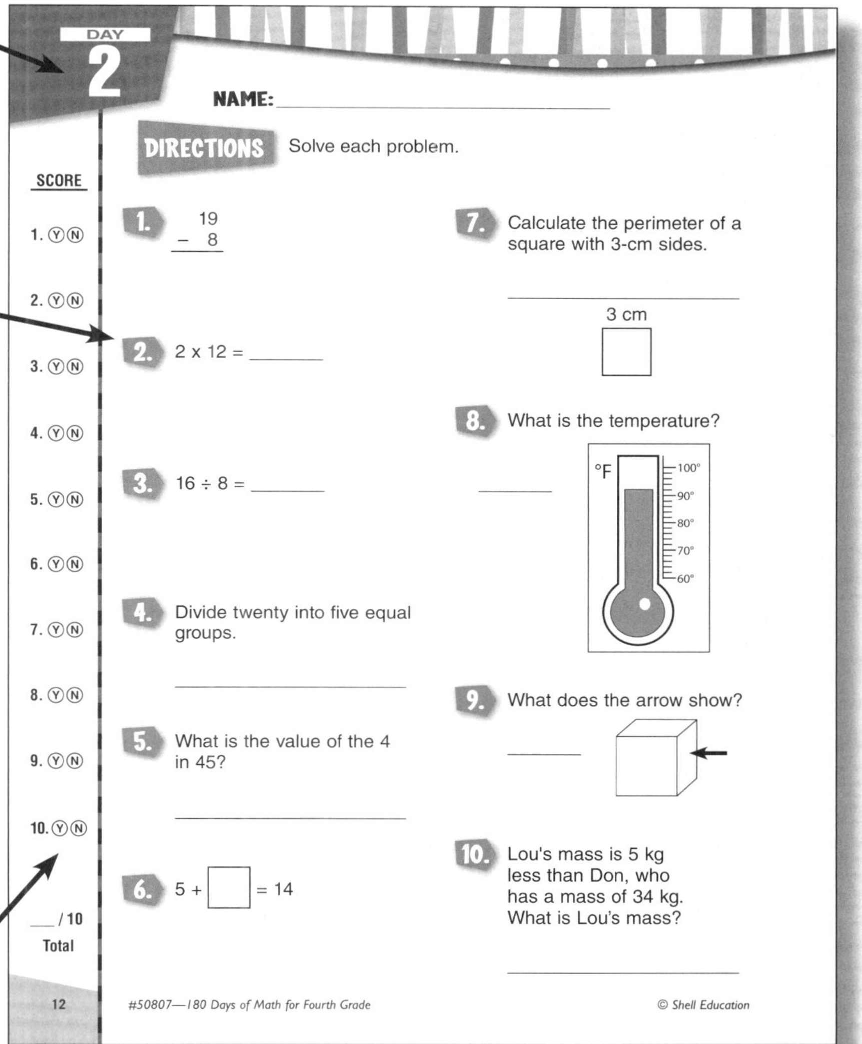

DAY 2

NAME: ____________

DIRECTIONS Solve each problem.

SCORE

1. Ⓨ Ⓝ
2. Ⓨ Ⓝ
3. Ⓨ Ⓝ
4. Ⓨ Ⓝ
5. Ⓨ Ⓝ
6. Ⓨ Ⓝ
7. Ⓨ Ⓝ
8. Ⓨ Ⓝ
9. Ⓨ Ⓝ
10. Ⓨ Ⓝ

___ / 10 Total

1. $19 - 8$
2. 2 x 12 = ______
3. 16 ÷ 8 = ______
4. Divide twenty into five equal groups. ______
5. What is the value of the 4 in 45? ______
6. 5 + ☐ = 14
7. Calculate the perimeter of a square with 3-cm sides. ______ (3 cm)
8. What is the temperature? ______ (°F; 100°, 90°, 80°, 70°, 60°)
9. What does the arrow show? ______
10. Lou's mass is 5 kg less than Don, who has a mass of 34 kg. What is Lou's mass? ______

12 #50807—180 Days of Math for Fourth Grade © Shell Education

Using the Scoring Guide

Use the scoring guide along the side of each practice page to check answers and see at a glance which skills may need more reinforcement.

Fill in the appropriate circle for each problem to indicate correct (Y) or incorrect (N) responses. You might wish to indicate only incorrect responses to focus on those skills. (For example, if students consistently miss numbers 2 and 6, they may need additional help with those concepts as outlined in the table on page 4.) Use the answer key at the back of the book to score the problems, or you may call out answers to have students self-score or peer-score their work.

HOW TO USE THIS BOOK *(cont.)*

Diagnostic Assessment

Teachers can use the practice pages as diagnostic assessments. The data analysis tools included with the book enable teachers or parents to quickly score students' work and monitor their progress. Teachers and parents can see at a glance which mathematics concepts or skills students may need to target in order to develop proficiency.

After students complete a practice page, grade each page using the answer key (pages 191–206). Then, complete the *Practice Page Item Analysis* (page 7) for the whole class, or the *Student Item Analysis* (page 8) for individual students. These charts are also provided in the digital resources (filenames: G4_practicepage_analysis.pdf, G4_student_analysis.pdf). Teachers can input data into the electronic files directly on the computer or they can print the pages and analyze students' work using paper and pencil.

To complete the Practice Page Item Analysis:

- Write or type students' names in the far-left column. Depending on the number of students, more than one copy of the form may be needed or you may need to add rows.
- The question numbers are included across the top of the chart. Each item correlates with the matching question number from the practice page.
- For each student, record an *X* in the column if the student has the item incorrect. If the item is correct, leave the item blank.
- Count the *X*s in each row and column and fill in the correct boxes.

To complete the Student Item Analysis:

- Write or type the student's name on the top row. This form tracks the ongoing progress of each student, so one copy per student is necessary.
- The question numbers are included across the top of the chart. Each item correlates with the matching question number from the practice page.
- For each day, record an *X* in the column if the student has the item incorrect. If the item is correct, leave the item blank.
- Count the *X*s in each row and column and fill in the correct boxes.

Practice Page Item Analysis

Directions: Record an *X* in cells to indicate where students have missed questions. Add up the totals. You can view: (1) which questions/concepts were missed per student; (2) the total correct score for each student; and (3) the total number of students who missed each question.

Day: ______ Question #	1	2	3	4	5	6	7	8	9	10	# correct
Student Name											
Sample Student		X			X	X				X	6/10
# of students missing each question											

HOW TO USE THIS BOOK *(cont.)*

Student Item Analysis

Directions: Record an *X* in cells to indicate where the student has missed questions. Add up the totals. You can view: (1) which questions/concepts the student missed; (2) the total correct score per day; and (3) the total number of times each question/concept was missed.

Student Name: Sample Student											
Question	**1**	**2**	**3**	**4**	**5**	**6**	**7**	**8**	**9**	**10**	**# correct**
Day											
1		X			X						8/10
Total											

HOW TO USE THIS BOOK *(cont.)*

Using the Results to Differentiate Instruction

Once results are gathered and analyzed, teachers can use the results to inform the way they differentiate instruction. The data can help determine which concepts are the most difficult for students and which need additional instructional support and continued practice. Depending on how often the practice pages are scored, results can be considered for instructional support on a daily or weekly basis.

Whole-Class Support

The results of the diagnostic analysis may show that the entire class is struggling with a particular concept or group of concepts. If these concepts have been taught in the past, this indicates that further instruction or reteaching is necessary. If these concepts have not been taught in the past, this data is a great pre-assessment and demonstrates that students do not have a working knowledge of the concepts. Thus, careful planning for the length of the unit(s) or lesson(s) must be considered, and extra frontloading may be required.

Small-Group or Individual Support

The results of the diagnostic analysis may show that an individual or small group of students is struggling with a particular concept or group of concepts. If these concepts have been taught in the past, this indicates that further instruction or reteaching is necessary. Consider pulling aside these students while others are working independently to instruct further on the concept(s). Teachers can also use the results to help identify individuals or groups of proficient students who are ready for enrichment or above-grade level instruction. These students may benefit from independent learning contracts or more challenging activities. Students may also benefit from extra practice using games or computer-based resources.

Digital Resources

Reference page 208 for information about accessing the digital resources and an overview of the contents.

HOW TO USE THIS BOOK *(cont.)*

NCTM Standards

The lessons in this book are aligned to the National Council of Teachers of Mathematics (NCTM) standards. The standards listed on page 4 support the concepts and skills that are consistently presented on each of the practice pages.

Standards Correlations

Shell Education is committed to producing educational materials that are research and standards based. In this effort, we have correlated all of our products to the academic standards of all 50 states, the District of Columbia, and the Department of Defense Dependent Schools, as well as to the college and career readiness standards.

How to Find Standards Correlations

To print a customized correlation report of this product for your state, visit our website at **www.tcmpub.com/shell-education** and follow the on-screen directions. If you require assistance in printing correlation reports, please contact Customer Service at 1-877-777-3450.

Purpose and Intent of Standards

The No Child Left Behind legislation mandates that all states adopt academic standards that identify the skills students will learn in kindergarten through grade twelve. While many states had already adopted academic standards prior to NCLB, the legislation set requirements to ensure the standards were detailed and comprehensive.

Standards are designed to focus instruction and guide adoption of curricula. Standards are statements that describe the criteria necessary for students to meet specific academic goals. They define the knowledge, skills, and content students should acquire at each level. Standards are also used to develop standardized tests to evaluate students' academic progress.

Teachers are required to demonstrate how their lessons meet state standards. State standards are used in development of all of our products, so educators can be assured they meet the academic requirements of each state.

NAME: ______________________

DIRECTIONS Solve each problem.

1. 18 + 5 = ______

2. Color $\frac{4}{5}$ of the rectangle.

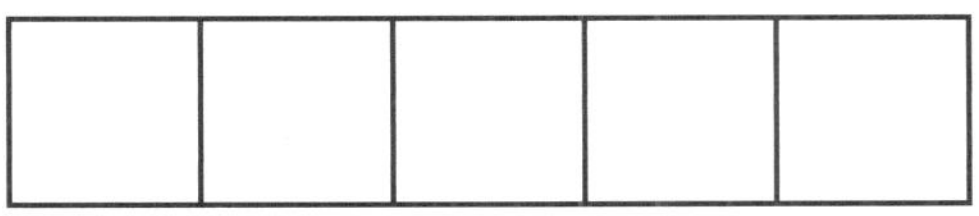

3. Share 8 equally between 2.

____

4. 8 ÷ 4 = ______

5. Is 15 smaller than 51?

____

6. Fill in the missing number.

45, 50, 55, ______, 65, 70

7. Write the line length in centimeters.

____

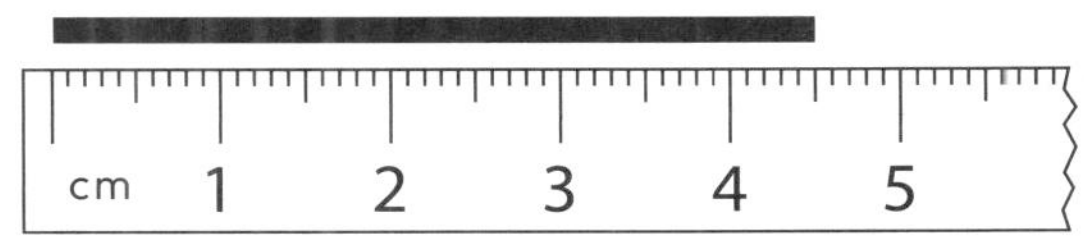

8. Do you use A.M. or P.M. to write 7:00 in the morning?

____

9. How many sides does a pentagon have?

____

10. Complete the addition grid.

+	8	14	17	19	22	36
19						
29						
39						

SCORE

1. Ⓨ Ⓝ
2. Ⓨ Ⓝ
3. Ⓨ Ⓝ
4. Ⓨ Ⓝ
5. Ⓨ Ⓝ
6. Ⓨ Ⓝ
7. Ⓨ Ⓝ
8. Ⓨ Ⓝ
9. Ⓨ Ⓝ
10. Ⓨ Ⓝ

___ / 10 Total

NAME: ____________________

DIRECTIONS Solve each problem.

SCORE

1. Ⓨ Ⓝ
2. Ⓨ Ⓝ
3. Ⓨ Ⓝ
4. Ⓨ Ⓝ
5. Ⓨ Ⓝ
6. Ⓨ Ⓝ
7. Ⓨ Ⓝ
8. Ⓨ Ⓝ
9. Ⓨ Ⓝ
10. Ⓨ Ⓝ

___ / 10

Total

1.

$$\begin{array}{r} 19 \\ -\ \ 8 \\ \hline \end{array}$$

2. 2 x 12 = ________

3. 16 ÷ 8 = ________

4. Divide twenty into five equal groups.

____

5. What is the value of the 4 in 45?

____

6. 5 + ☐ = 14

7. Calculate the perimeter of a square with 3-cm sides.

____

3 cm

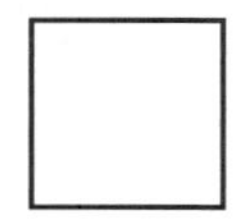

8. What is the temperature?

____

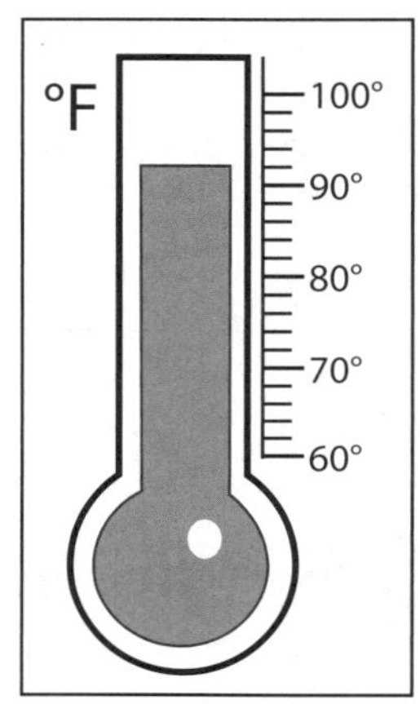

9. What does the arrow show?

____

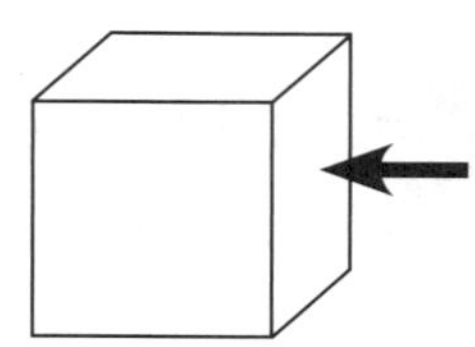

10. Lou's mass is 5 kg less than Don, who has a mass of 34 kg. What is Lou's mass?

____

NAME: ____________________________

DIRECTIONS Solve each problem.

1.

$$\begin{array}{r} 500 \\ +\ 400 \\ \hline \end{array}$$

2. $\frac{1}{2}$ of 16 is ________.

3. Divide 18 into 9 equal groups.

____

4. $16 \div 2 =$ ________

5. Circle the smallest number.

471 741 417

6. $8 = 10 - \square$

7. Write the time.

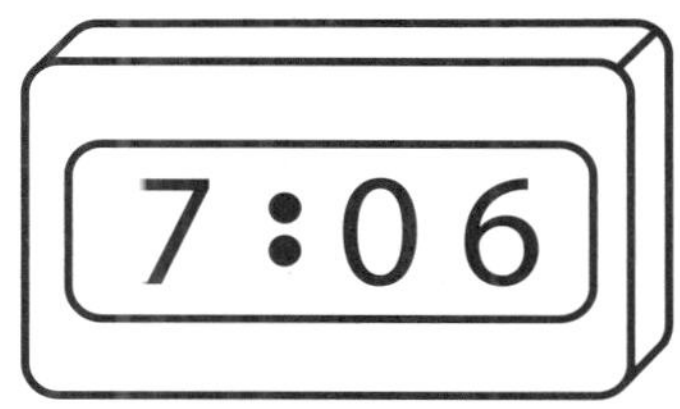

________ past ________

8. How many seconds are in 1 minute?

____

9. Do parallel lines intersect?

____

10. Rex bought 4 pens at $1.50 each. How much did he spend?

____

SCORE

1. Ⓨ Ⓝ
2. Ⓨ Ⓝ
3. Ⓨ Ⓝ
4. Ⓨ Ⓝ
5. Ⓨ Ⓝ
6. Ⓨ Ⓝ
7. Ⓨ Ⓝ
8. Ⓨ Ⓝ
9. Ⓨ Ⓝ
10. Ⓨ Ⓝ

___ / 10 Total

DAY 4

NAME: ______________________

DIRECTIONS Solve each problem.

SCORE

1. Ⓨ Ⓝ
2. Ⓨ Ⓝ
3. Ⓨ Ⓝ
4. Ⓨ Ⓝ
5. Ⓨ Ⓝ
6. Ⓨ Ⓝ
7. Ⓨ Ⓝ
8. Ⓨ Ⓝ
9. Ⓨ Ⓝ
10. Ⓨ Ⓝ

___ / 10 Total

1. 26 – 9 = ______

2.

$$\begin{array}{r} \$2.00 \\ +\ \$1.25 \\ \hline \end{array}$$

3. $8\overline{)40}$

4. 32 ÷ 4 = ______

5. 6 tens + 4 ones = ______

6. 7 x ☐ = 28

7. What is the term for the amount of space inside a container?

____

8. ______ quarts = 1 gallon

9. Name this shape.

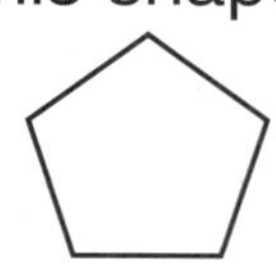

____

10. $\frac{1}{10}$ of 20 = 2, so $\frac{3}{10}$ of 20 =

____

NAME: ______________________

DIRECTIONS Solve each problem.

1. 20 + 80 = ______

2.

$$\begin{array}{r} 5 \\ \times\ 8 \\ \hline \end{array}$$

3. $8\overline{)12}$

4. How many groups of 10 are in 40?

____

5. Write 306 in words.

____

6. 9 + ☐ = 10

7. Circle the best estimate for the area of a door.

2 m^2 40 m^2

8. What day comes after Sunday?

____

9. Record the data in the chart using numbers.

Number of Pets				
Tyrone	Melissa	Aubrey	Mitch	Cara

Tyrone has 3 pets.

Melissa has 6 pets.

Aubrey has no pets.

Mitch has 2 pets.

Cara has 3 pets.

10. Complete the multiplication wheel.

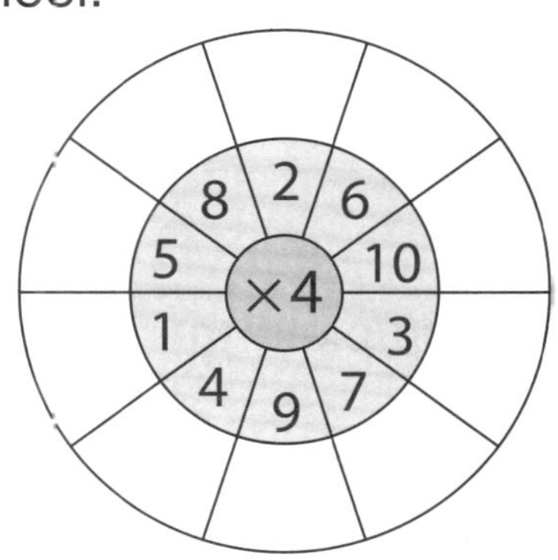

SCORE

1. Ⓨ Ⓝ
2. Ⓨ Ⓝ
3. Ⓨ Ⓝ
4. Ⓨ Ⓝ
5. Ⓨ Ⓝ
6. Ⓨ Ⓝ
7. Ⓨ Ⓝ
8. Ⓨ Ⓝ
9. Ⓨ Ⓝ
10. Ⓨ Ⓝ

___ / 10 Total

DAY 6

NAME: ____________________

DIRECTIONS Solve each problem.

SCORE

1. Ⓨ Ⓝ
2. Ⓨ Ⓝ
3. Ⓨ Ⓝ
4. Ⓨ Ⓝ
5. Ⓨ Ⓝ
6. Ⓨ Ⓝ
7. Ⓨ Ⓝ
8. Ⓨ Ⓝ
9. Ⓨ Ⓝ
10. Ⓨ Ⓝ

___ / 10 Total

1. $\begin{array}{r} 24 \\ -\ 13 \\ \hline \end{array}$

2. $\frac{1}{2}$ of 18 is ________.

3. Divide 28 into 4 equal groups.

____

4. $8\overline{)63}$

5. What is the value of the 3 in 352?

____

6. Complete the pattern.

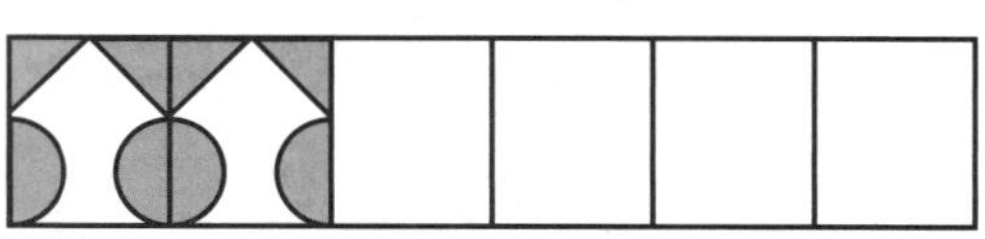

7. How many buckets of water are needed to fill the tub?

____

8. ________ inches = 1 foot

9. Name the shape of the cross-section.

____

10. Beverly had 475 pennies which she divided into stacks of 5. How many stacks did she have?

____

NAME: ____________________

DIRECTIONS Solve each problem.

1.
$$\begin{array}{r} 6 \\ 4 \\ +\ 5 \\ \hline \end{array}$$

2. Color $\frac{1}{4}$ of the pentagons.

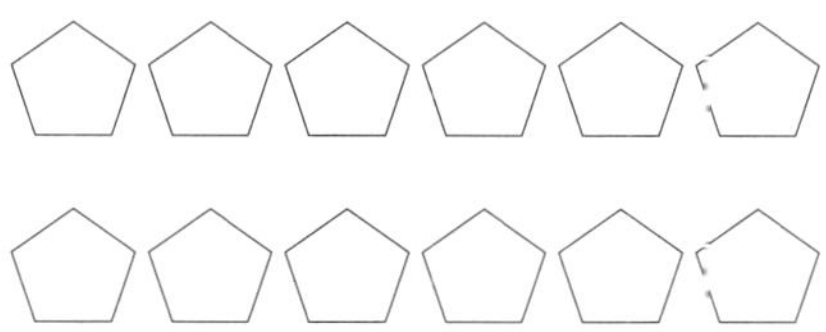

3. $2\overline{)18}$

4. 12 shared equally by 6 is

____________________.

5. Write 247 in expanded notation.

____

6. 6 x ☐ = 24

7. What is the date of the first Monday in February?

____

FEBRUARY						
Sun	Mon	Tue	Wed	Thu	Fri	Sat
		1	2	3	4	5
6	7	8	9	10	11	12
13	14	15	16	17	18	19
20	21	22	23	24	25	26
27	28	29				

8. What is the month before October?

____

9. Is the angle below a right angle?

____

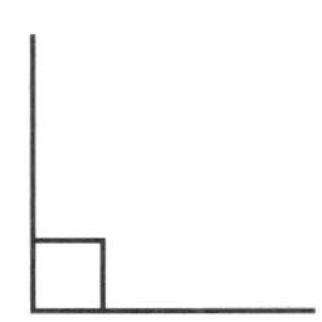

10. If you add 9 to me, the sum is 43. What number am I?

____

SCORE

1. Ⓨ Ⓝ
2. Ⓨ Ⓝ
3. Ⓨ Ⓝ
4. Ⓨ Ⓝ
5. Ⓨ Ⓝ
6. Ⓨ Ⓝ
7. Ⓨ Ⓝ
8. Ⓨ Ⓝ
9. Ⓨ Ⓝ
10. Ⓨ Ⓝ

___ / 10 Total

NAME: ____________________

DIRECTIONS Solve each problem.

SCORE

1. Ⓨ Ⓝ
2. Ⓨ Ⓝ
3. Ⓨ Ⓝ
4. Ⓨ Ⓝ
5. Ⓨ Ⓝ
6. Ⓨ Ⓝ
7. Ⓨ Ⓝ
8. Ⓨ Ⓝ
9. Ⓨ Ⓝ
10. Ⓨ Ⓝ

___ / 10
Total

1. $50 - 15 =$ ________

2. Is $\frac{1}{2}$ equal to 0.5?

____

3. $16 \div 4 =$ ________

4. $56 \div 8 =$ ________

5. Is 42 greater than 24?

____

6. $1 \times \square = 8$

7. Record the liquid amount in the pitcher in liters.

____

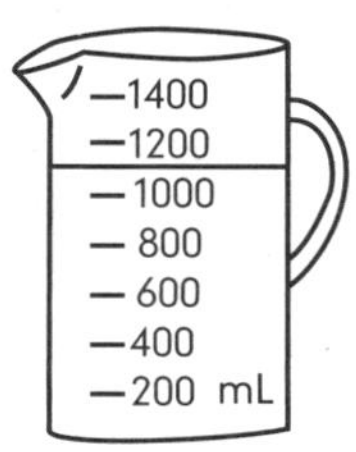

8. Write the length in inches.

________ inches

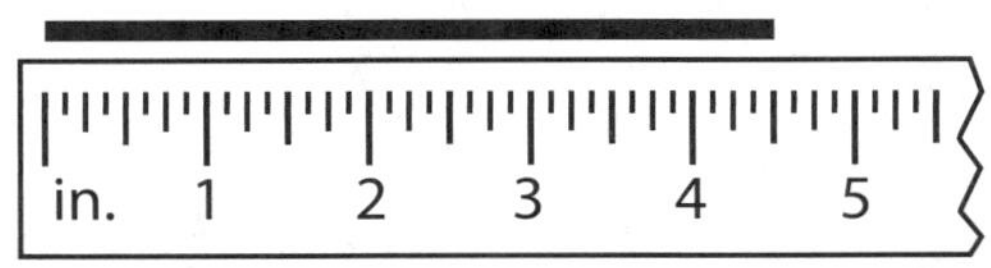

9. Do the pencils show a *reflection*, *translation*, or *rotation*?

____

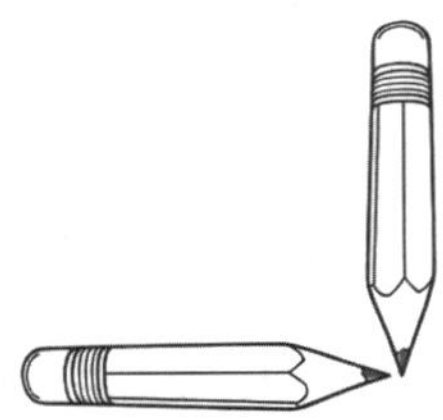

10. Estimate the number of dots in the square. Then check by counting.

Estimate: ________

Actual Number: ________

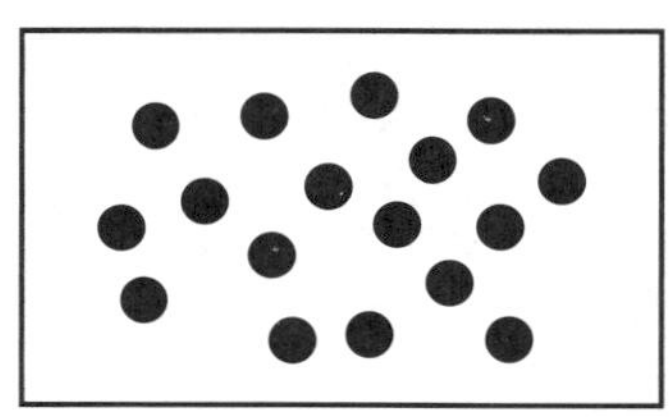

NAME: ______________________________

DIRECTIONS Solve each problem.

1. Calculate the sum of 12, 4, and 8.

____

2. How many eighths are in one whole?

____

3. Divide 16 into 4 equal groups.

____

4. 36 ÷ 4 = ________

5. Circle the largest number.

639 963 936

6. 2 x ☐ = 12

7. ________ mm = 1 cm

8. Which would be the best measuring tool for the length of a shoelace: a yardstick, a scale, or a clock?

____

9. Color the polygons.

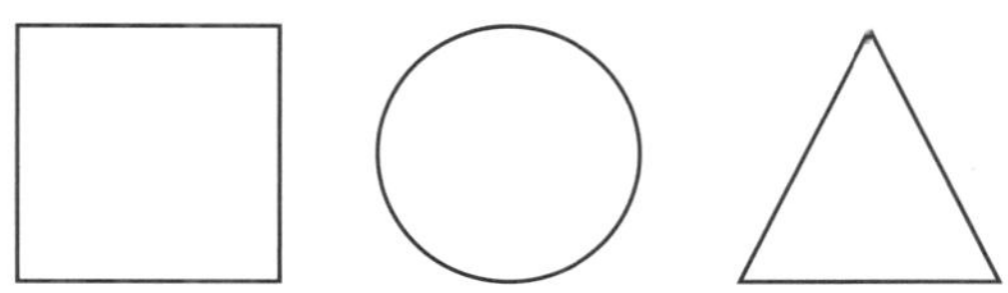

10. Last year Nick was 58 cm tall. He has grown 13 cm. What is his height now?

____

SCORE

1. Ⓨ Ⓝ
2. Ⓨ Ⓝ
3. Ⓨ Ⓝ
4. Ⓨ Ⓝ
5. Ⓨ Ⓝ
6. Ⓨ Ⓝ
7. Ⓨ Ⓝ
8. Ⓨ Ⓝ
9. Ⓨ Ⓝ
10. Ⓨ Ⓝ

___ / 10
Total

NAME: ____________________

DIRECTIONS Solve each problem.

SCORE

1. Ⓨ Ⓝ
2. Ⓨ Ⓝ
3. Ⓨ Ⓝ
4. Ⓨ Ⓝ
5. Ⓨ Ⓝ
6. Ⓨ Ⓝ
7. Ⓨ Ⓝ
8. Ⓨ Ⓝ
9. Ⓨ Ⓝ
10. Ⓨ Ⓝ

___ / 10 Total

1. $\begin{array}{r} 27 \\ -\ 8 \\ \hline \end{array}$

2. 6 x 9 = ________

3. $3\overline{)24}$

4. 12 shared equally by 4 is

____________________.

5. What is the value in the ones place in 36?

____

6. 10 x ☐ = 20

7. Is the total distance around the outside of a shape perimeter or volume?

____________________.

8. 8 quarts = ☐ gallons

9. Draw a line from the real-life object to the matching solid.

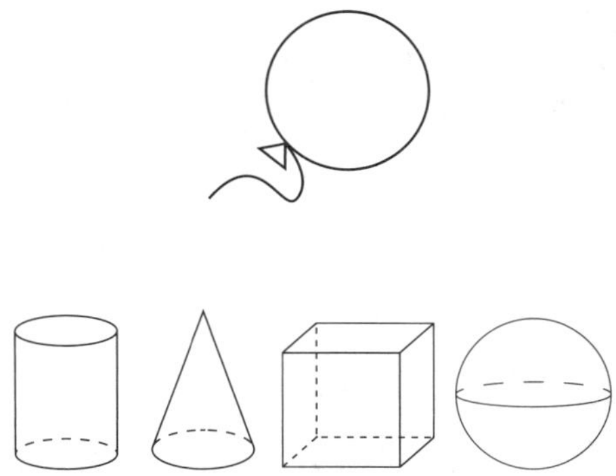

10. Circle the card that shows the same fraction as the example on top.

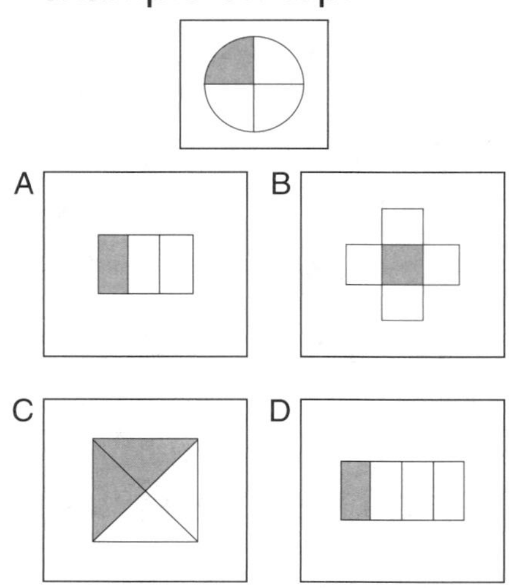

NAME: ____________________

DIRECTIONS Solve each problem.

1.

$$\begin{array}{r} 17 \\ 5 \\ +\ 3 \\ \hline \end{array}$$

2. Is $\frac{1}{2}$ equal to $\frac{5}{10}$? ________

3. $16 \div 2 =$ ________

4. $6\overline{)12}$

5. What is the number right after 46?

____

6. Fill in the missing number.

3, 6, 9, ________, 15, 18

7. Write the length in millimeters.

____

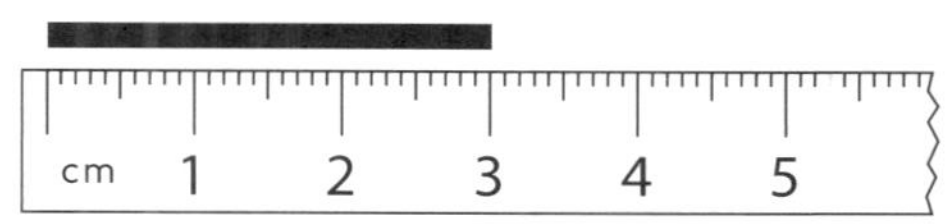

8. Tom left home at 7:40 A.M. and reached school at 8:05 A.M. How many minutes did it take him to get to school?

____

9. Mark the parallel lines with an X.

10. Write two odd numbers that total the even number 12.

____

SCORE

1. Ⓨ Ⓝ
2. Ⓨ Ⓝ
3. Ⓨ Ⓝ
4. Ⓨ Ⓝ
5. Ⓨ Ⓝ
6. Ⓨ Ⓝ
7. Ⓨ Ⓝ
8. Ⓨ Ⓝ
9. Ⓨ Ⓝ
10. Ⓨ Ⓝ

___ / 10
Total

DAY 12

NAME: ____________________

DIRECTIONS Solve each problem.

SCORE

1. Ⓨ Ⓝ
2. Ⓨ Ⓝ
3. Ⓨ Ⓝ
4. Ⓨ Ⓝ
5. Ⓨ Ⓝ
6. Ⓨ Ⓝ
7. Ⓨ Ⓝ
8. Ⓨ Ⓝ
9. Ⓨ Ⓝ
10. Ⓨ Ⓝ

___ / 10
Total

1. $36 - 7 =$ ________

2. $\frac{1}{4}$ of 28 is ________.

3. Divide 24 into equal groups of 4.

____

4. $28 \div 4 =$ ________

5. What is the value of the 1 in 312?

____

6. $5 + \square = 25$

7. Calculate the area of the square.

____

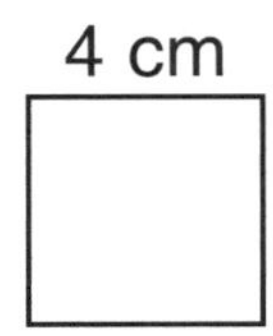

8. Would you use a scale or ruler to measure weight?

____

9. What is the area of a rectangle that measures 4 cm by 12 cm?

____

10. There are 16 boys. A coach wants to form 4 equal teams. How many boys will be on each team?

____

DAY 13

NAME: ______________________________

DIRECTIONS Solve each problem.

1. 22 + 5 = ________

2. Is 0.7 equal to $\frac{7}{100}$?

____

3. If 18 pens are divided into 9 equal rows, how many pens are in each row?

____

4. $7\overline{)14}$

5. What is the place value of 7 in 71?

____

6. 36 ÷ ☐ = 9

7. Write the time.

________ to ________

8. 1 day = ________ hours

9. Name this shape.

____

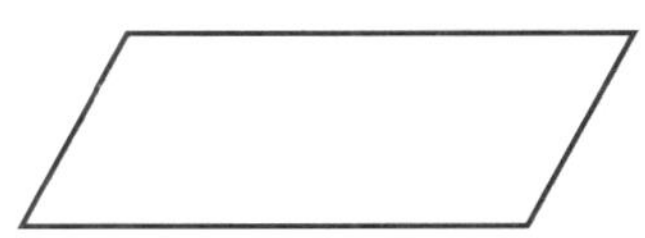

10. Mel spent $20 on 5 tickets. How much is one ticket?

____

SCORE

1. Ⓨ Ⓝ
2. Ⓨ Ⓝ
3. Ⓨ Ⓝ
4. Ⓨ Ⓝ
5. Ⓨ Ⓝ
6. Ⓨ Ⓝ
7. Ⓨ Ⓝ
8. Ⓨ Ⓝ
9. Ⓨ Ⓝ
10. Ⓨ Ⓝ

___ / 10 Total

DAY 14

NAME: ______________________________

DIRECTIONS Solve each problem.

SCORE

1. Ⓨ Ⓝ
2. Ⓨ Ⓝ
3. Ⓨ Ⓝ
4. Ⓨ Ⓝ
5. Ⓨ Ⓝ
6. Ⓨ Ⓝ
7. Ⓨ Ⓝ
8. Ⓨ Ⓝ
9. Ⓨ Ⓝ
10. Ⓨ Ⓝ

___ / 10 Total

1.

$$\begin{array}{r} 43 \\ -\ \ 8 \\ \hline \end{array}$$

2. Is $\frac{1}{2}$ less than $\frac{1}{4}$?

____

3. $5 \overline{)40}$

4. How many 4s are in 20?

____

5. Order the numbers from smallest to largest.

43, 73, 33

________ ________ ________

6. 45 – $\square$ = 39

7. Would you use kilograms or grams to measure the mass of a banana?

____

8. ________ pints = 1 quart

9. Circle the solids that have a rectangular top view.

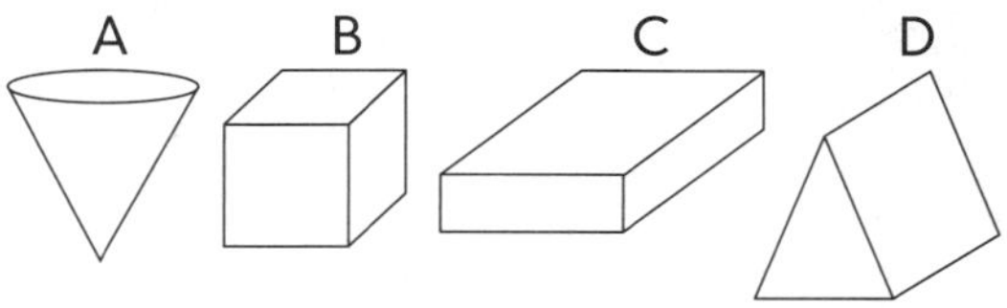

10. Complete the chart. Round the number 423.

Tens	
Hundreds	

NAME: ______________________________

DIRECTIONS Solve each problem.

1.

$$\begin{array}{r} 24 \\ +\ 7 \\ \hline \end{array}$$

2. Calculate the product of 9 and 6.

____

3. 40 ÷ 10 = ________

4. Divide 36 into 4 equal groups.

____

5. What is the value of the 9 in 892,135?

____

6. ☐ x 4 = 24

7. Is the distance around a polygon called perimeter?

____

8. ________ feet = 1 yard

9. Circle the triangle that has 3 equal sides.

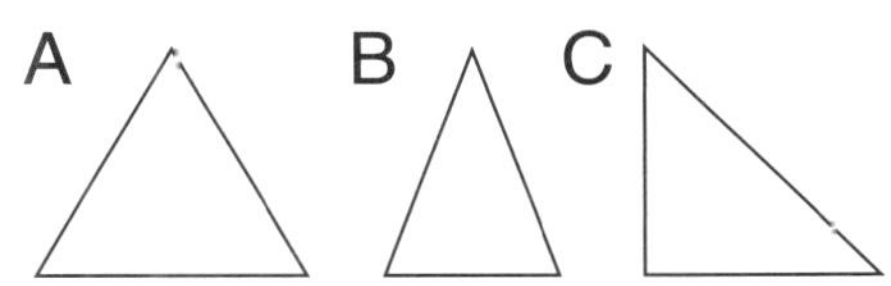

10. Use different colors to color pairs of numbers that equal the product shown in the center.

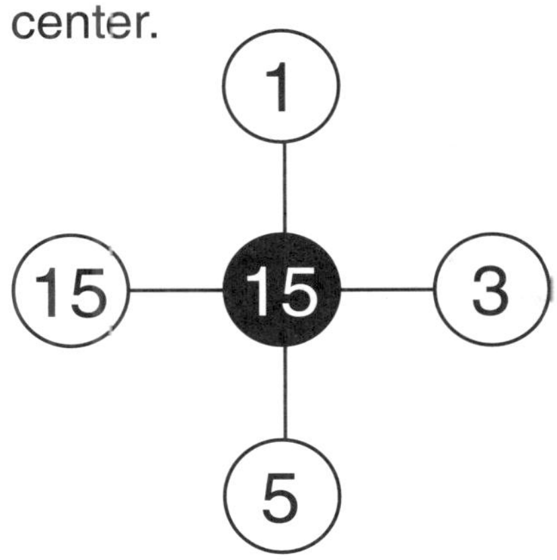

SCORE

1. Ⓨ Ⓝ
2. Ⓨ Ⓝ
3. Ⓨ Ⓝ
4. Ⓨ Ⓝ
5. Ⓨ Ⓝ
6. Ⓨ Ⓝ
7. Ⓨ Ⓝ
8. Ⓨ Ⓝ
9. Ⓨ Ⓝ
10. Ⓨ Ⓝ

___ / 10 Total

DAY 16

NAME: ______________________

DIRECTIONS Solve each problem.

SCORE

1. Ⓨ Ⓝ
2. Ⓨ Ⓝ
3. Ⓨ Ⓝ
4. Ⓨ Ⓝ
5. Ⓨ Ⓝ
6. Ⓨ Ⓝ
7. Ⓨ Ⓝ
8. Ⓨ Ⓝ
9. Ⓨ Ⓝ
10. Ⓨ Ⓝ

___ / 10
Total

1. 32 – 7 = ________

2. Calculate one-tenth of 40.

____

3. How many groups of 7 are in 14?

____

4. $9\overline{)36}$

5. Write 563 in expanded notation.

____

6. Fill in the missing number.

49, ________, 29, 19, 9

7. You can put either a ball or a brick into a bucket of water. Circle the one that would raise the water level higher.

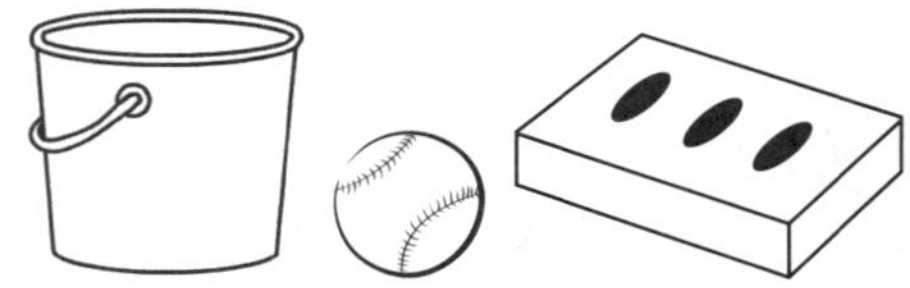

8. How many days are in January?

____

9. **Dollars Earned in May**

Audrey	$15
Dameon	$23
Jason	$12
Lauren	$18

How much money did Lauren earn?

____

10. A bus leaves Oakton at 12:30 P.M. and arrives at Rockville at 4:18 P.M. How long is the trip?

____

DAY 17

NAME: ____________________

DIRECTIONS Solve each problem.

1. 33 + 19 = ________

2. How many fourths are in 1?

____

3. If you share 20 cups equally among 10 people, how many cups will each person get?

____

4. $2\overline{)12}$

5. What is the value of the tens place in 62?

____

6. 12 x ☐ = 24

7. What is the date of the third Monday in February?

____

FEBRUARY						
Sun	Mon	Tue	Wed	Thu	Fri	Sat
		1	2	3	4	5
6	7	8	9	10	11	12
13	14	15	16	17	18	19
20	21	22	23	24	25	26
27	28	29				

8. Would you use a ruler or a yardstick to measure a flag pole?

____

9. Are parallel lines always the same distance apart?

____

10. If you subtract 14 from me, the difference is 32. What number am I?

____

SCORE

1. Ⓨ Ⓝ
2. Ⓨ Ⓝ
3. Ⓨ Ⓝ
4. Ⓨ Ⓝ
5. Ⓨ Ⓝ
6. Ⓨ Ⓝ
7. Ⓨ Ⓝ
8. Ⓨ Ⓝ
9. Ⓨ Ⓝ
10. Ⓨ Ⓝ

___ / 10
Total

NAME: ____________________

DIRECTIONS Solve each problem.

SCORE

1. Ⓨ Ⓝ
2. Ⓨ Ⓝ
3. Ⓨ Ⓝ
4. Ⓨ Ⓝ
5. Ⓨ Ⓝ
6. Ⓨ Ⓝ
7. Ⓨ Ⓝ
8. Ⓨ Ⓝ
9. Ⓨ Ⓝ
10. Ⓨ Ⓝ

___ / 10
Total

1.
$$\begin{array}{r} 20 \\ -\ 5 \\ \hline \end{array}$$

2. Write $\frac{25}{100}$ as a decimal.

____

3. Divide 40 into 10 equal groups.

____

4. $80 \div 8 =$ ________

5. What is the next even number after 68?

____

6. $24 \div \square = 6$

7. Can containers with a capacity of 1 liter have different shapes?

____

8. Circle the most likely mass of a dog.

5 grams

5 kilograms

5 kilometers

9. Name the shape of the shaded face.

____

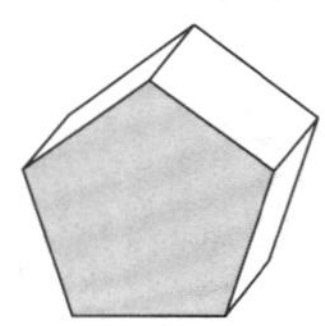

10. Look at the first tile. Continue the pattern by translating the tile three times.

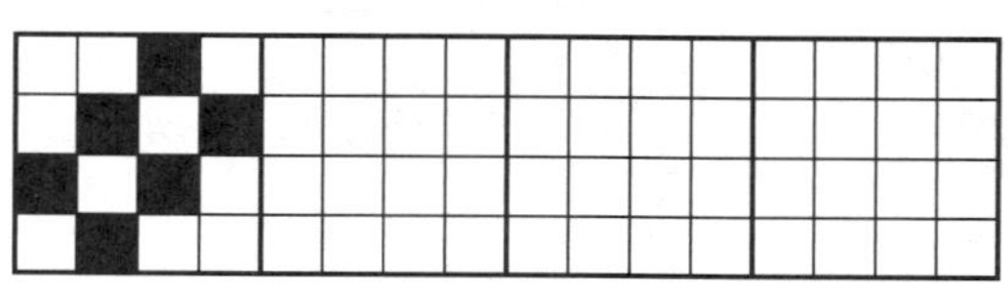

NAME: ______________________________

DIRECTIONS Solve each problem.

1.
```
  21
+ 14
----
```

2. $\frac{1}{4}$ of 24 is ________

3. $3 \overline{)12}$

4. What is 48 books shared equally among 4 classes?

____

5. Which is larger: 6 or 0.6?

____

6. 15 + $\square$ = 37

7. Each cube has 1-cm sides. What is the volume of the model?

____

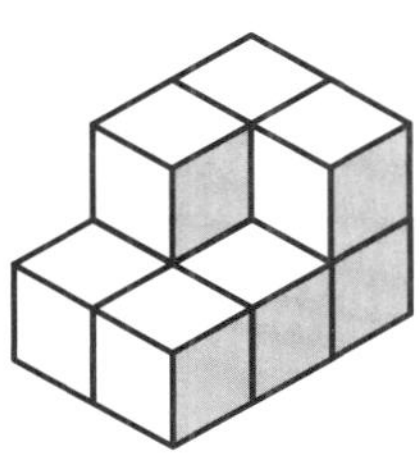

8. Do you leave for school in the A.M. or P.M.?

____

9. **Books Read in March**

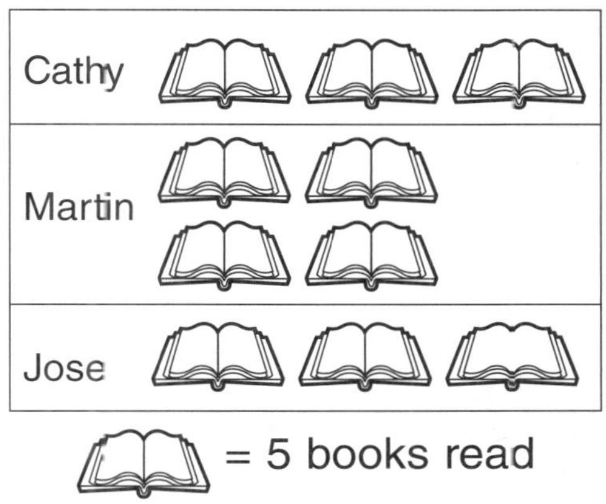

How many books did Cathy read?

____

10. It takes Dad 20 minutes to drive to work. How long does he spend driving to and from work every day?

____

SCORE

1. Ⓨ Ⓝ
2. Ⓨ Ⓝ
3. Ⓨ Ⓝ
4. Ⓨ Ⓝ
5. Ⓨ Ⓝ
6. Ⓨ Ⓝ
7. Ⓨ Ⓝ
8. Ⓨ Ⓝ
9. Ⓨ Ⓝ
10. Ⓨ Ⓝ

___ / 10
Total

DAY 20

NAME: ____________________

DIRECTIONS Solve each problem.

SCORE

1. Ⓨ Ⓝ
2. Ⓨ Ⓝ
3. Ⓨ Ⓝ
4. Ⓨ Ⓝ
5. Ⓨ Ⓝ
6. Ⓨ Ⓝ
7. Ⓨ Ⓝ
8. Ⓨ Ⓝ
9. Ⓨ Ⓝ
10. Ⓨ Ⓝ

___ / 10
Total

1. 30 – 15 = ________

2.
$$\begin{array}{r} 8 \\ \times\ 8 \\ \hline \end{array}$$

3. 40 ÷ 4 = ________

4. 18 divided into 9 equal groups is

____________________.

5. Fill in the missing number.

63, 64, 65, ________

6. 9 x ☐ = 18

7. Would the area of a stamp most likely be measured in cm^2 or m^2?

____

8. 60 minutes equals how many hours?

____

9. Which numbers are inside the circle but not in the rectangle or triangle?

____

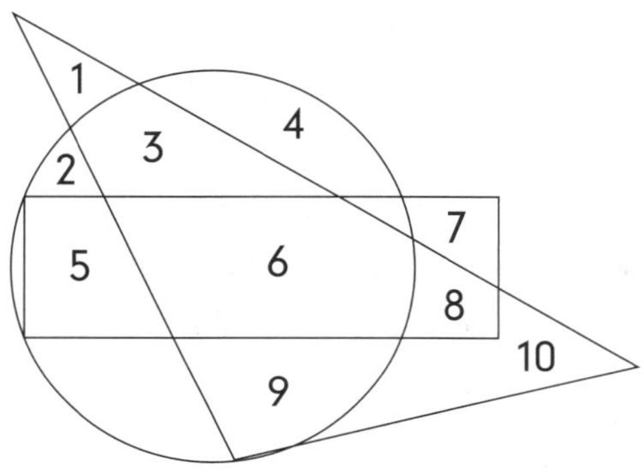

10. Color half of the area so that both the shaded and unshaded parts have the same shape.

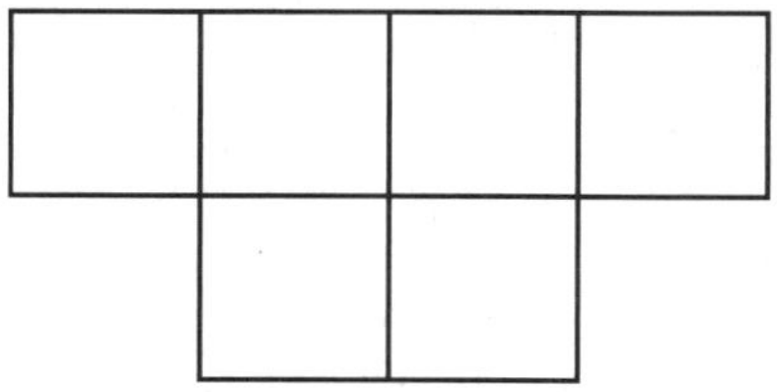

NAME: ________________________________

DIRECTIONS Solve each problem.

1. 26 + 13 = ________

2. $\frac{1}{8}$ of 24 is ________

3. $5\overline{)20}$

4. 56 ÷ 8 = ________

5. What is the place value of 9 in 918?

____

6. Fill in the missing number.

8, 12, 16, ________, 24

7. Write the line length in centimeters.

____

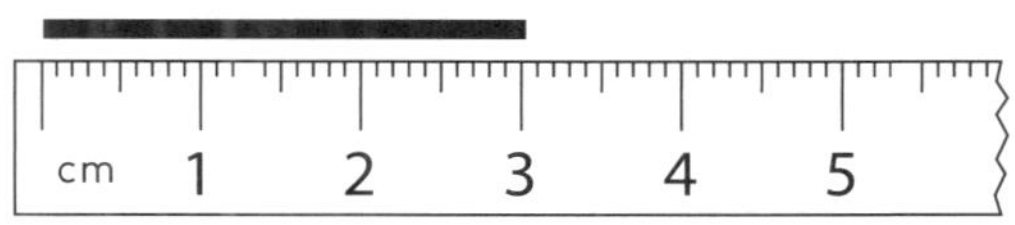

8. If you wanted a glass of water, would you pour a cup or a gallon of water?

____

9. Draw the axes of symmetry.

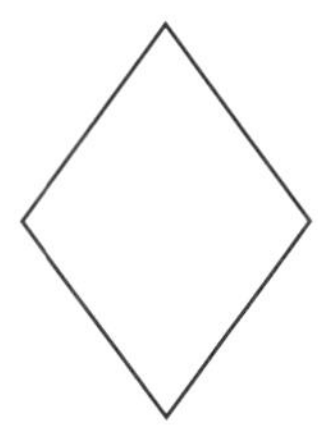

10. Write two odd numbers that total the even number 8.

____

SCORE

1. Ⓨ Ⓝ
2. Ⓨ Ⓝ
3. Ⓨ Ⓝ
4. Ⓨ Ⓝ
5. Ⓨ Ⓝ
6. Ⓨ Ⓝ
7. Ⓨ Ⓝ
8. Ⓨ Ⓝ
9. Ⓨ Ⓝ
10. Ⓨ Ⓝ

___ / 10

Total

DAY 22

NAME: ____________________

DIRECTIONS Solve each problem.

SCORE

1. Ⓨ Ⓝ
2. Ⓨ Ⓝ
3. Ⓨ Ⓝ
4. Ⓨ Ⓝ
5. Ⓨ Ⓝ
6. Ⓨ Ⓝ
7. Ⓨ Ⓝ
8. Ⓨ Ⓝ
9. Ⓨ Ⓝ
10. Ⓨ Ⓝ

___ / 10 Total

1.

$$\begin{array}{r} 24 \\ -\ 18 \\ \hline \end{array}$$

2. Which is greater: 0.3 or 0.29?

____

3. Divide 28 into 4 equal groups.

____

4. $8\overline{)48}$

5. Is 102 greater than 120?

____

6. 13 + ☐ = 15

7. Calculate the perimeter of the rectangle.

____

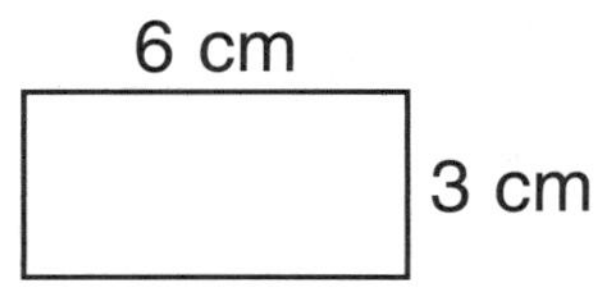

8. What is the temperature?

____

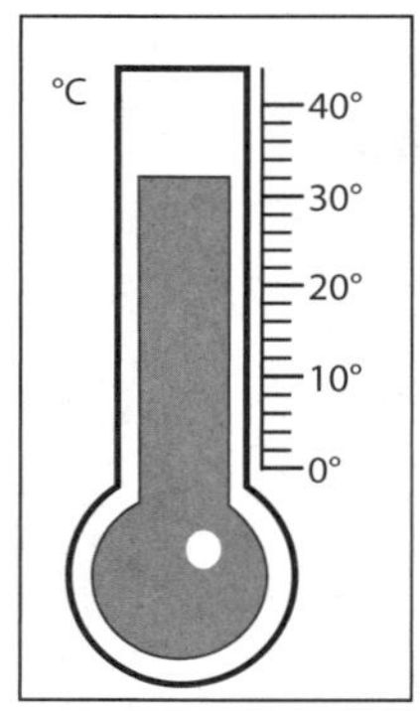

9. What solid figure is a globe?

____

10. One bag of cookies has a mass of 350 g. What is the mass of 2 bags?

____

DAY 23

NAME: ______________________________

DIRECTIONS Solve each problem.

1.

$$\begin{array}{r} 35 \\ +\ 14 \\ \hline \end{array}$$

2. Write the decimal for $\frac{35}{100}$.

____

3. $16 \div 4 =$ ________

4. How many equal groups of 8 are in 32?

____

5. Write the smallest 2-digit number using 8, 3, and 4.

____

6. $24 \div \square = 4$

7. Fill in the blanks for the time shown.

4: ______
____ past 4

8. 7 days = ________ week

9.

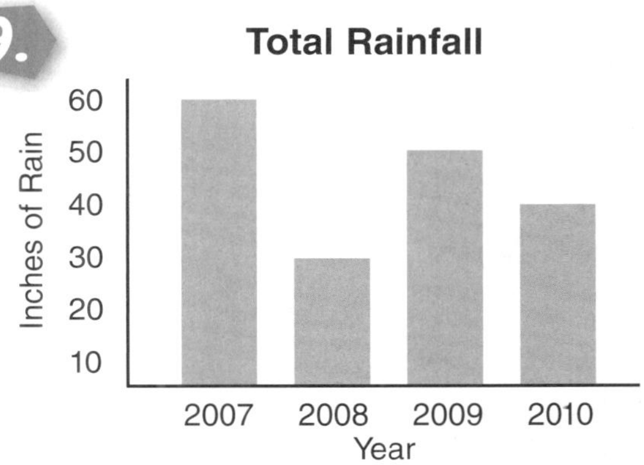

Which year received the most rainfall?

____

10. If 1 kg of apples costs $1.25, what do 5 kg of apples cost?

____

SCORE

1. Ⓨ Ⓝ
2. Ⓨ Ⓝ
3. Ⓨ Ⓝ
4. Ⓨ Ⓝ
5. Ⓨ Ⓝ
6. Ⓨ Ⓝ
7. Ⓨ Ⓝ
8. Ⓨ Ⓝ
9. Ⓨ Ⓝ
10. Ⓨ Ⓝ

___ / 10
Total

DAY 24

NAME: ____________________

DIRECTIONS Solve each problem.

SCORE

1. Ⓨ Ⓝ
2. Ⓨ Ⓝ
3. Ⓨ Ⓝ
4. Ⓨ Ⓝ
5. Ⓨ Ⓝ
6. Ⓨ Ⓝ
7. Ⓨ Ⓝ
8. Ⓨ Ⓝ
9. Ⓨ Ⓝ
10. Ⓨ Ⓝ

___ / 10 Total

1. 20 – 17 = ________

2. Write the fraction for 0.27.

____

3. 54 ÷ 6 = ________

4. $7\overline{)14}$

5. 300 + 80 + 6 = ________

6. ☐ – 4 = 12

7. Circle the best estimate for the weight of the object.

100 g   2 kg   5 kg   10 kg

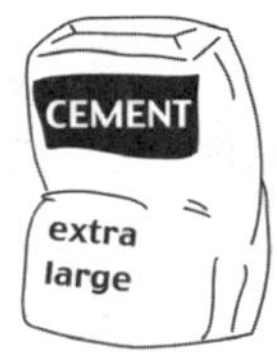

8. ________ pints = 1 gallon

9. Name the polygon with three vertices.

____

10. Show the amount shaded as a fraction, decimal, and percentage.

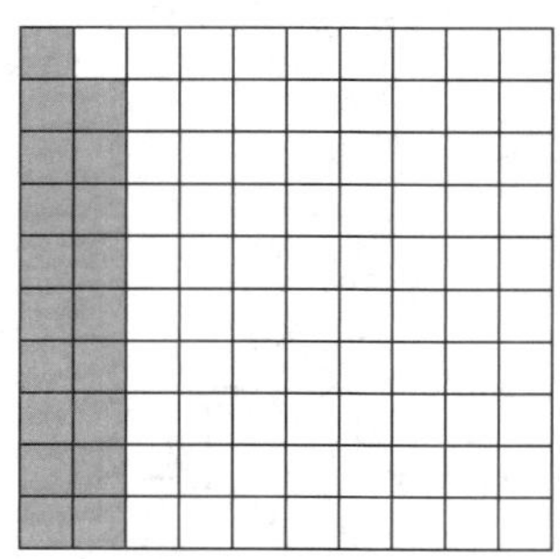

$\frac{}{100}$	0.	%

NAME: ______________________________

DIRECTIONS Solve each problem.

1. 32 + 26 = ________

2. 4 × 3 = ____

3. How many groups of three are in 30?

____

4. $7\overline{)70}$

5. Write 1,061 in expanded notation.

____

6. 4 x ☐ = 40

7. How many millimeters are in 5 centimeters?

____

8. ________ inches = 1 yard

9. A parallelogram has:

________ angles

________ axes of symmetry

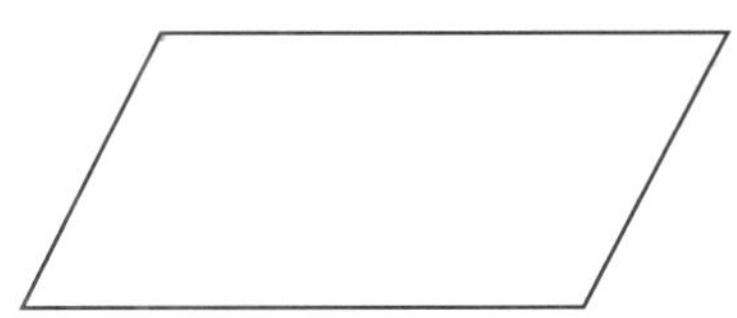

10. Color the multiples of 4.

1	2	3	4	5	6	7	8	9	10
11	12	13	14	15	16	17	18	19	20
21	22	23	24	25	26	27	28	29	30
31	32	33	34	35	36	37	38	39	40

SCORE

1. Ⓨ Ⓝ
2. Ⓨ Ⓝ
3. Ⓨ Ⓝ
4. Ⓨ Ⓝ
5. Ⓨ Ⓝ
6. Ⓨ Ⓝ
7. Ⓨ Ⓝ
8. Ⓨ Ⓝ
9. Ⓨ Ⓝ
10. Ⓨ Ⓝ

___ / 10 Total

DAY
26

NAME: ____________________

DIRECTIONS Solve each problem.

SCORE

1. Ⓨ Ⓝ
2. Ⓨ Ⓝ
3. Ⓨ Ⓝ
4. Ⓨ Ⓝ
5. Ⓨ Ⓝ
6. Ⓨ Ⓝ
7. Ⓨ Ⓝ
8. Ⓨ Ⓝ
9. Ⓨ Ⓝ
10. Ⓨ Ⓝ

___ / 10
Total

1.
$$\begin{array}{r} 20 \\ -\ 15 \\ \hline \end{array}$$

2. Which is smaller:
0.6 or 0.16?

____

3. How many groups of 6 are in 42?

____

4. 25 ÷ 5 = ________

5. Is 75 less than 57?

____

6. Fill in the missing number.

112, 102, ________, 82, 72

7. If 2  fill a  and

3  fill a , then

________  fill a .

8. Which month has only 28 days?

____

9. **School Awards**

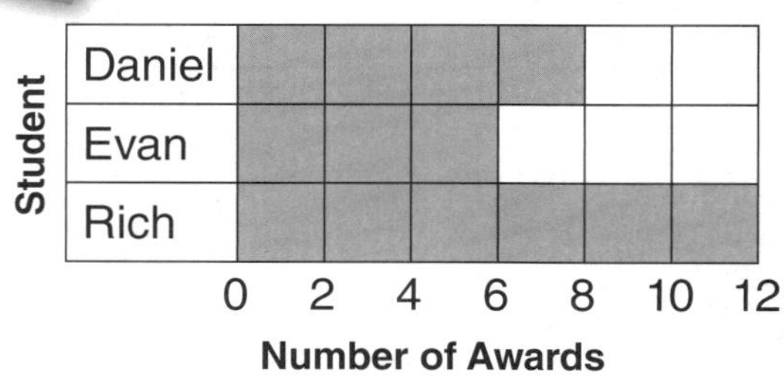

Who has won the most awards?

____

10. Ms. Nielson's class has an ant farm. There are 1,235 male and 2,628 worker ants. How many ants are there in the farm?

____

DAY 27

NAME: ______________________

DIRECTIONS Solve each problem.

1. 26 + 35 = ________

2. $\frac{1}{2}$ of 18 = ________

3. $8\overline{)24}$

4. 9 ÷ 3 = ________

5. What number is 100 more than 1,468?

____

6. 18 + ☐ = 20

7. On what day of the week does January end?

____

JANUARY						
Sun	Mon	Tue	Wed	Thu	Fri	Sat
		1	2	3	4	5
6	7	8	9	10	11	12
13	14	15	16	17	18	19
20	21	22	23	24	25	26
27	28	29	30	31		

8. Write the length in inches.

________________ inches

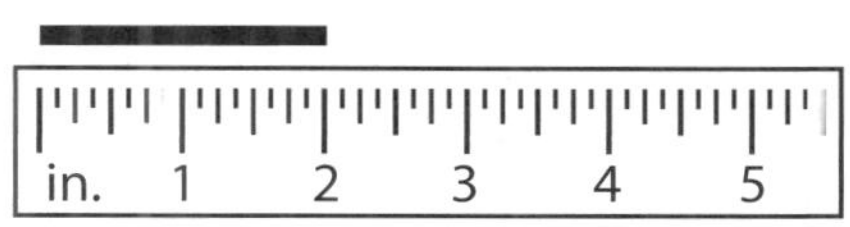

9. Circle the solids that have a circular top view.

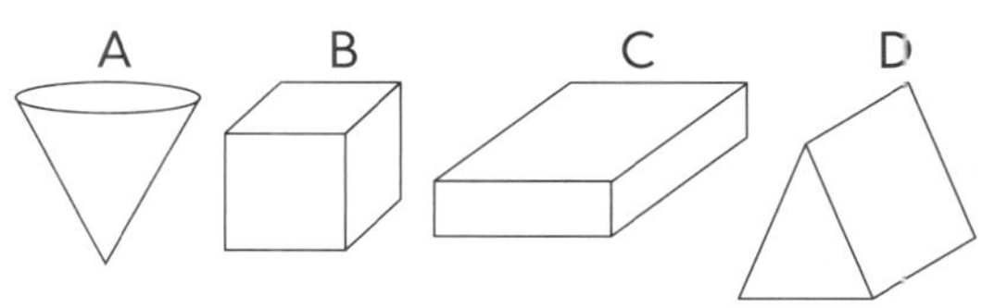

10. Our sum is 11. The difference between us is 1. What numbers are we?

____

SCORE

1. Ⓨ Ⓝ
2. Ⓨ Ⓝ
3. Ⓨ Ⓝ
4. Ⓨ Ⓝ
5. Ⓨ Ⓝ
6. Ⓨ Ⓝ
7. Ⓨ Ⓝ
8. Ⓨ Ⓝ
9. Ⓨ Ⓝ
10. Ⓨ Ⓝ

___ / 10 Total

DAY
28

NAME: ____________________________

DIRECTIONS Solve each problem.

SCORE

1. Ⓨ Ⓝ
2. Ⓨ Ⓝ
3. Ⓨ Ⓝ
4. Ⓨ Ⓝ
5. Ⓨ Ⓝ
6. Ⓨ Ⓝ
7. Ⓨ Ⓝ
8. Ⓨ Ⓝ
9. Ⓨ Ⓝ
10. Ⓨ Ⓝ

___ / 10

Total

1. 32 – 15 = ________

2. How many fourths are in 3?

____

3. Divide 8 by 2.

____

4. 14 ÷ 7 = ________

5. What is the place value of 7 in 1,709?

____

6. ☐ x 4 = 20

7. I put 700 mL of water in the jug. Next I put a toy in the jug. How much water was displaced by the toy?
________ mL was displaced.

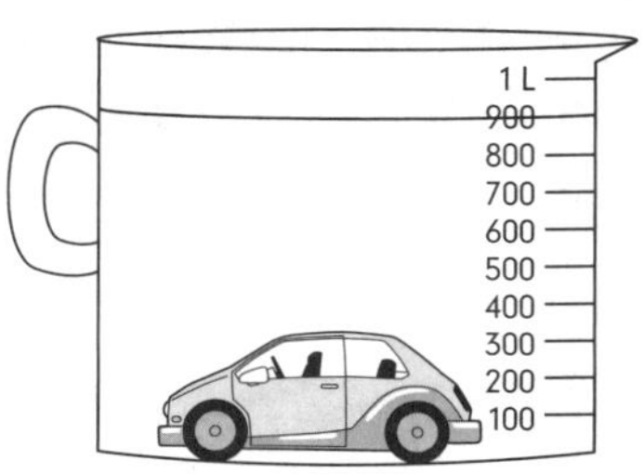

8. Which would be the best tool for measuring the length of a book: a ruler, a yardstick, or a scale?

____

9. Does this shape tessellate?

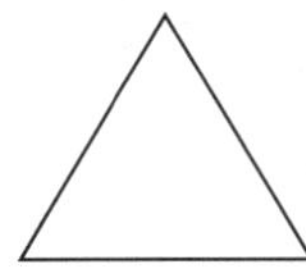
____

10. Draw a triangle on the coordinate (G,3).

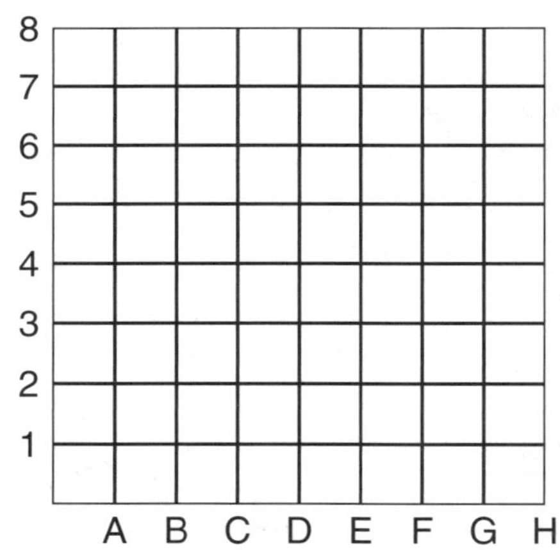

DAY
29

NAME: ____________________________________

DIRECTIONS Solve each problem.

1. 25 + 27 = ________

2. Write the decimal for $\frac{1}{2}$.

____

3. How many groups of 2 are in 16?

____

4. $6\overline{)24}$

5. 100 + 40 + 7 = ________

6. 18 ÷ ☐ = 9

7. What unit of measure is used for volume?

____

8. Jan left home at 7:35 A.M. and reached school at 8:10 A.M. How many minutes did she travel?

____

9. Draw in the axes of symmetry.

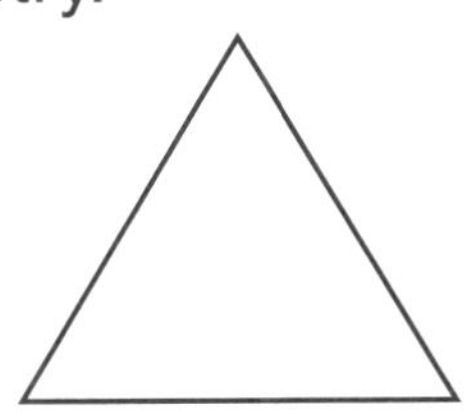

10. Carole's mom gave her $14.00. She wants to buy 3 charm bracelets that cost $5.00 each. Does she have enough money to buy the 3 bracelets?

____

SCORE

1. Ⓨ Ⓝ
2. Ⓨ Ⓝ
3. Ⓨ Ⓝ
4. Ⓨ Ⓝ
5. Ⓨ Ⓝ
6. Ⓨ Ⓝ
7. Ⓨ Ⓝ
8. Ⓨ Ⓝ
9. Ⓨ Ⓝ
10. Ⓨ Ⓝ

___ / 10
Total

DAY 30

NAME: ____________________

DIRECTIONS Solve each problem.

SCORE

1. Ⓨ Ⓝ
2. Ⓨ Ⓝ
3. Ⓨ Ⓝ
4. Ⓨ Ⓝ
5. Ⓨ Ⓝ
6. Ⓨ Ⓝ
7. Ⓨ Ⓝ
8. Ⓨ Ⓝ
9. Ⓨ Ⓝ
10. Ⓨ Ⓝ

___ / 10 Total

1.

$$\begin{array}{r} 30 \\ -\ \ 9 \\ \hline \end{array}$$

2. 5 x 7 = ________

3. Divide 16 into 4 equal groups.

____

4. 28 ÷ 7 = ________

5. Is 63 closer to 60 or 70?

____

6. ☐ x 6 = 36

7. The area of the flower bed is 12 m^2 and the area of the grass is 24 m^2. What is their combined area?

____

8. Is 12:00 P.M. a reasonable bedtime?

____

9. **Sports Played Each Year**

	1st Trimester	2nd Trimester	3rd Trimester
Troy	soccer	basketball	baseball
Jessica	golf	basketball	track
Allison	soccer	diving	swimming

Which sport does Troy play in the 3rd trimester?

____

10. $\frac{1}{10}$ of 60 = 6, so $\frac{7}{10}$ of 60 =

____

DAY 31

NAME: ____________________

DIRECTIONS Solve each problem.

1.
$$\begin{array}{r} 12 \\ +\ 14 \\ \hline \end{array}$$

2. $\frac{1}{4}$ of 36 is ________

3. Divide 20 by 5. ________

4. $8\overline{)40}$

5. Write the smallest 4-digit numeral using 0, 2, 8, and 7.

____

6. Fill in the missing number.

20, 40, 60, ________, 100

7. Write the length in millimeters.

____

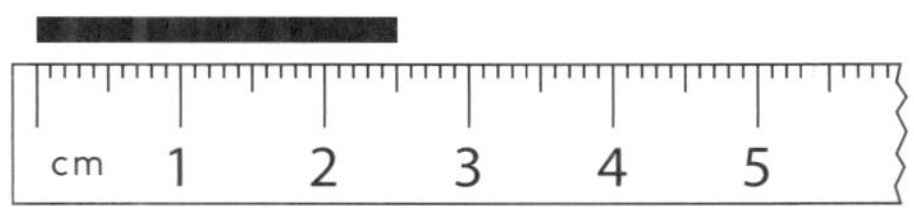

8. If the temperature were 89 degrees Fahrenheit, would you wear a bathing suit or a jacket?

____

9. What type of prism is shown?

____

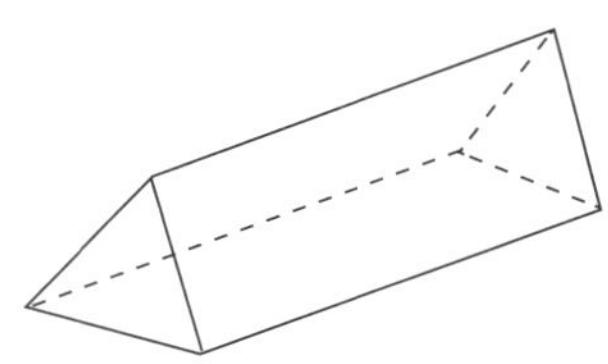

10. Complete the subtraction grid.

–	44	48	53	61	72	75
19						
29						
39						

SCORE

1. Ⓨ Ⓝ
2. Ⓨ Ⓝ
3. Ⓨ Ⓝ
4. Ⓨ Ⓝ
5. Ⓨ Ⓝ
6. Ⓨ Ⓝ
7. Ⓨ Ⓝ
8. Ⓨ Ⓝ
9. Ⓨ Ⓝ
10. Ⓨ Ⓝ

___ / 10 Total

DAY 32

NAME: ______________________________

DIRECTIONS Solve each problem.

1. 43 – 17 = ________

2. Which is smaller: 0.4 or $\frac{3}{10}$?

____

3. 15 ÷ 5 = ________

4. $3\overline{)18}$

5. Write 3,426 in expanded notation.

____

____

6. 25 + ☐ = 36

7. Calculate the area of a square with 3 cm sides.

________ 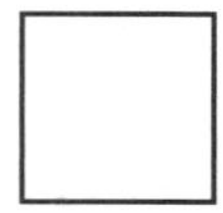 3 cm

8. How many weeks are in one year?

____

9. Circle the set of lines that are parallel.

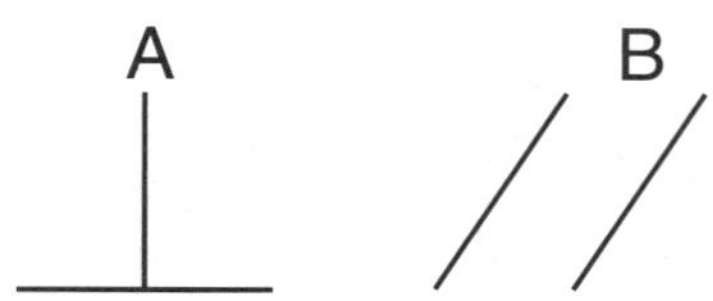

10. Sam found one dollar. He kept half and spent the rest. How much did he spend?

____

SCORE

1. Ⓨ Ⓝ
2. Ⓨ Ⓝ
3. Ⓨ Ⓝ
4. Ⓨ Ⓝ
5. Ⓨ Ⓝ
6. Ⓨ Ⓝ
7. Ⓨ Ⓝ
8. Ⓨ Ⓝ
9. Ⓨ Ⓝ
10. Ⓨ Ⓝ

___ / 10 Total

NAME: ____________________

DIRECTIONS Solve each problem.

1. 23 + 7 = ______

2. Color $\frac{1}{2}$.

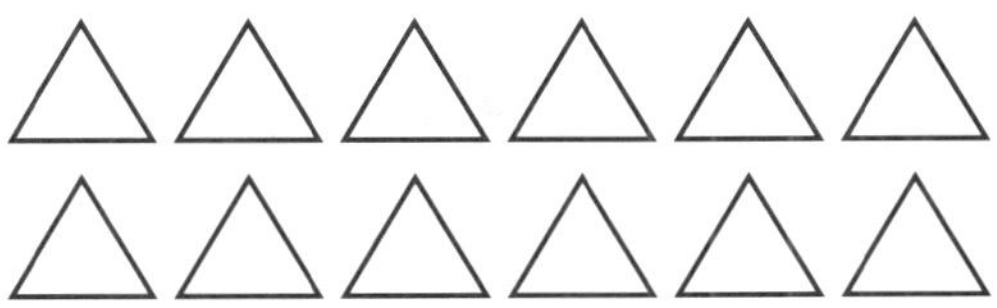

3. The quotient of 40 and 10 is

____________________.

4. 56 ÷ 7 = ______

5. Write 2,467 in words.

____

____

____

6. 42 – ☐ = 15

7. Show 20 to 3 on both clocks.

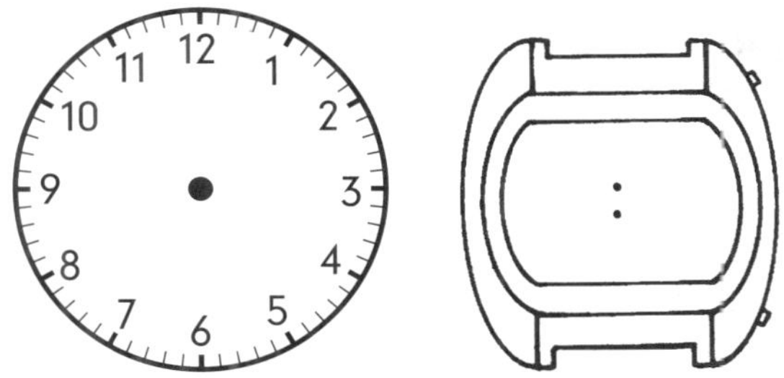

8. ______ pints = $\frac{1}{2}$ gallon

9. Record the data in the chart.

	Pizza	Tacos
Sharon		
Sue		

Sue likes pizza.

Sharon and Sue like tacos.

Sharon does not like pizza.

10. Joe found one dollar. He kept a quarter and spent the rest. How much did he spend?

____

SCORE

1. Ⓨ Ⓝ
2. Ⓨ Ⓝ
3. Ⓨ Ⓝ
4. Ⓨ Ⓝ
5. Ⓨ Ⓝ
6. Ⓨ Ⓝ
7. Ⓨ Ⓝ
8. Ⓨ Ⓝ
9. Ⓨ Ⓝ
10. Ⓨ Ⓝ

___ / 10

Total

DAY 34

NAME: ____________________________

DIRECTIONS Solve each problem.

SCORE

1. Ⓨ Ⓝ
2. Ⓨ Ⓝ
3. Ⓨ Ⓝ
4. Ⓨ Ⓝ
5. Ⓨ Ⓝ
6. Ⓨ Ⓝ
7. Ⓨ Ⓝ
8. Ⓨ Ⓝ
9. Ⓨ Ⓝ
10. Ⓨ Ⓝ

___ / 10 Total

1. 16 – 5 = ________

2. Write the decimal for $\frac{60}{100}$.

____

3. $5\overline{)30}$

4. 28 ÷ 2 = ________

5. Is 573 less than 537?

____

6. $\square$ + 3 = 18

7. Dan's mass is double the mass of Tim, whose mass is 39 kg. What is Dan's mass?

____

8. ________ inches = 4 feet

9. Label with *reflection*, *translation*, or *rotation*.

____

10. Add 4 tens and 3 ones to the number 38.

____

DAY 35

NAME: ____________________________________

DIRECTIONS Solve each problem.

1.
$$\begin{array}{r} 32 \\ +\ 29 \\ \hline \end{array}$$

2. $5 \times 9 =$ ________

3. How many groups of nine are in the number twenty-seven?

____

4. $7\overline{)14}$

5. Is 357 closer to 300 or 400?

____

6. $4 \times \square = 16$

7. Is 1 m^2 greater than 1 cm^2?

____

8. What month comes after May?

____

9. Circle the quadrilaterals.

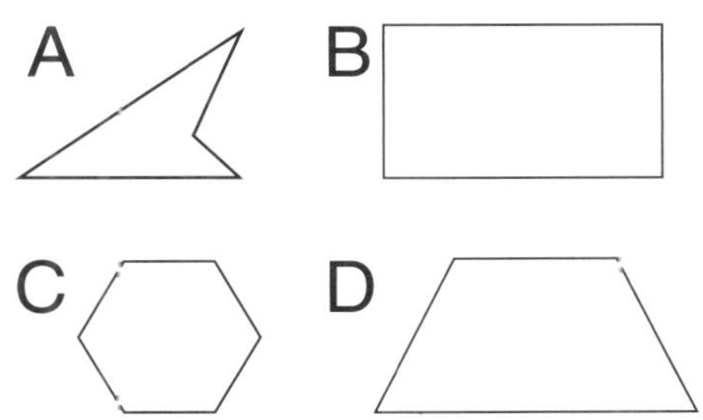

10. Use different colors to color pairs of numbers that equal the product shown in the center.

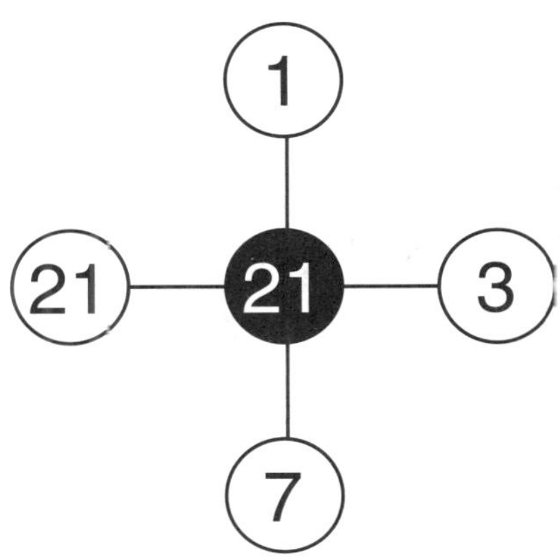

SCORE

1. (Y) (N)

2. (Y) (N)

3. (Y) (N)

4. (Y) (N)

5. (Y) (N)

6. (Y) (N)

7. (Y) (N)

8. (Y) (N)

9. (Y) (N)

10. (Y) (N)

___ / 10
Total

DAY 36

NAME: ______________________

DIRECTIONS Solve each problem.

SCORE

1. Ⓨ Ⓝ
2. Ⓨ Ⓝ
3. Ⓨ Ⓝ
4. Ⓨ Ⓝ
5. Ⓨ Ⓝ
6. Ⓨ Ⓝ
7. Ⓨ Ⓝ
8. Ⓨ Ⓝ
9. Ⓨ Ⓝ
10. Ⓨ Ⓝ

___ / 10 Total

1. 27 – 15 = ________

2. $\frac{1}{4}$ of 28 is ________

3. 40 ÷ 4 = ________

4. List all the factors of 6.

____

5. What is 200 more than 694?

____

6. Fill in the missing number.

650, 700, ________, 800, 850

7. How many liters are in 7,000 milliliters?

____

8. Would you use a ruler or a yardstick to measure the length of your shoe?

____

9. Draw the top view of this solid.

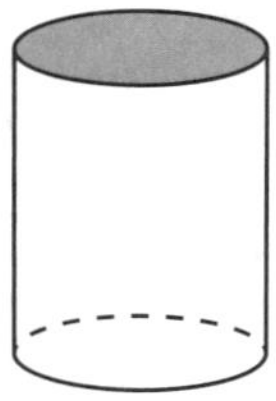

10. Omar has a licorice rope that is 48 inches long. He gives a 9-inch length to Ruby, an 8-inch length to Shen, and 10-inch lengths to both Nita and Paco. How long is Omar's licorice rope now?

____

DAY 37

NAME: ____________________

DIRECTIONS Solve each problem.

1. 35 + 37 = ______

2. Write the decimal for $\frac{3}{4}$.

____

3. $7\overline{)14}$

4. How many groups of 9 are in 81?

____

5. Is 847 closer to 800 or 900?

____

6. 15 ÷ ☐ = 5

7. Look at the calendar below. What day of the week is January 31?

____

FEBRUARY						
Sun	Mon	Tue	Wed	Thu	Fri	Sat
		1	2	3	4	5
6	7	8	9	10	11	12
13	14	15	16	17	18	19
20	21	22	23	24	25	26
27	28	29				

8. Circle the most likely height of a door.

6 inches

6 feet

6 centimeters

9. Draw an obtuse angle.

10. If you add me to 246, the sum is 473. What number am I?

____

SCORE

1. Ⓨ Ⓝ
2. Ⓨ Ⓝ
3. Ⓨ Ⓝ
4. Ⓨ Ⓝ
5. Ⓨ Ⓝ
6. Ⓨ Ⓝ
7. Ⓨ Ⓝ
8. Ⓨ Ⓝ
9. Ⓨ Ⓝ
10. Ⓨ Ⓝ

___ / 10 Total

DAY
38

NAME: ____________________

DIRECTIONS Solve each problem.

SCORE

1. Ⓨ Ⓝ
2. Ⓨ Ⓝ
3. Ⓨ Ⓝ
4. Ⓨ Ⓝ
5. Ⓨ Ⓝ
6. Ⓨ Ⓝ
7. Ⓨ Ⓝ
8. Ⓨ Ⓝ
9. Ⓨ Ⓝ
10. Ⓨ Ⓝ

___ / 10
Total

1.
$$\begin{array}{r} 24 \\ -\ 12 \\ \hline \end{array}$$

2. Write the fraction for 0.1.

____

3. 16 ÷ 4 = ________

4. How many groups of 7 are in 42?

____

5. 1,000 + 300 + 70 + 4 =

____

6. 56 − ☐ = 36

7. How many milliliters are in 7 liters?

____

8. Do you go home from school in the A.M. or P.M.?

____

9. Name the quadrilateral with only one set of parallel sides.

____

10. Follow the directions and color the path of the counter.

Directions

Move: 3 right, 3 up, 6 right, 4 down, 2 right, 2 down, 10 left, 1 down.

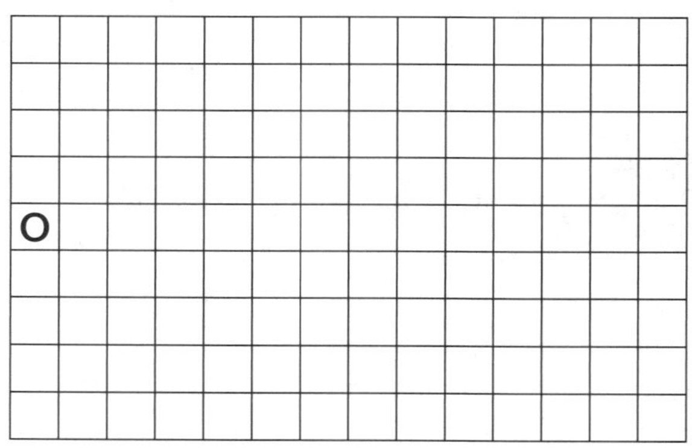

DAY
39

NAME: ____________________

DIRECTIONS Solve each problem.

1.
$$\begin{array}{r} 22 \\ +\ 19 \\ \hline \end{array}$$

2. $\frac{1}{4}$ of 20 is ________

3. $6\overline{)36}$

4. List all the factors of 4.

____

5. Is 265 less than 256?

____

6. $\square$ x 5 = 30

7. 100 ________ = 1 m

8. If the outdoor temperature is 85°F, is it a warm or cold day?

____

9. How many right angles does a rectangle have?

____

10. There are 8 squares. If 25% of the squares are red and the rest of them are blue, how many squares are red?

____

SCORE

1. Ⓨ Ⓝ
2. Ⓨ Ⓝ
3. Ⓨ Ⓝ
4. Ⓨ Ⓝ
5. Ⓨ Ⓝ
6. Ⓨ Ⓝ
7. Ⓨ Ⓝ
8. Ⓨ Ⓝ
9. Ⓨ Ⓝ
10. Ⓨ Ⓝ

___ / 10
Total

DAY 40

NAME: ______________________________

DIRECTIONS Solve each problem.

SCORE

1. Ⓨ Ⓝ
2. Ⓨ Ⓝ
3. Ⓨ Ⓝ
4. Ⓨ Ⓝ
5. Ⓨ Ⓝ
6. Ⓨ Ⓝ
7. Ⓨ Ⓝ
8. Ⓨ Ⓝ
9. Ⓨ Ⓝ
10. Ⓨ Ⓝ

___ / 10 Total

1. What is the difference between 24 and 7?

______________________.

2. Calculate the product of 7 and 6.

____

3. $35 \div 7 =$ ________

4. $6\overline{)12}$

5. $1{,}000 + 300 + 20 =$

____

6. $\square \times 4 = 32$

7. ________________ is the longest dimension of an object.

8. 12 months = ______ year(s)

9. A cylinder has:

________ surfaces

________ edges

10. If the shaded area is equal to one, what is the area of the dotted region?

____

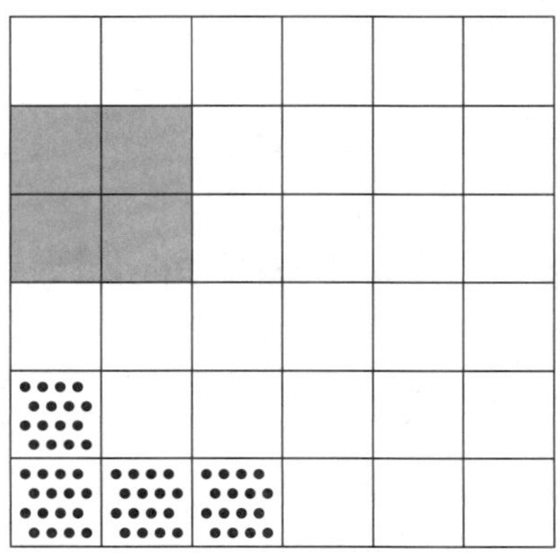

NAME: ____________________

DIRECTIONS Solve each problem.

1. 35 + 18 = ______

2. Which is larger: 0.6 or 0.16?

   ____

3. List all the factors of 9.

   ____

4. 70 ÷ 7 = ______

5. How many digits are in 600?

   ____

6. Fill in the missing number.

   32, 40, 48, ______, 64

7. Write the length in centimeters.

   ____

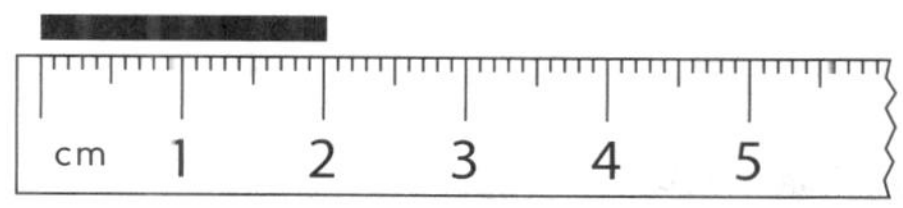

8. ______ quarts = 2 gallons

9. **Dollars Earned in May**

Audrey	$15
Dameon	$23
Jason	$12
Lauren	$18

   Who earned the most money?

   ____

10. Write two odd numbers that total the even number 20.

   ____

SCORE

1. Ⓨ Ⓝ
2. Ⓨ Ⓝ
3. Ⓨ Ⓝ
4. Ⓨ Ⓝ
5. Ⓨ Ⓝ
6. Ⓨ Ⓝ
7. Ⓨ Ⓝ
8. Ⓨ Ⓝ
9. Ⓨ Ⓝ
10. Ⓨ Ⓝ

___ / 10
Total

DAY

42

NAME: ____________________________

DIRECTIONS Solve each problem.

SCORE

1. Ⓨ Ⓝ
2. Ⓨ Ⓝ
3. Ⓨ Ⓝ
4. Ⓨ Ⓝ
5. Ⓨ Ⓝ
6. Ⓨ Ⓝ
7. Ⓨ Ⓝ
8. Ⓨ Ⓝ
9. Ⓨ Ⓝ
10. Ⓨ Ⓝ

___ / 10

Total

1. $\begin{array}{r} 46 \\ -\ 25 \\ \hline \end{array}$

2. Color $\frac{3}{10}$.

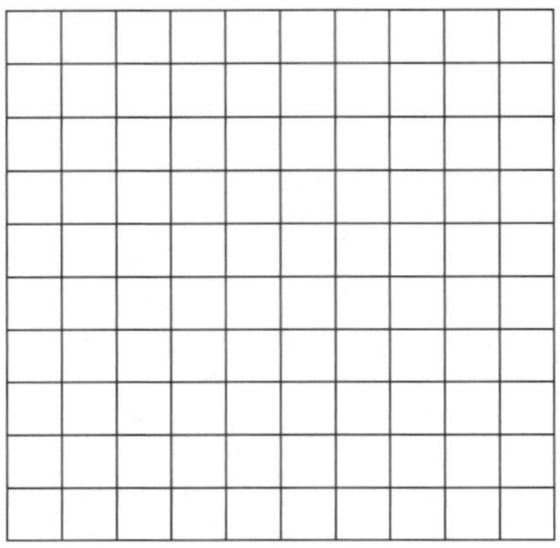

3. $9\overline{)18}$

4. List all the factors of 12.

____

5. Write the ordinal number after sixteenth.

____

6. 7 x ☐ = 21

7. Calculate the perimeter of a square with 5 cm sides.

____

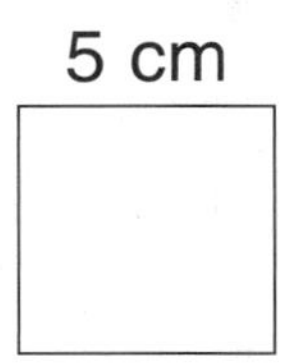

8. ________ inches = $\frac{1}{2}$ foot

9. True or false? Plane shapes are 3-dimensional.

____

10. Jack is 87 cm tall. Joe is 13 cm taller. How tall is Joe?

____

DAY 43

NAME: ____________________

DIRECTIONS Solve each problem.

1. $\begin{array}{r} 22 \\ +\ 17 \\ \hline \end{array}$

2. $\frac{1}{8}$ of 48 is ________

3. List all the factors of 16.

____

4. $8\overline{)64}$

5. Which is greater: 0.03 or 0.3?

____

6. 48 ÷ ☐ = 12

7. Fill in the blanks for the time shown.

12: ________
_____ past 12

8. How many days are in April?

____

9. Draw in the axes of symmetry.

10. Dad bought 4 hats that cost \$2.50 each. How much did he spend?

____

SCORE

1. Ⓨ Ⓝ
2. Ⓨ Ⓝ
3. Ⓨ Ⓝ
4. Ⓨ Ⓝ
5. Ⓨ Ⓝ
6. Ⓨ Ⓝ
7. Ⓨ Ⓝ
8. Ⓨ Ⓝ
9. Ⓨ Ⓝ
10. Ⓨ Ⓝ

___ / 10 Total

DAY
44

NAME: ____________________

DIRECTIONS Solve each problem.

SCORE

1. Ⓨ Ⓝ
2. Ⓨ Ⓝ
3. Ⓨ Ⓝ
4. Ⓨ Ⓝ
5. Ⓨ Ⓝ
6. Ⓨ Ⓝ
7. Ⓨ Ⓝ
8. Ⓨ Ⓝ
9. Ⓨ Ⓝ
10. Ⓨ Ⓝ

___ / 10 Total

1. 37 – 23 = ______

2. Shade 0.53.

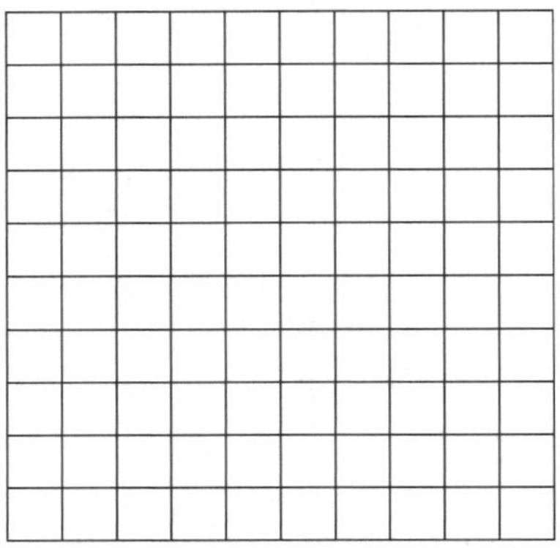

3. How many sevens are in twenty-eight?

____

4. 24 ÷ 3 = ______

5. What is the value of the digit 6 in 1,564?

____

6. ☐ x 8 = 24

7. Does a slice of pizza have a mass of more than 1 kilogram?

____

8. Write the length in inches.

______ inches

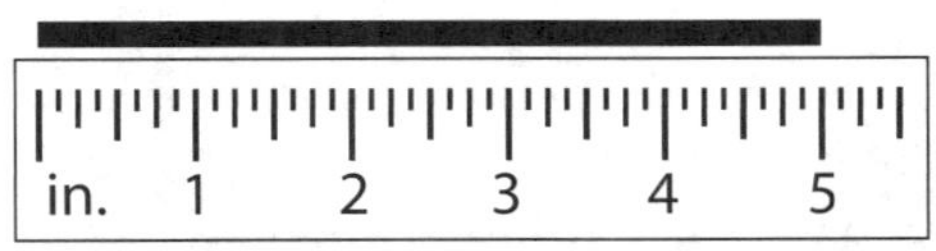

9. The cross-section will be a

____________________.

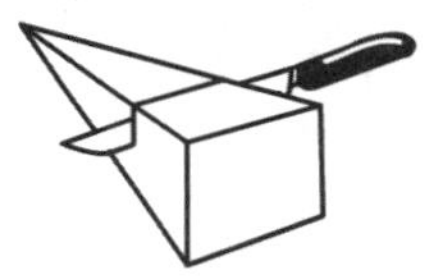

10. Choose a number:
Add 6.
Double the result.
Subtract 4.
Halve the result.
Subtract the number with which you began.
Write your ending number.

____________________.

NAME: ______________________

DIRECTIONS Solve each problem.

1. Calculate the sum of 23 and 15.

____

2.

$$\begin{array}{r} 6 \\ \times\ 5 \\ \hline \end{array}$$

3. $3 \overline{)27}$

4. List all the factors of 18.

____

5. 2,000 + 900 + 70 + 5 =

____

6. 4 x ☐ = 36

7. What is the abbreviation for cubic centimeter?

____

8. Which would be the best tool for measuring the temperature of water: a scale, a thermometer, or a meter stick?

____

9.

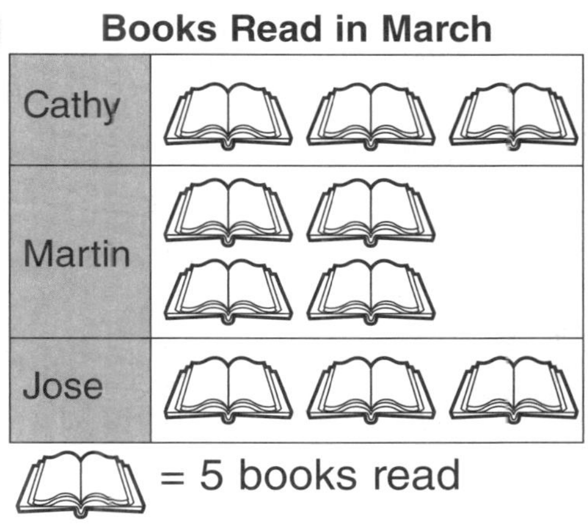

Which children read the same number of books?

____

10. Complete the multiplication wheel.

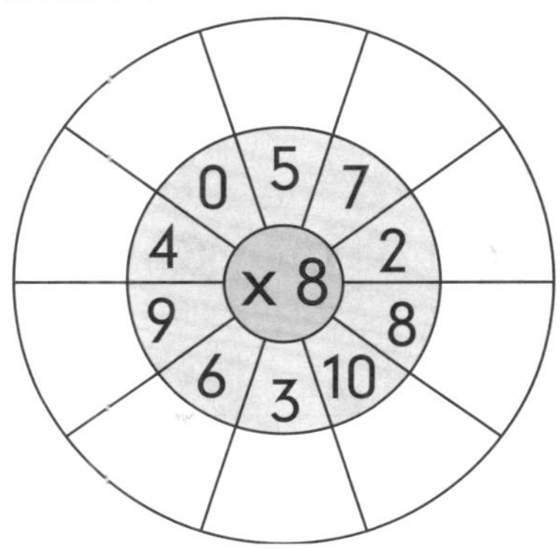

SCORE

1. Ⓨ Ⓝ
2. Ⓨ Ⓝ
3. Ⓨ Ⓝ
4. Ⓨ Ⓝ
5. Ⓨ Ⓝ
6. Ⓨ Ⓝ
7. Ⓨ Ⓝ
8. Ⓨ Ⓝ
9. Ⓨ Ⓝ
10. Ⓨ Ⓝ

___ / 10 Total

DAY

46

NAME: ____________________

DIRECTIONS Solve each problem.

SCORE

1. Ⓨ Ⓝ
2. Ⓨ Ⓝ
3. Ⓨ Ⓝ
4. Ⓨ Ⓝ
5. Ⓨ Ⓝ
6. Ⓨ Ⓝ
7. Ⓨ Ⓝ
8. Ⓨ Ⓝ
9. Ⓨ Ⓝ
10. Ⓨ Ⓝ

___ / 10

Total

1.

$$\begin{array}{r} 13 \\ -\ \ 6 \\ \hline \end{array}$$

2. 0.5 of 18 is ________.

3. How many groups of 6 are in the number 36?

____

4. 48 ÷ 6 = ________

5. What is the even number right before 36?

____

6. Fill in the missing number.

129, 139, 149, ________, 169

7. How many full oil bottles can be poured into the bucket?

____

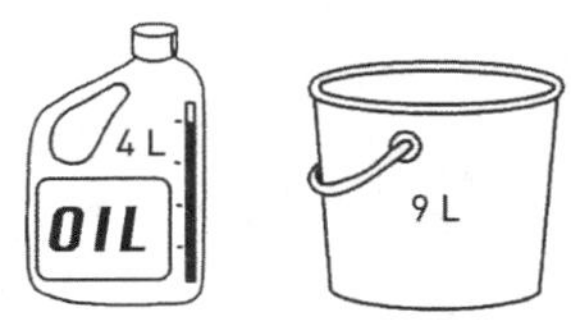

8. ________ inches = 2 feet

9. A regular octagon has:

________ angles

________ sides

________ axes of symmetry

10. What fraction must be added to $\frac{3}{4}$ of a pizza to make 1 whole pizza?

____

DAY 47

NAME: ______________________________

DIRECTIONS Solve each problem.

1. 4 + 7 + 6 = ________

2. What decimal is shaded?

____

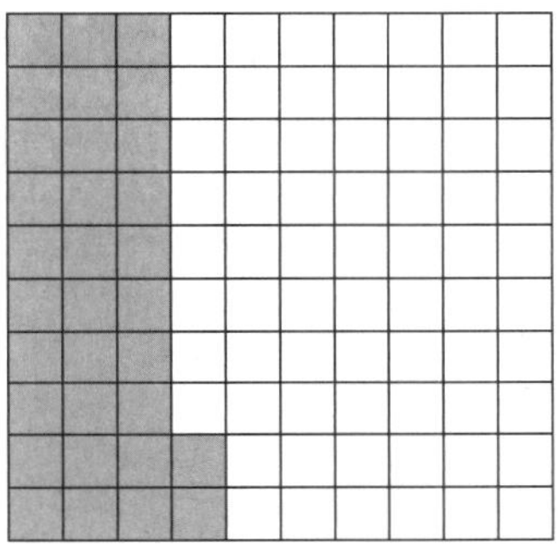

3. How many threes are in 21?

____

4. $6 \overline{)60}$

5. Is 42 smaller than 24?

____

6. ☐ x 2 = 18

7. What is the date of the first Monday in March?

____

FEBRUARY						
Sun	Mon	Tue	Wed	Thu	Fri	Sat
		1	2	3	4	5
6	7	8	9	10	11	12
13	14	15	16	17	18	19
20	21	22	23	24	25	26
27	28	29				

8. A movie starts at 3:15 P.M. and ends at 5:30 P.M. How long is the movie?

____

9. How many pairs of opposite parallel sides does a parallelogram have?

____

10. Our product is 72. The difference between us is 1. What numbers are we?

________ ________

SCORE

1. Ⓨ Ⓝ
2. Ⓨ Ⓝ
3. Ⓨ Ⓝ
4. Ⓨ Ⓝ
5. Ⓨ Ⓝ
6. Ⓨ Ⓝ
7. Ⓨ Ⓝ
8. Ⓨ Ⓝ
9. Ⓨ Ⓝ
10. Ⓨ Ⓝ

___ / 10 Total

NAME: ______________________

DIRECTIONS Solve each problem.

SCORE

1. Ⓨ Ⓝ
2. Ⓨ Ⓝ
3. Ⓨ Ⓝ
4. Ⓨ Ⓝ
5. Ⓨ Ⓝ
6. Ⓨ Ⓝ
7. Ⓨ Ⓝ
8. Ⓨ Ⓝ
9. Ⓨ Ⓝ
10. Ⓨ Ⓝ

___ / 10 Total

1. $33 - 7 =$ ________

2. $\frac{1}{5}$ of 15 is ________.

3. How many rows of 7 are in 49?

____

4. $42 \div 6 =$ ________

5. Is 0.6 less than 0.06?

____

6. $\square \div 7 = 6$

7. It took 4 buckets of water to fill a 20-liter tub. How many liters are in each bucket?

____

8. What is the temperature?

____

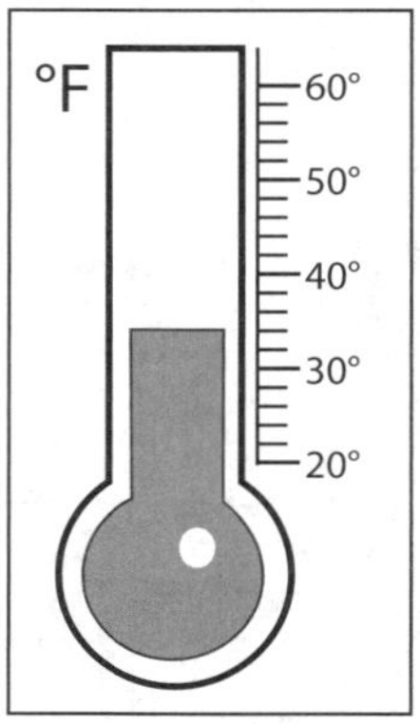

9.

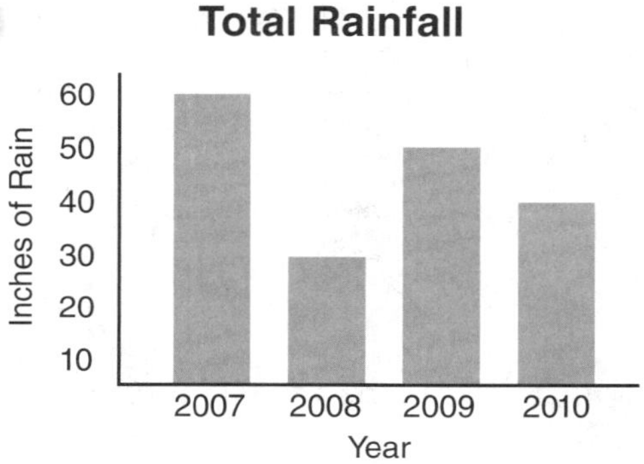

Which year received the least rainfall?

____

10. Use the same three colors for each flag. Color each flag in a different way.

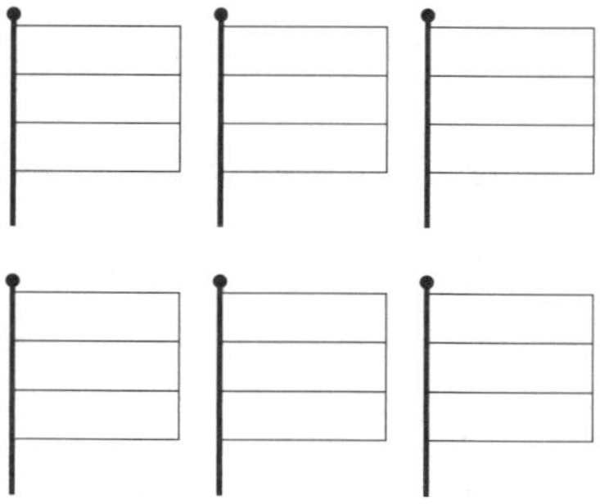

NAME: ______________________________

DIRECTIONS Solve each problem.

1.
$$\begin{array}{r} 16 \\ +\ \ 8 \\ \hline \end{array}$$

2. $\frac{1}{4}$ of 36 is ________.

3. List all the factors of 8.

____

4. $9\overline{)45}$

5. What is the value of the digit 4 in 10,472?

____

6. 36 + ☐ = 40

7. Each cube has 1-cm sides. What is the volume of the model?

____

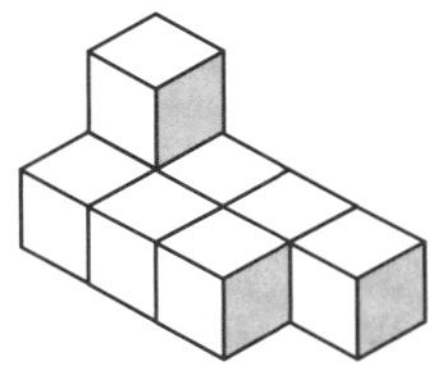

8. 2 hours = ________ minutes

9. Which solid has a square for the top, front, and side views?

____

10. Shawn is 36 in. tall. His mom is twice as tall as he is. How tall is Shawn's mom?

____

SCORE

1. Ⓨ Ⓝ
2. Ⓨ Ⓝ
3. Ⓨ Ⓝ
4. Ⓨ Ⓝ
5. Ⓨ Ⓝ
6. Ⓨ Ⓝ
7. Ⓨ Ⓝ
8. Ⓨ Ⓝ
9. Ⓨ Ⓝ
10. Ⓨ Ⓝ

___ / 10 Total

NAME: ____________________

DIRECTIONS Solve each problem.

SCORE

1. Ⓨ Ⓝ
2. Ⓨ Ⓝ
3. Ⓨ Ⓝ
4. Ⓨ Ⓝ
5. Ⓨ Ⓝ
6. Ⓨ Ⓝ
7. Ⓨ Ⓝ
8. Ⓨ Ⓝ
9. Ⓨ Ⓝ
10. Ⓨ Ⓝ

___ / 10 Total

1.

$$\begin{array}{r} 28 \\ -\ \ 9 \\ \hline \end{array}$$

2. 9 x 6 = ________

3. How many twos are in 18?

____

4. List all the factors of 24.

____

5. What is the number after 3,899?

____

6. 24 ÷ ☐ = 4

7. How many mm are in 2 cm?

____

8. ________ quarts = $\frac{1}{2}$ gallon

9. Circle the right angles.

A. B. C.

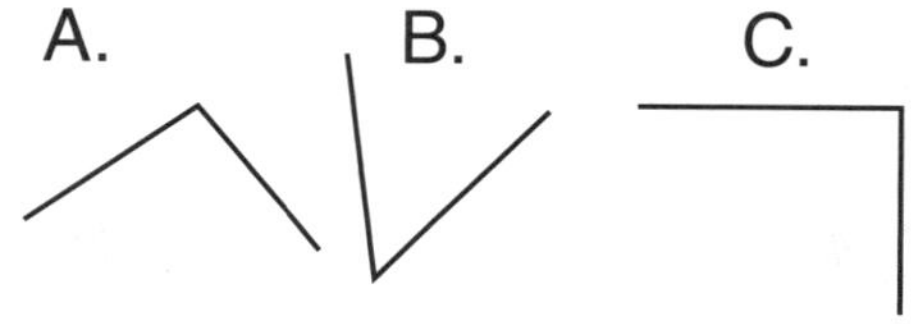

10. $\frac{1}{5}$ of 45 is 9, so $\frac{4}{5}$ of 45 is

____

DAY 51

NAME: ______________________

DIRECTIONS Solve each problem.

1. 16 + 8 + 14 = ________

2. Is $\frac{3}{10}$ larger than $\frac{29}{100}$?

____

3. $9\overline{)81}$

4. 54 divided by 9 is ________

5. What is the next odd number after 421?

____

6. Write the number that comes next in the pattern.
41, 31, 21, 11,

____

7. Write the line length in millimeters.

____

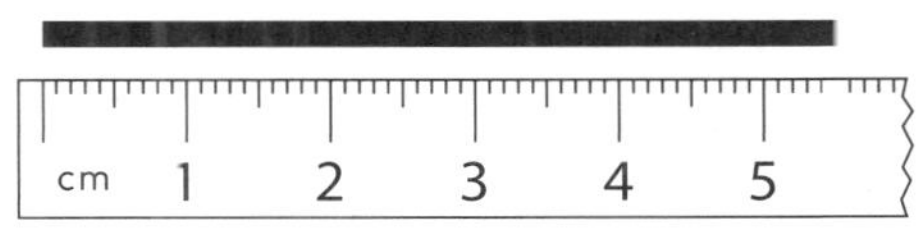

8. ________ yard = 18 inches

9. Draw in the diagonals for the shape.

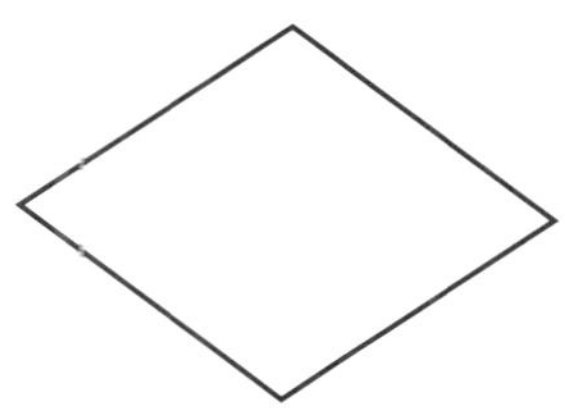

10. Write two odd numbers that total the even number 16.

____

SCORE

1. Ⓨ Ⓝ
2. Ⓨ Ⓝ
3. Ⓨ Ⓝ
4. Ⓨ Ⓝ
5. Ⓨ Ⓝ
6. Ⓨ Ⓝ
7. Ⓨ Ⓝ
8. Ⓨ Ⓝ
9. Ⓨ Ⓝ
10. Ⓨ Ⓝ

___ / 10
Total

DAY 52

NAME: ____________________

DIRECTIONS Solve each problem.

SCORE

1. Ⓨ Ⓝ
2. Ⓨ Ⓝ
3. Ⓨ Ⓝ
4. Ⓨ Ⓝ
5. Ⓨ Ⓝ
6. Ⓨ Ⓝ
7. Ⓨ Ⓝ
8. Ⓨ Ⓝ
9. Ⓨ Ⓝ
10. Ⓨ Ⓝ

___ / 10 Total

1. 41 – 8 = ________

2. $1.50 + $1.25 = ________

3. How many sixes are in 30?

____

4. 72 ÷ 9 = ________

5. Circle the larger number.

2,463   2,634

6. ☐ x 4 = 24

7. Calculate the area of a square with 9-cm sides.

____

8. How many months are in a year?

____

9.

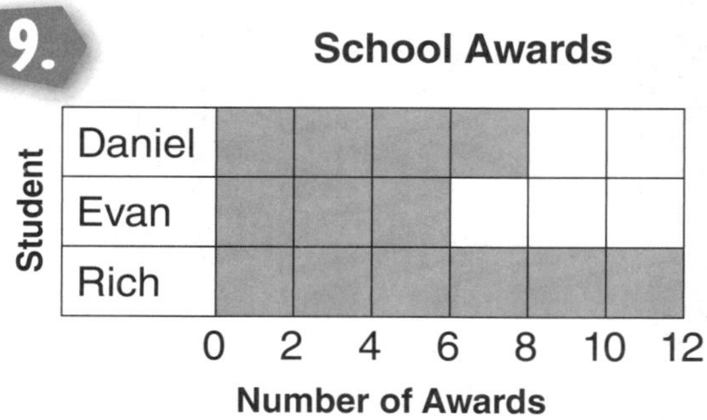

How many awards did Daniel win?

____

10. Follow the pattern in the first circle to complete the second circle.

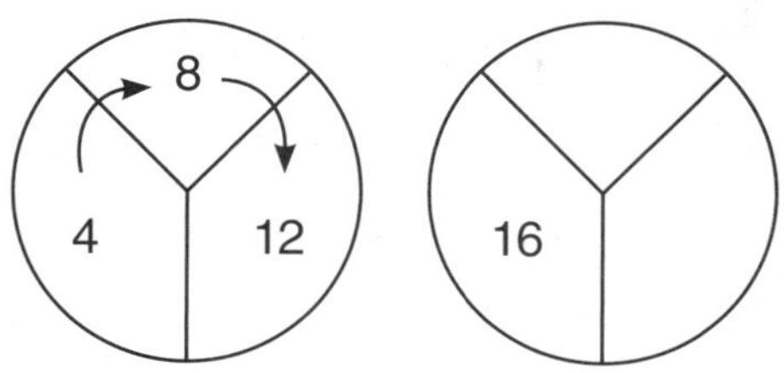

NAME: ______________________________

DIRECTIONS Solve each problem.

1.

$$\begin{array}{r} 24 \\ +\ 9 \\ \hline \end{array}$$

2. $\frac{4}{5}$ of 30 is ________

3. Divide 36 in 4 equal rows.

____

4. $7\overline{)28}$

5. What is the value of the tens place in 1,906?

____

6. ☐ ÷ 5 = 6

7. Draw and write the time that is 15 minutes later.

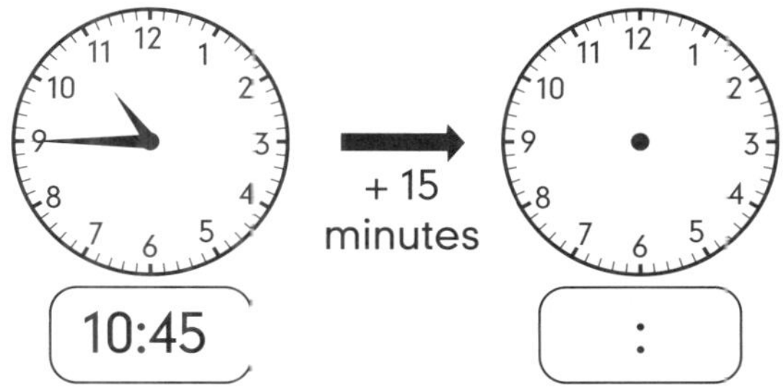

8. Would you use square inches or square feet to measure the area of a piece of paper?

____

9. What does the arrow show?

____

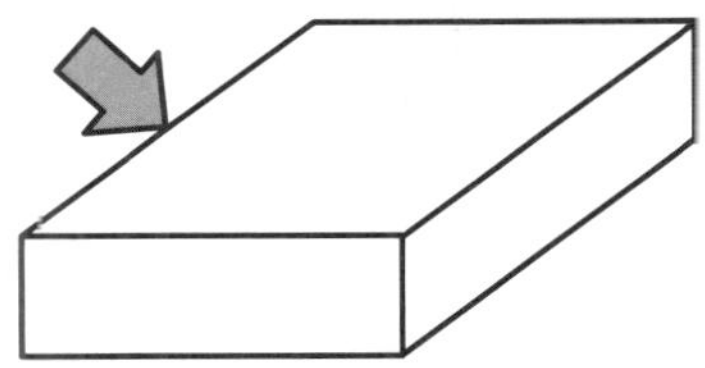

10. If one ticket costs $3.75, how much do 4 tickets cost?

____

SCORE

1. Ⓨ Ⓝ
2. Ⓨ Ⓝ
3. Ⓨ Ⓝ
4. Ⓨ Ⓝ
5. Ⓨ Ⓝ
6. Ⓨ Ⓝ
7. Ⓨ Ⓝ
8. Ⓨ Ⓝ
9. Ⓨ Ⓝ
10. Ⓨ Ⓝ

___ / 10
Total

NAME: ______________________________

DIRECTIONS Solve each problem.

SCORE

1. Ⓨ Ⓝ
2. Ⓨ Ⓝ
3. Ⓨ Ⓝ
4. Ⓨ Ⓝ
5. Ⓨ Ⓝ
6. Ⓨ Ⓝ
7. Ⓨ Ⓝ
8. Ⓨ Ⓝ
9. Ⓨ Ⓝ
10. Ⓨ Ⓝ

___ / 10 Total

1. $\begin{array}{r} 45 \\ -\ \ 7 \\ \hline \end{array}$

2. Write 0.67 as a fraction.

____

3. 56 ÷ 7 = ________

4. Divide 63 into 9 equal groups.

____

5. Write the ordinal number for 36.

____

6. 36 ÷ ☐ = 6

7. Would you use kilograms or grams to measure the mass of a watermelon?

____

8. Circle the most likely distance to the store from your house.

1 kilometer

1 meter

1 gram

9. Label with *reflection*, *translation*, or *rotation*.

____

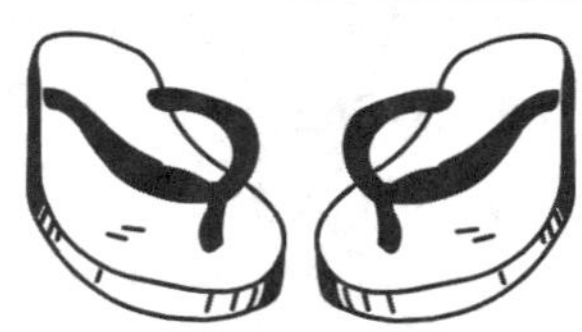

10. Complete the chart. Round the number 872.

Tens	
Hundreds	

NAME: ______________________________

DIRECTIONS Solve each problem.

1. Find the sum of 496 and 784

____

2.
```
   3
 x 8
-----
```

3. 7 ⟌ 14

4. Divide 54 into 6 equal groups.

____

5. Is 36 an even number?

____

6. To find 12 ÷ 4, we say

☐ x 4 = 12

7. Ezra takes 2 steps to cover a meter. She walks 500 meters to the bus stop. How many steps does she take?

____

8. 24 inches = ______ feet

9. **Sports Played Each Year**

	1st Trimester	2nd Trimester	3rd Trimester
Troy	soccer	basketball	baseball
Jessica	golf	basketball	track
Allison	soccer	diving	swimming

Which 3 sports does Allison play?

____

____

10. Use different colors to color pairs of numbers that equal the product shown in the center.

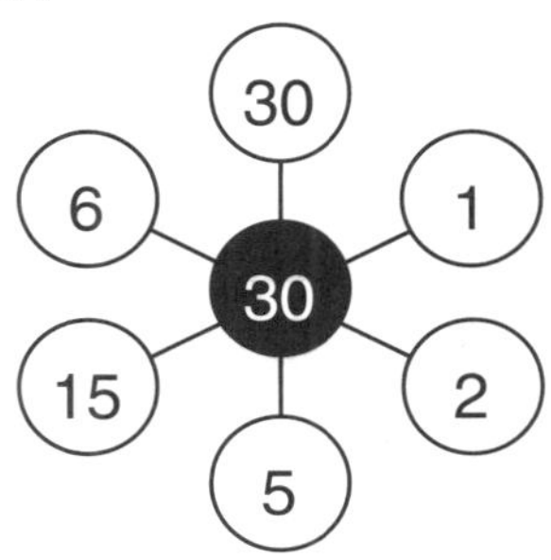

SCORE

1. Ⓨ Ⓝ
2. Ⓨ Ⓝ
3. Ⓨ Ⓝ
4. Ⓨ Ⓝ
5. Ⓨ Ⓝ
6. Ⓨ Ⓝ
7. Ⓨ Ⓝ
8. Ⓨ Ⓝ
9. Ⓨ Ⓝ
10. Ⓨ Ⓝ

___ / 10 Total

DAY 56

NAME: ______________________________

DIRECTIONS Solve each problem.

SCORE

1. Ⓨ Ⓝ
2. Ⓨ Ⓝ
3. Ⓨ Ⓝ
4. Ⓨ Ⓝ
5. Ⓨ Ⓝ
6. Ⓨ Ⓝ
7. Ⓨ Ⓝ
8. Ⓨ Ⓝ
9. Ⓨ Ⓝ
10. Ⓨ Ⓝ

___ / 10 Total

1. $62 - 8 =$ ________

2. Color $\frac{3}{100}$.

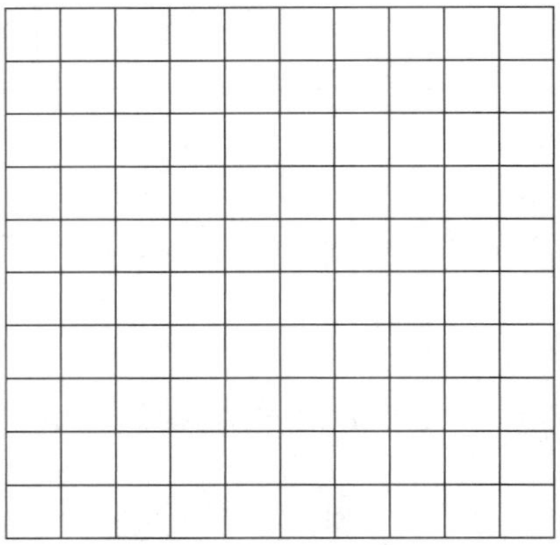

3. How many groups of 6 are in 42?

____

4. $5 \overline{)50}$

5. What is the place value of 3 in 3,916?

____

6. Fill in the missing number.

18, 24, ________, 36, 42

7. Circle the model that when placed in the bucket would raise the water level most.

____

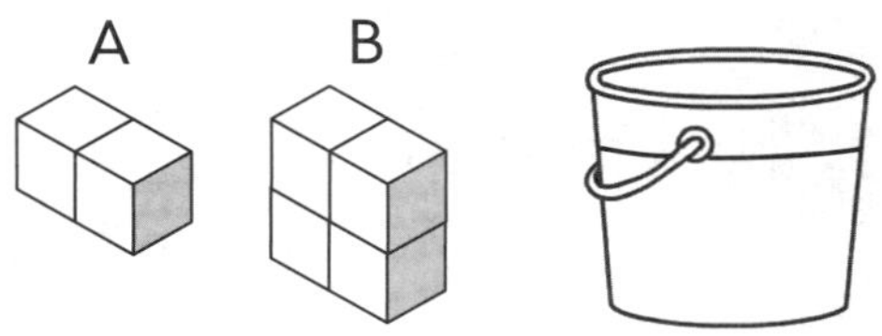

8. If today is Tuesday, what day of the week is 15 days later?

____

9. Draw the axes of symmetry.

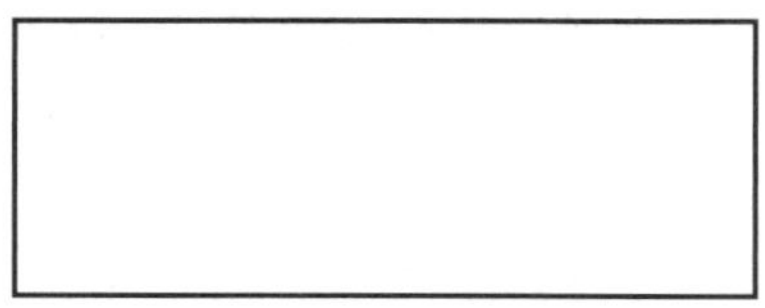

10. Javier is cutting 10 feet long pieces of string. How many pieces of string can he cut if he has 79 feet of string?

____

NAME: ______________________________

DIRECTIONS Solve each problem.

SCORE

1.
$$\begin{array}{r} 59 \\ +\ 9 \\ \hline \end{array}$$

2. \$5.00 - \$2.25 = ________

3. Share 63 equally among 7.

____

4. 49 ÷ 7 = ________

5. Round 132 to the nearest ten.

____

6. 18 + ☐ = 25

7. On what day of the week is March 15th?

____

FEBRUARY						
Sun	Mon	Tue	Wed	Thu	Fri	Sat
		1	2	3	4	5
6	7	8	9	10	11	12
13	14	15	16	17	18	19
20	21	22	23	24	25	26
27	28	29				

8. Do you go to bed in the A.M. or P.M.?

____

9. Draw a line from the real-life object to the solid.

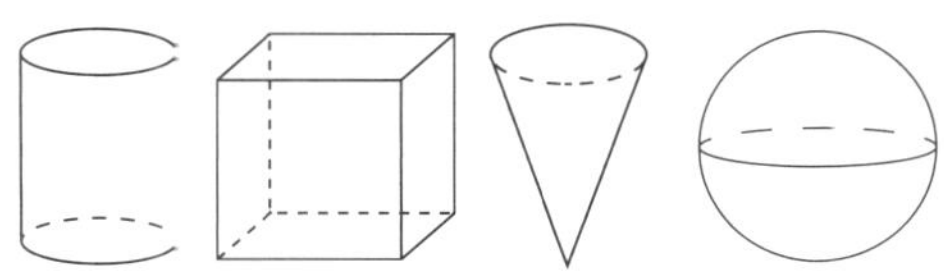

10. If you add me to 493, the sum is 1,221. What number am I?

____

1. Ⓨ Ⓝ
2. Ⓨ Ⓝ
3. Ⓨ Ⓝ
4. Ⓨ Ⓝ
5. Ⓨ Ⓝ
6. Ⓨ Ⓝ
7. Ⓨ Ⓝ
8. Ⓨ Ⓝ
9. Ⓨ Ⓝ
10. Ⓨ Ⓝ

___ / 10

Total

DAY 58

NAME: ____________________

DIRECTIONS Solve each problem.

SCORE

1. Ⓨ Ⓝ
2. Ⓨ Ⓝ
3. Ⓨ Ⓝ
4. Ⓨ Ⓝ
5. Ⓨ Ⓝ
6. Ⓨ Ⓝ
7. Ⓨ Ⓝ
8. Ⓨ Ⓝ
9. Ⓨ Ⓝ
10. Ⓨ Ⓝ

___ / 10 Total

1.

$$\begin{array}{r} 53 \\ -\ \ 7 \\ \hline \end{array}$$

2. Write 0.99 as a fraction.

____

3. $8\overline{)24}$

4. How many sevens are in 70?

____

5. Write the smallest 3-digit number using 2, 8, and 1.

____

6. 72 ÷ ☐ = 9

7. Record in milliliters.

________ mL

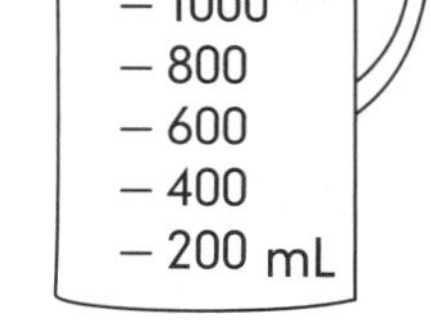

8. What is the temperature?

____

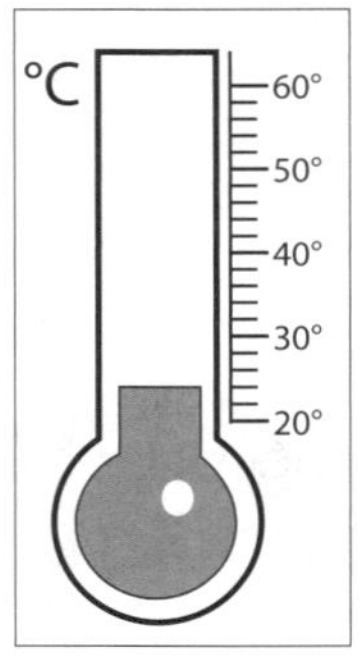

9. Record the data in the chart.

Child's Name	Number of CDs

Jahir has 23 music CDs.
Olivia has 15 music CDs.
Gerald has 35 music CDs.
Mimi has 3 music CDs.

10. Plot each set of coordinates to make a rectangle.
(A, 2); (A, 5); (E, 2); (E, 5)

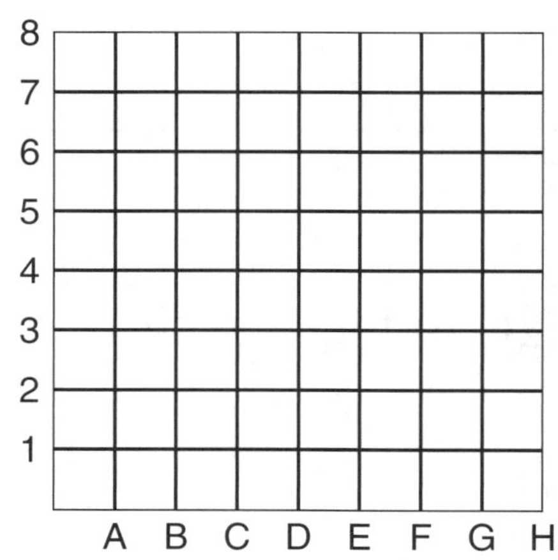

NAME: ______________________________

DIRECTIONS Solve each problem.

1. 35 + 8 = ________

2. $\frac{8}{10}$ of 90 = ________

3. Share 35 equally by 5.

____

4. 54 ÷ 9 = ________

5. Round 1,874 to the nearest hundred.

____

6. ☐ − 16 = 23

7. Each cube has 1-cm sides. What is the volume of the model?

____

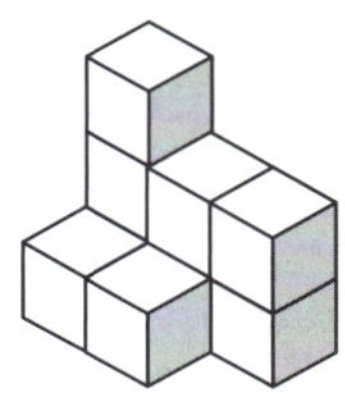

8. 120 seconds = ________ minutes

9. Does this shape tessellate?

____

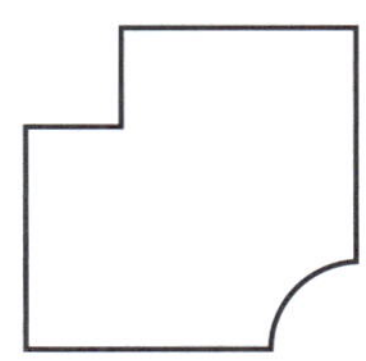

10. Bananas cost 19¢ each. How much will 6 bananas cost?

____

SCORE

1. Ⓨ Ⓝ
2. Ⓨ Ⓝ
3. Ⓨ Ⓝ
4. Ⓨ Ⓝ
5. Ⓨ Ⓝ
6. Ⓨ Ⓝ
7. Ⓨ Ⓝ
8. Ⓨ Ⓝ
9. Ⓨ Ⓝ
10. Ⓨ Ⓝ

___ / 10 Total

DAY 60

NAME: ______________________________

DIRECTIONS Solve each problem.

SCORE

1. Ⓨ Ⓝ

2. Ⓨ Ⓝ

3. Ⓨ Ⓝ

4. Ⓨ Ⓝ

5. Ⓨ Ⓝ

6. Ⓨ Ⓝ

7. Ⓨ Ⓝ

8. Ⓨ Ⓝ

9. Ⓨ Ⓝ

10. Ⓨ Ⓝ

___ / 10

Total

1. 28 – 19 = ________

2.

$$\begin{array}{r} 7 \\ \times\ 3 \\ \hline \end{array}$$

3. $8\overline{)32}$

4. Divide 45 into 5 equal groups.

____

5. What is the value of the tens place in 3,571?

____

6. 72 – ☐ = 12

7. Is the area of a handprint measured in cm^2 or m^2?

____

8. ________ pints = 2 quarts

9.

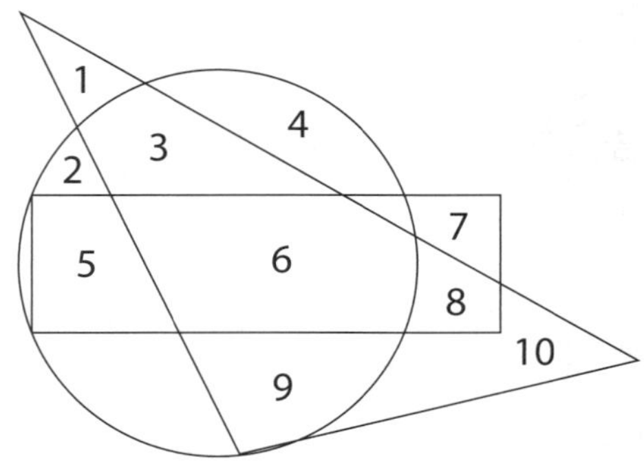

Which numbers are inside the triangle but not in the circle or rectangle?

____

10. Circle the card that shows the same fraction as the example on top.

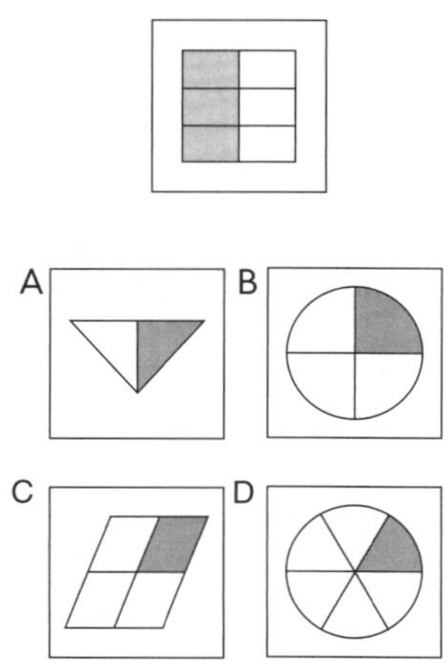

NAME: ______________________________

DIRECTIONS Solve each problem.

1.
$$\begin{array}{r} 56 \\ +\ \ 8 \\ \hline \end{array}$$

2. Color $\frac{30}{100}$.

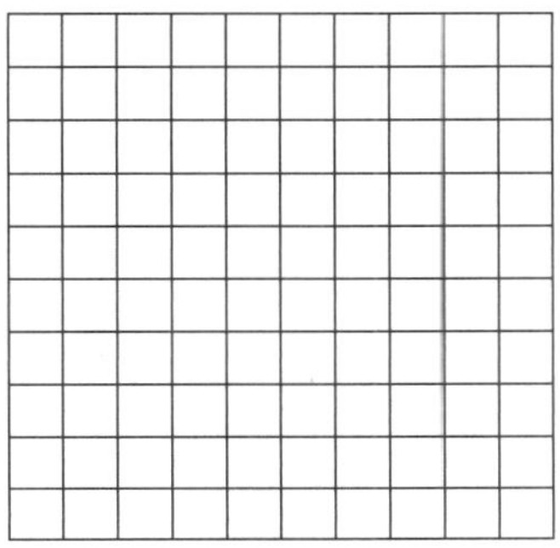

3. $50 \div 5 =$ ________

4. $63 \div 9 =$ ________

5. What is the first odd number before 81?

____

6. Fill in the missing number.

200, 400, _____, 800, 1,000

7. Write the length in centimeters.

____

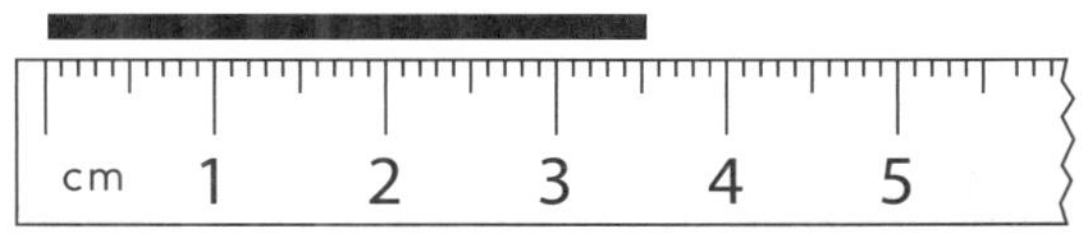

8. ________ yards = 72 inches

9. What shape is the base of a cylinder?

____

10. Complete the addition grid.

+	7	15	18	23	25	28
19						
29						
39						

SCORE

1. Ⓨ Ⓝ
2. Ⓨ Ⓝ
3. Ⓨ Ⓝ
4. Ⓨ Ⓝ
5. Ⓨ Ⓝ
6. Ⓨ Ⓝ
7. Ⓨ Ⓝ
8. Ⓨ Ⓝ
9. Ⓨ Ⓝ
10. Ⓨ Ⓝ

___ / 10
Total

DAY
62

NAME: ____________________

DIRECTIONS Solve each problem.

SCORE

1. Ⓨ Ⓝ
2. Ⓨ Ⓝ
3. Ⓨ Ⓝ
4. Ⓨ Ⓝ
5. Ⓨ Ⓝ
6. Ⓨ Ⓝ
7. Ⓨ Ⓝ
8. Ⓨ Ⓝ
9. Ⓨ Ⓝ
10. Ⓨ Ⓝ

___ / 10
Total

1.

$$\begin{array}{r} 17 \\ -\ \ 9 \\ \hline \end{array}$$

2. Circle the greater number.

0.02   0.2

3. $12\overline{)84}$

4. $36 \div 6 =$ ________

5. Write 2,365 in expanded notation.

____

____

6. $23 + \square = 50$

7. Calculate the perimeter of a square with 2-cm sides.

____

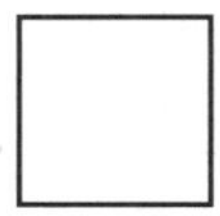

2 cm

8. How many faces does a rectangular prism have?

____

9. Draw intersecting lines.

10. It takes 5 bottles of juice to fill a 20-liter tank. How many liters are in each bottle?

____

NAME: ______________________________

DIRECTIONS Solve each problem.

1. $13 + 4 + 17 =$ ________

2. $\frac{8}{10}$ of 70 is ________

3. $60 \div 6 =$ ________

4. $63 \div 7 =$ ________

5. What is the value of the digit 5 in 42,562?

____

6. $\square \times 5 = 10$

7. Complete the labels for the time shown.

7: ______
____ past 7

8. Write the length in inches.

________ inches

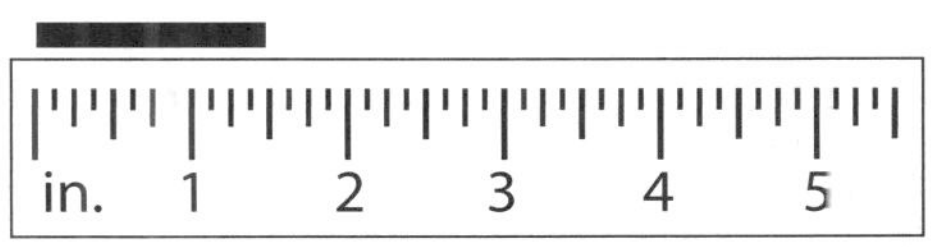

9. Are these lines perpendicular? ________

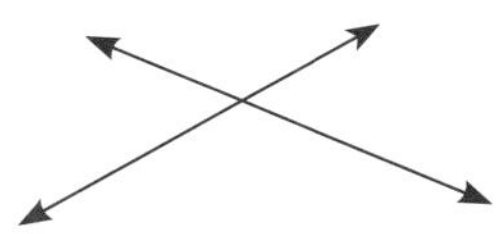

10. Michael buys 1 notebook and 5 pencils. If the notebook costs $3.50 and the pencils are 25¢ each, what is the total he spent?

____

SCORE

1. Ⓨ Ⓝ
2. Ⓨ Ⓝ
3. Ⓨ Ⓝ
4. Ⓨ Ⓝ
5. Ⓨ Ⓝ
6. Ⓨ Ⓝ
7. Ⓨ Ⓝ
8. Ⓨ Ⓝ
9. Ⓨ Ⓝ
10. Ⓨ Ⓝ

___ / 10
Total

DAY 64

NAME: ____________________

DIRECTIONS Solve each problem.

SCORE

1. Ⓨ Ⓝ
2. Ⓨ Ⓝ
3. Ⓨ Ⓝ
4. Ⓨ Ⓝ
5. Ⓨ Ⓝ
6. Ⓨ Ⓝ
7. Ⓨ Ⓝ
8. Ⓨ Ⓝ
9. Ⓨ Ⓝ
10. Ⓨ Ⓝ

___ / 10
Total

1. Subtract 19 from 36.

____

2. Is 0.4 less than 0.04?

____

3. 81 ÷ 9 = ________

4. Divide 27 into 3 equal groups.

____

5. Order the numbers from smallest to largest.
1,624; 1,264; 1,426

______ ______ ______

6. 8 x ☐ = 64

7. Circle the best estimate for the weight of the object.

100 g 2 kg 5 kg 10 kg

8. Which would be the best measure for the width of your pointer finger: a foot, a degree, or a centimeter?

____

9. Does an angle get bigger if you make its lines longer?

____

10. Complete the chart below to represent the shaded part of the hundred grid.

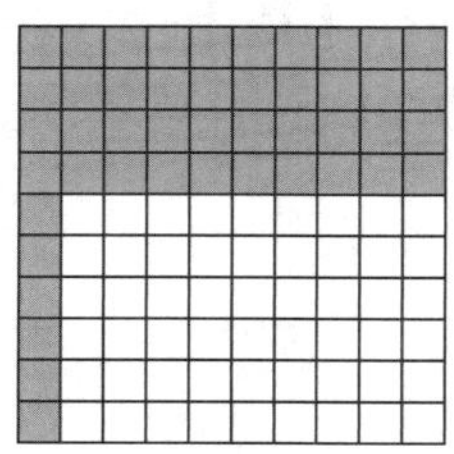

$\frac{\quad}{100}$	0.	%

NAME: ______________________________

DIRECTIONS Solve each problem.

1.
$$\begin{array}{r} 18 \\ +\ 13 \\ \hline \end{array}$$

2. 10 rows of 6 is ________.

3. $5\overline{)45}$

4. 56 ÷ 7 = ________

5. Is 2,509 less than 2,590?

____

6. 12 x ☐ = 36

7. Circle the best estimate for the area of a handprint.

75 cm^2 750 cm^2

8. 108 inches equals how many yards?

____

9. What type of prism is shown?

____

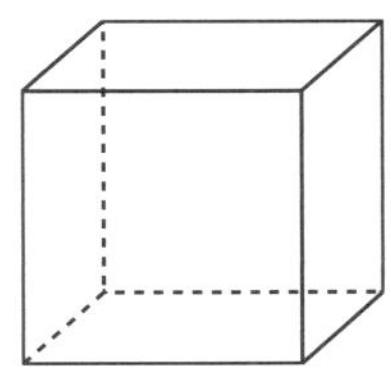

10. Complete the multiplication wheel.

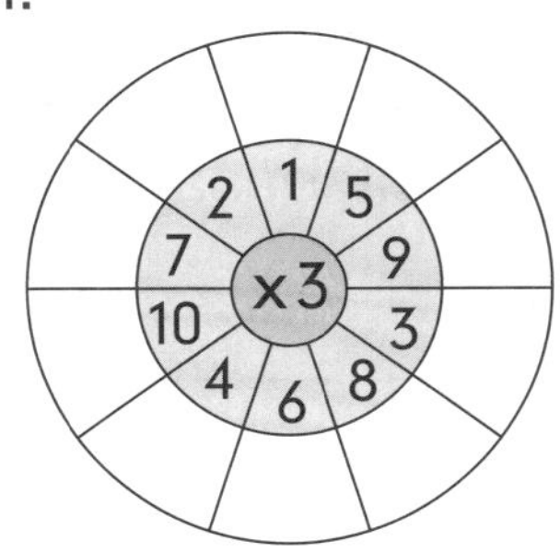

SCORE

1. Ⓨ Ⓝ
2. Ⓨ Ⓝ
3. Ⓨ Ⓝ
4. Ⓨ Ⓝ
5. Ⓨ Ⓝ
6. Ⓨ Ⓝ
7. Ⓨ Ⓝ
8. Ⓨ Ⓝ
9. Ⓨ Ⓝ
10. Ⓨ Ⓝ

___ / 10
Total

DAY 66

NAME: ____________________

DIRECTIONS Solve each problem.

SCORE

1. Ⓨ Ⓝ
2. Ⓨ Ⓝ
3. Ⓨ Ⓝ
4. Ⓨ Ⓝ
5. Ⓨ Ⓝ
6. Ⓨ Ⓝ
7. Ⓨ Ⓝ
8. Ⓨ Ⓝ
9. Ⓨ Ⓝ
10. Ⓨ Ⓝ

___ / 10 Total

1.

$$\begin{array}{r} 43 \\ -\ 29 \\ \hline \end{array}$$

2. $\frac{3}{5}$ of 35 is ________

3. The quotient of 35 and 7 is

____________________.

4. $9\overline{)72}$

5. Write the numeral for two thousand three.

____

6. Fill in the missing number.

4, 8, ________, 16, 20

7. How many 250-milliliter bottles are needed to fill a 5-liter bucket?

____

8. Calculate the number of seconds there are in 2 minutes.

____

9. **Dollars Earned in May**

Audrey	$15
Dameon	$23
Jason	$12
Lauren	$18

How much more did Audrey earn than Jason?

____

10. Find the perimeter of a figure with these 4 sides: 3 cm, 5 cm, 7 cm, 4 cm.

____

DAY 67

NAME: ______________________________

DIRECTIONS Solve each problem.

1. 23 + 17 = ________

2. $\frac{1}{2}$ of 14 is ________

3. 14 ÷ 2 = ________

4. Divide 50 by 10. ________

5. How many digits are in the number 2,967?

____

6. 45 – ☐ = 40

7. How many Mondays are in February?

____

FEBRUARY						
Sun	Mon	Tue	Wed	Thu	Fri	Sat
		1	2	3	4	5
6	7	8	9	10	11	12
13	14	15	16	17	18	19
20	21	22	23	24	25	26
27	28	29				

8. Trish starts to watch TV at 7:30 P.M. and ends at 8:10 P.M. How long did she watch?

____

9. Name this shape.

____

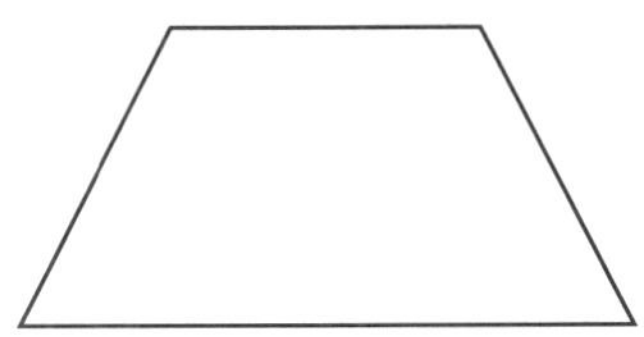

10. Our sum is 13. The difference between us is 1. What numbers are we?

____

SCORE

1. Ⓨ Ⓝ
2. Ⓨ Ⓝ
3. Ⓨ Ⓝ
4. Ⓨ Ⓝ
5. Ⓨ Ⓝ
6. Ⓨ Ⓝ
7. Ⓨ Ⓝ
8. Ⓨ Ⓝ
9. Ⓨ Ⓝ
10. Ⓨ Ⓝ

___ / 10

Total

DAY 68

NAME: ______________________________

DIRECTIONS Solve each problem.

SCORE

1. Ⓨ Ⓝ
2. Ⓨ Ⓝ
3. Ⓨ Ⓝ
4. Ⓨ Ⓝ
5. Ⓨ Ⓝ
6. Ⓨ Ⓝ
7. Ⓨ Ⓝ
8. Ⓨ Ⓝ
9. Ⓨ Ⓝ
10. Ⓨ Ⓝ

___ / 10 Total

1. 18 – 9 = ________

2. What decimal is shaded?

____

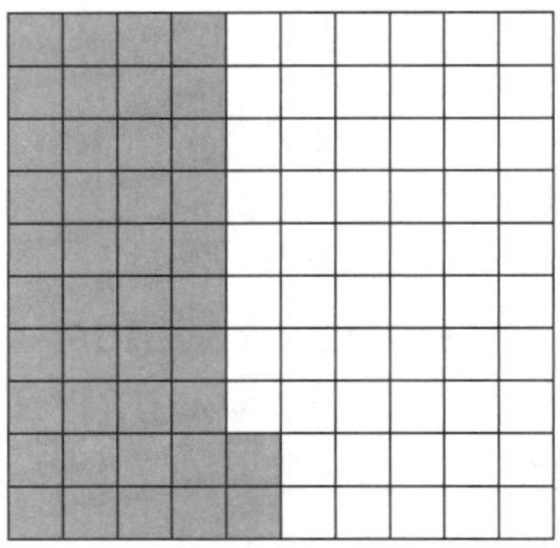

3. $6\overline{)96}$

4. 55 ÷ 11 = ________

5. What is the value in the hundreds place in 1,463?

____

6. 6 x ☐ = 42

7. How many cups of ice cream will fill the tub of ice cream?

____

8. Which months make up the third quarter of the year?

____

____

____

9. Draw the axes of symmetry.

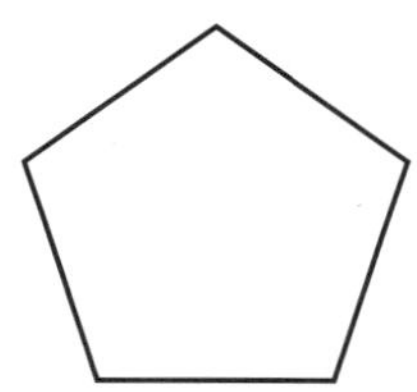

10. If tile A is rotated, which tile would it *not* look like?

____

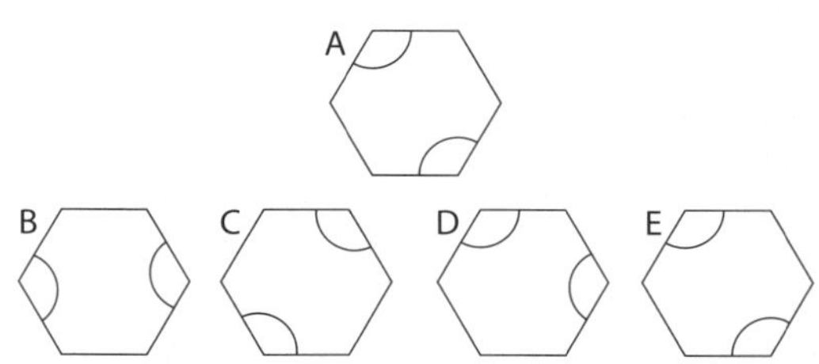

NAME: ______________________________

DIRECTIONS Solve each problem.

1.

$$\begin{array}{r} 42 \\ +\ 19 \\ \hline \end{array}$$

2. $\frac{1}{4}$ of 28 = ________

3. How many threes are in the number twelve?

____

4. 58 ÷ 6 = ________

5. Write the largest 4-digit number using 3, 7, 2, and 5.

____

6. 70 – ☐ = 55

7. Is this a leap year?

____

FEBRUARY						
Sun	Mon	Tue	Wed	Thu	Fri	Sat
		1	2	3	4	5
6	7	8	9	10	11	12
13	14	15	16	17	18	19
20	21	22	23	24	25	26
27	28	29				

8. If the outdoor temperature were 32°F, would you more likely build a snowman or go swimming in the ocean?

____

9. Color the solids that have a triangle for a front view.

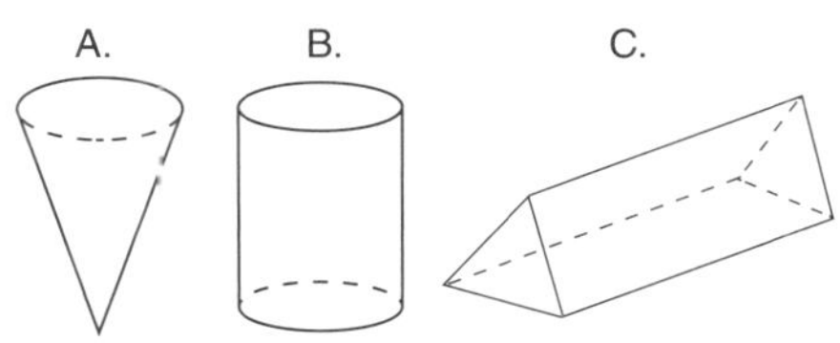

10. It takes David 15 minutes to ride his bike around the block. How many times can he ride around the block in 45 minutes?

____

SCORE

1. Ⓨ Ⓝ
2. Ⓨ Ⓝ
3. Ⓨ Ⓝ
4. Ⓨ Ⓝ
5. Ⓨ Ⓝ
6. Ⓨ Ⓝ
7. Ⓨ Ⓝ
8. Ⓨ Ⓝ
9. Ⓨ Ⓝ
10. Ⓨ Ⓝ

___ / 10
Total

NAME: ______________________________

DIRECTIONS Solve each problem.

SCORE

1. Ⓨ Ⓝ
2. Ⓨ Ⓝ
3. Ⓨ Ⓝ
4. Ⓨ Ⓝ
5. Ⓨ Ⓝ
6. Ⓨ Ⓝ
7. Ⓨ Ⓝ
8. Ⓨ Ⓝ
9. Ⓨ Ⓝ
10. Ⓨ Ⓝ

___ / 10 Total

1.

$$\begin{array}{r} 45 \\ -\ 19 \\ \hline \end{array}$$

2. 9 x 9 = ________

3. $3\overline{)24}$

4. 48 ÷ 6 = ________

5. Is 1,442 closer to 1,400 or 1,500?

____

6. Complete the chart to find the cost of 7 pens at 10¢ each.

1 Pen	2 Pens	3 Pens	4 Pens
10¢			
5 Pens	6 Pens	7 Pens	8 Pens

7. A classroom is 48 m^2 and the coat room is 12 m^2. What is the total area?

____

8. 1 hour = ________ minutes

9. Color the polygons.

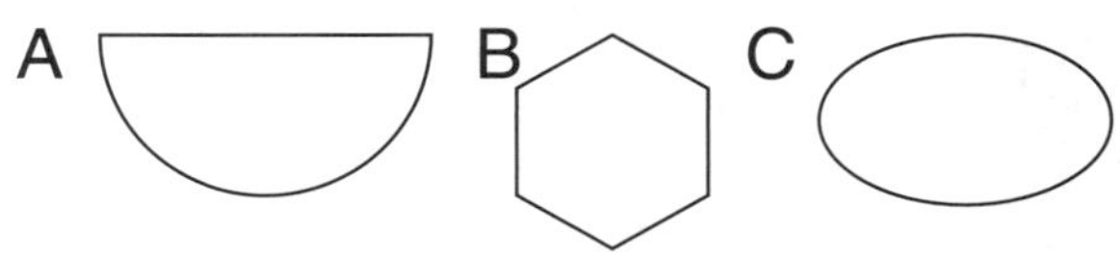

10. Shade half of the area so that both the shaded and unshaded parts have the same shape.

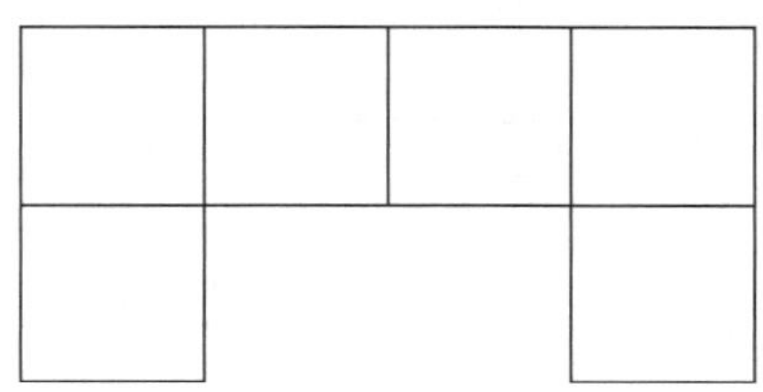

NAME: ____________________

DIRECTIONS Solve each problem.

1. 54 + 1 = ______

2. $\frac{1}{8}$ of 64 is ______

3. How many sixes are in 24?

____

4. 36 ÷ 4 = ______

5. Write 2,047 in words.

____

____

6. Fill in the missing number.

6, 12, 18, ______, 30

7. Measure in centimeters.

____

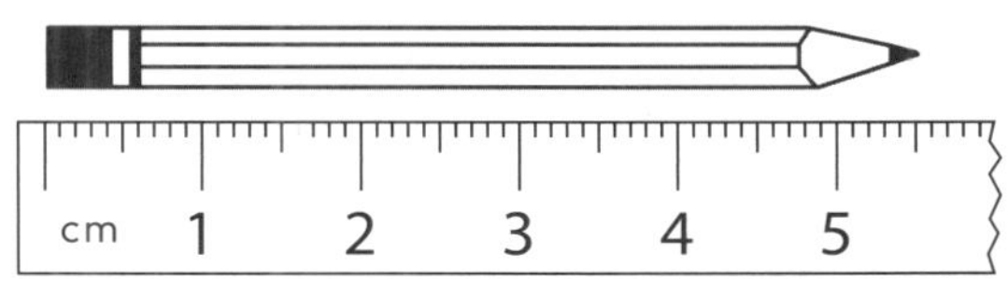

8. ______ pints = 2 gallons

9.

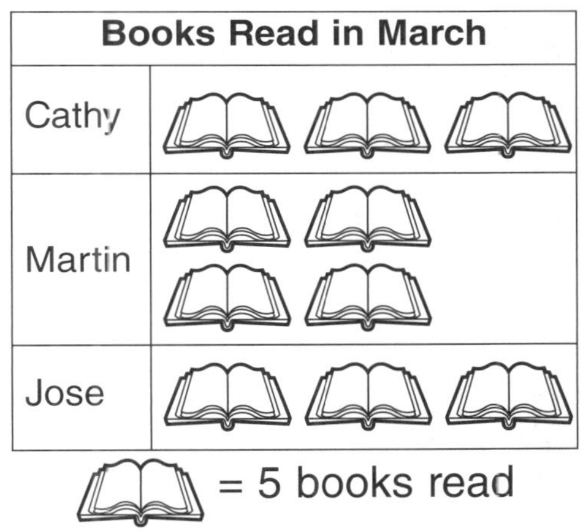

How many more books did Martin read than Cathy?

____

10. Write two odd numbers that total the even number 24.

____

SCORE

1. Ⓨ Ⓝ
2. Ⓨ Ⓝ
3. Ⓨ Ⓝ
4. Ⓨ Ⓝ
5. Ⓨ Ⓝ
6. Ⓨ Ⓝ
7. Ⓨ Ⓝ
8. Ⓨ Ⓝ
9. Ⓨ Ⓝ
10. Ⓨ Ⓝ

___ / 10
Total

DAY
72

NAME: ____________________________

DIRECTIONS Solve each problem.

SCORE

1. Ⓨ Ⓝ
2. Ⓨ Ⓝ
3. Ⓨ Ⓝ
4. Ⓨ Ⓝ
5. Ⓨ Ⓝ
6. Ⓨ Ⓝ
7. Ⓨ Ⓝ
8. Ⓨ Ⓝ
9. Ⓨ Ⓝ
10. Ⓨ Ⓝ

___ / 10
Total

1. 34 – 19 = ________

2. Write 0.3 as a fraction.

____

3. Divide 64 into eight groups.

____

4. $3\overline{)24}$

5. Order the numbers from largest to smallest.

2,097; 2,079; 2,907

______ ______ ______

6. 4 x ☐ = 28

7. Calculate the area of a square with 6-cm sides.

____

6 cm

8. 3 yards = ________ feet

9. Name the angle found at the corner of this page.

____

10. Follow the pattern in the first circle to complete the second circle.

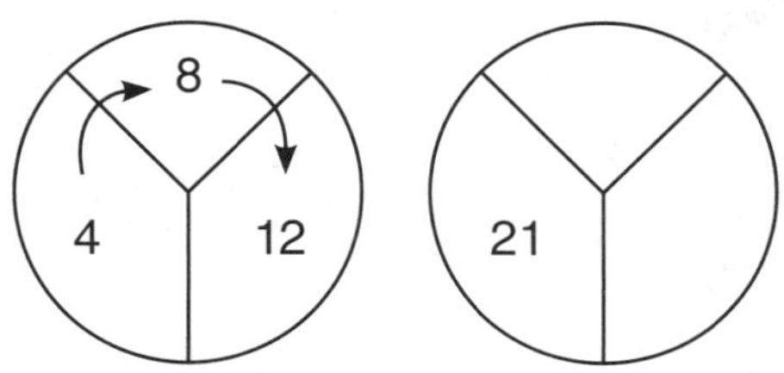

NAME: ____________________

DIRECTIONS Solve each problem.

1. 28 + 12 = ______

2. Shade 0.65.

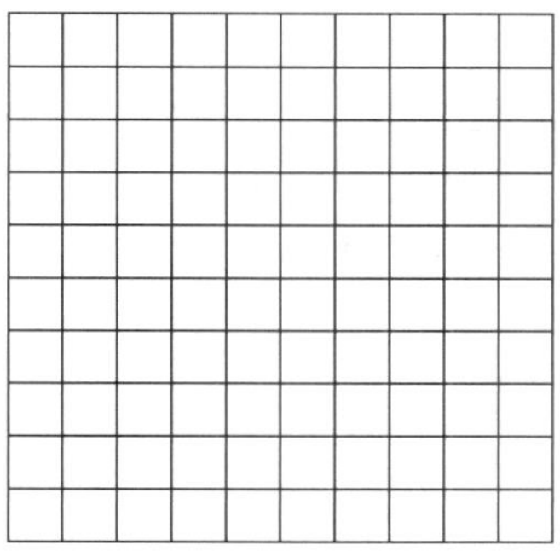

3. Divide 26 by 7. ______

4. 15 ÷ 3 = ______

5. What is the value of the digit 2 in 3,245?

____

6. 4 x ☐ = 28

7. Draw the time that is 10 minutes later.

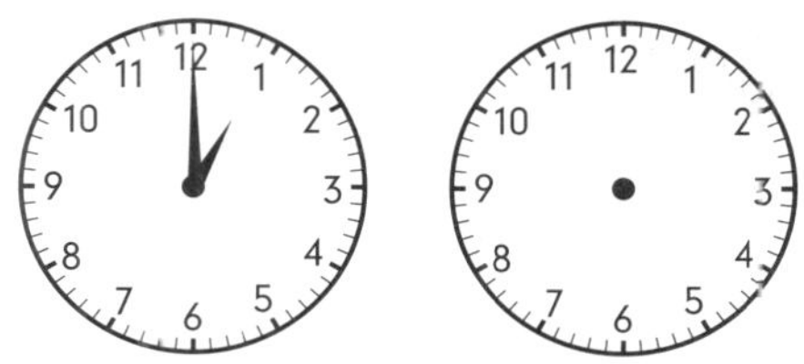

8. How many months are in 2 years?

____

9. What shape is the cross-section?

____

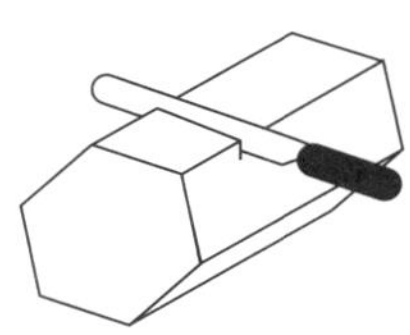

10. Tina has $12.00. She spends $7.50 at the movies. How much money does she have left to spend on lunch?

____

SCORE

1. Ⓨ Ⓝ
2. Ⓨ Ⓝ
3. Ⓨ Ⓝ
4. Ⓨ Ⓝ
5. Ⓨ Ⓝ
6. Ⓨ Ⓝ
7. Ⓨ Ⓝ
8. Ⓨ Ⓝ
9. Ⓨ Ⓝ
10. Ⓨ Ⓝ

___ / 10 **Total**

DAY 74

NAME: ____________________

DIRECTIONS Solve each problem.

SCORE

1. Ⓨ Ⓝ
2. Ⓨ Ⓝ
3. Ⓨ Ⓝ
4. Ⓨ Ⓝ
5. Ⓨ Ⓝ
6. Ⓨ Ⓝ
7. Ⓨ Ⓝ
8. Ⓨ Ⓝ
9. Ⓨ Ⓝ
10. Ⓨ Ⓝ

___ / 10 Total

1. $\begin{array}{r} 46 \\ -\ 29 \\ \hline \end{array}$

2. Is 0.3 equal to $\frac{3}{100}$?

____

3. How many sixes are in 24?

____

4. $3\overline{)16}$

5. How many digits are in the number 3,090?

____

6. $36 \div \square = 6$

7. Jon's mass is half the mass of Nick, whose mass is 86 kg. What is Jon's mass?

____

8. Each cube has 3-cm sides. What is the volume of the model?

____

9.

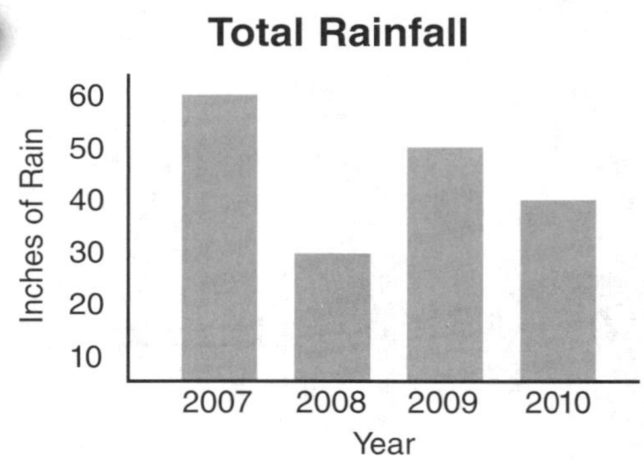

Which year received 60 inches of rainfall?

____

10. $\frac{1}{8}$ of 40 = 5, so $\frac{7}{8}$ of 40 =

____

DAY 75

NAME: ____________________

DIRECTIONS Solve each problem.

1.
$$\begin{array}{r} 34 \\ +\ 16 \\ \hline \end{array}$$

2. 8 x 9 = ________

3. 42 ÷ 6 = ________

4. How many groups of 8 are in 72?

____

5. Write 3,058 in words.

____

____

____

6. ☐ x 2 = 18

7. Is 100 cm equal to 1 m?

____

8. Would you use a ruler or a yardstick to measure the height of a person?

____

9. Are parallel lines always straight?

____

10. Use different colors to color pairs of numbers that equal the product shown in the center.

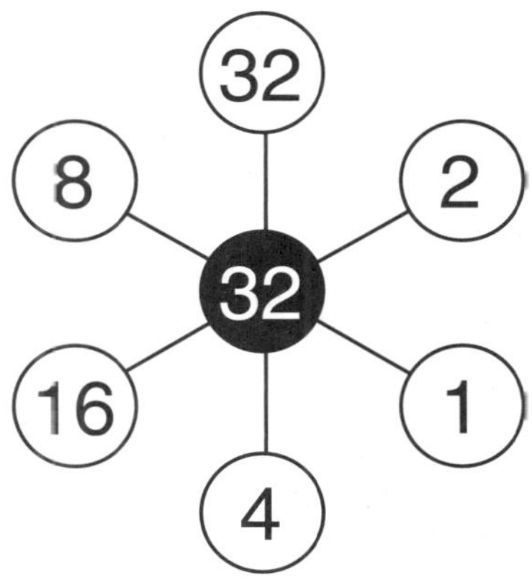

SCORE

1. Ⓨ Ⓝ
2. Ⓨ Ⓝ
3. Ⓨ Ⓝ
4. Ⓨ Ⓝ
5. Ⓨ Ⓝ
6. Ⓨ Ⓝ
7. Ⓨ Ⓝ
8. Ⓨ Ⓝ
9. Ⓨ Ⓝ
10. Ⓨ Ⓝ

___ / 10
Total

DAY
76

NAME: ______________________

DIRECTIONS Solve each problem.

SCORE

1. Ⓨ Ⓝ
2. Ⓨ Ⓝ
3. Ⓨ Ⓝ
4. Ⓨ Ⓝ
5. Ⓨ Ⓝ
6. Ⓨ Ⓝ
7. Ⓨ Ⓝ
8. Ⓨ Ⓝ
9. Ⓨ Ⓝ
10. Ⓨ Ⓝ

___ / 10
Total

1. $53 - 29 =$ ________

2. $\frac{1}{6}$ of 36 is ________

3. $6\overline{)54}$

4. How many groups of 4 are in 32?

____

5. What is the place value of 6 in 1,360?

____

6. Fill in the missing number.

60, 120, 180, ________, 300

7. What is the difference in capacity between the cream and the yogurt containers?

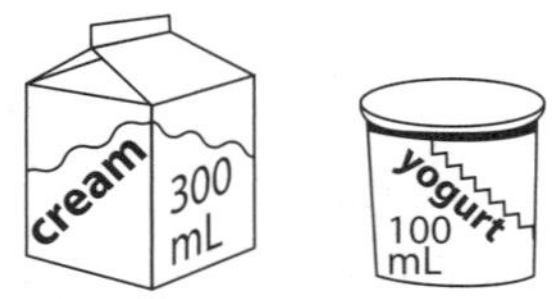

____

8. Which would be the best tool for measuring the height of a child: a calendar, a meter stick, or a watch?

____

9. A regular pentagon has:

________ angles

________ sides

________ axes of symmetry

10. Jill's soccer practice lasted from 3:25 P.M. until 6:15 P.M. How long was practice?

____

NAME: ______________________

DIRECTIONS Solve each problem.

1. 17 + 13 = ______

2. Write 0.53 as a fraction.

____

3. 45 ÷ 6 = ______

4. $5\overline{)30}$

5. Round 457 to the nearest hundred.

____

6. ☐ ÷ 5 = 9

7. What is the date of the third Monday in August?

____

August						
Sun	Mon	Tues	Wed	Thurs	Fri	Sat
				1	2	3
4	5	6	7	8	9	10
11	12	13	14	15	16	17
18	19	20	21	22	23	24
25	26	27	28	29	30	31

8. What is the length of a rectangle that has a width of 3 inches and an area of 12 in^2 ?

____

9. I have one curved surface, no edges, and no corners. What solid am I?

____

10. If you subtract me from 732, you get 173. What number am I?

____

SCORE

1. Ⓨ Ⓝ
2. Ⓨ Ⓝ
3. Ⓨ Ⓝ
4. Ⓨ Ⓝ
5. Ⓨ Ⓝ
6. Ⓨ Ⓝ
7. Ⓨ Ⓝ
8. Ⓨ Ⓝ
9. Ⓨ Ⓝ
10. Ⓨ Ⓝ

___ / 10

Total

NAME: ____________________

DIRECTIONS Solve each problem.

SCORE

1. Ⓨ Ⓝ
2. Ⓨ Ⓝ
3. Ⓨ Ⓝ
4. Ⓨ Ⓝ
5. Ⓨ Ⓝ
6. Ⓨ Ⓝ
7. Ⓨ Ⓝ
8. Ⓨ Ⓝ
9. Ⓨ Ⓝ
10. Ⓨ Ⓝ

___ / 10 Total

1.
$$\begin{array}{r} 19 \\ -\ 17 \\ \hline \end{array}$$

2. Is $\frac{1}{2}$ greater than $\frac{1}{3}$?

____

3. $34 \div 5 =$ ________

4. Divide 70 by 10. ________

5. Is 2,194 less than 2,914?

____

6. $81 \div \square = 9$

7. Does 1 liter equal 1,000 milliliters?

____

8. 3 yards = ________ inches

9. **School Awards**

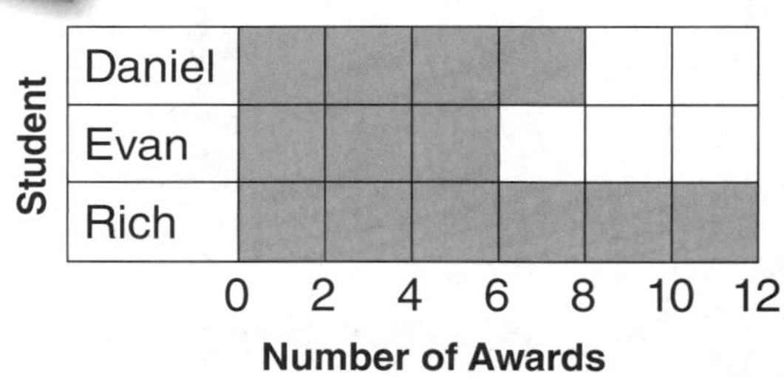

Who won exactly 6 awards?

____

10. Trace seven different paths from A to Z. One path has been done for you.

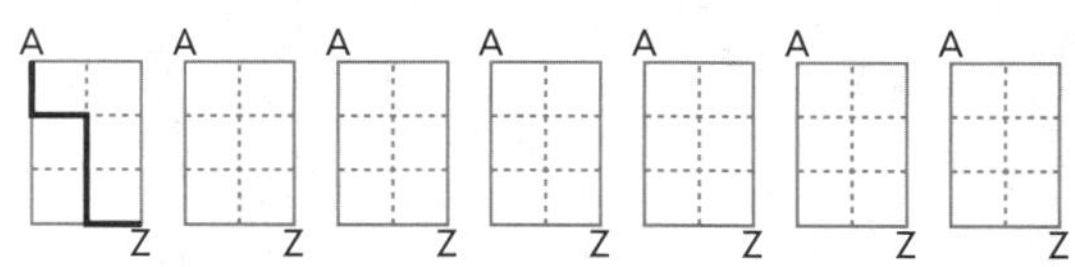

NAME: ______________________

DIRECTIONS Solve each problem.

1.
$$\begin{array}{r} 35 \\ +\ 25 \\ \hline \end{array}$$

2. Write $\frac{6}{10}$ as a decimal.

____

3. $10 \overline{)75}$

4. What is the quotient of 80 and 10?

____

5. What is the value of the tens place in 1,378?

____

6. $7 \times \square = 21$

7. Each cube has 2-cm sides. What is the volume of the model?

____

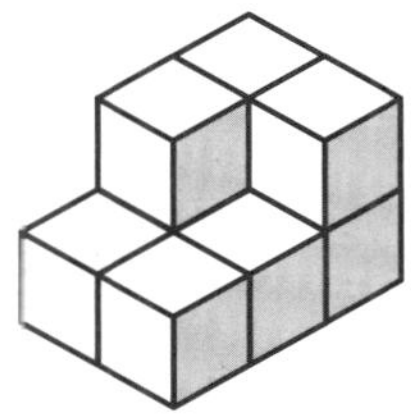

8. You wake up at 6:28 A.M. and go to bed at 9:30 P.M. How long are you awake?

____

9. If you turn around a given point, are you *reflecting*, *translating*, or *rotating*?

____

10. Three sisters are each making themselves one beaded necklace. They use 125 beads on each necklace. How many beads do they need?

____

SCORE

1. Ⓨ Ⓝ
2. Ⓨ Ⓝ
3. Ⓨ Ⓝ
4. Ⓨ Ⓝ
5. Ⓨ Ⓝ
6. Ⓨ Ⓝ
7. Ⓨ Ⓝ
8. Ⓨ Ⓝ
9. Ⓨ Ⓝ
10. Ⓨ Ⓝ

___ / 10 Total

NAME: ____________________

DIRECTIONS Solve each problem.

SCORE

1. Ⓨ Ⓝ
2. Ⓨ Ⓝ
3. Ⓨ Ⓝ
4. Ⓨ Ⓝ
5. Ⓨ Ⓝ
6. Ⓨ Ⓝ
7. Ⓨ Ⓝ
8. Ⓨ Ⓝ
9. Ⓨ Ⓝ
10. Ⓨ Ⓝ

___ / 10 Total

1. $24 - 6 =$ ________

2.

$$\begin{array}{r} 9 \\ \times\ 7 \\ \hline \end{array}$$

3. $2\overline{)10}$

4. $87 \div 10 =$ ________

5. Write the largest 4-digit numeral using 1, 0, 7, and 9.

____

6. $\square \times 8 = 32$

7. Is the area of the cover of a book measured in cm^2 or m^2?

____

8. Would you use a thermometer or a ruler to measure temperature?

____

9. Complete around the axis of symmetry.

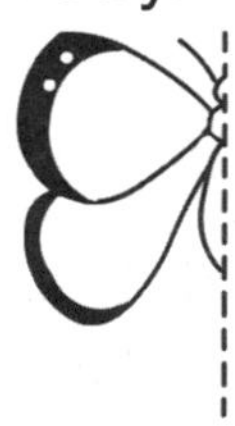

10. If the shaded area is equal to one, what is the area of the crossed region?

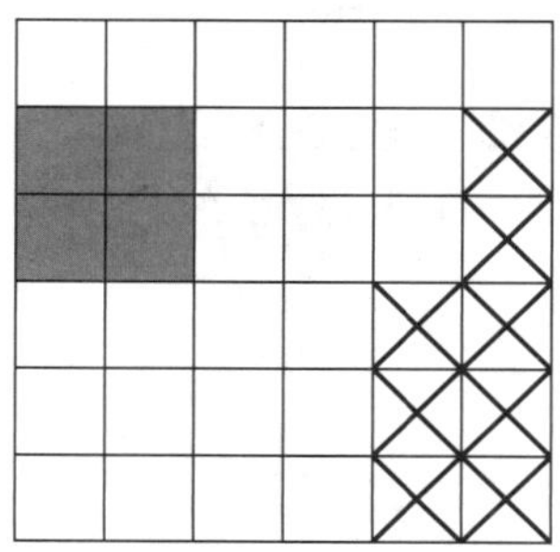

____

NAME: ______________________________

DIRECTIONS Solve each problem.

1. 31 + 29 = ________

2. Is $\frac{7}{10}$ equal to $\frac{7}{100}$?

____

3. Divide 50 into 10 equal groups.

____

4. 100 ÷ 10 = ________

5. What is the first odd number before 291?

____

6. Fill in the missing number.

60, 54, ________, 42, 36

7. Write the length in millimeters.

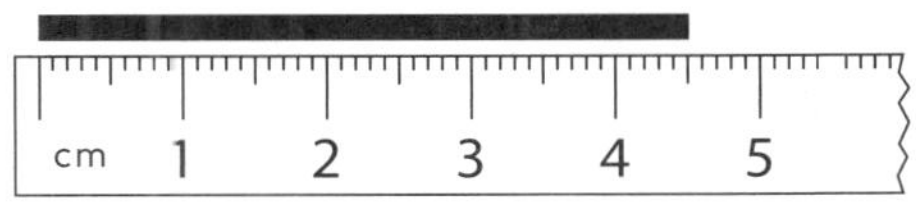

____

8. 2 hours = ________ minutes

9. A cylinder has:

________ faces

________ vertices

________ edges

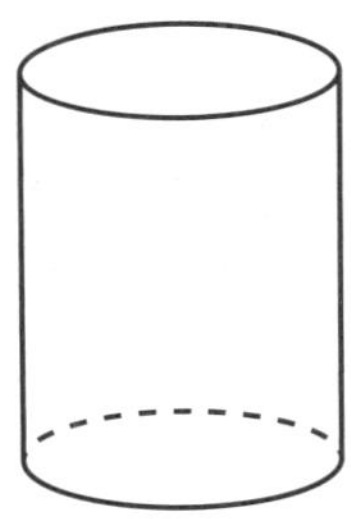

10. Write two odd numbers that total the even number 50.

____

SCORE

1. Ⓨ Ⓝ
2. Ⓨ Ⓝ
3. Ⓨ Ⓝ
4. Ⓨ Ⓝ
5. Ⓨ Ⓝ
6. Ⓨ Ⓝ
7. Ⓨ Ⓝ
8. Ⓨ Ⓝ
9. Ⓨ Ⓝ
10. Ⓨ Ⓝ

___ / 10
Total

NAME: ______________________

DIRECTIONS Solve each problem.

SCORE

1. Ⓨ Ⓝ
2. Ⓨ Ⓝ
3. Ⓨ Ⓝ
4. Ⓨ Ⓝ
5. Ⓨ Ⓝ
6. Ⓨ Ⓝ
7. Ⓨ Ⓝ
8. Ⓨ Ⓝ
9. Ⓨ Ⓝ
10. Ⓨ Ⓝ

___ / 10 Total

1. $41 - 8 =$ ________

2. $\frac{1}{2}$ of 40 is ________.

3. $7\overline{)44}$

4. $49 \div 7 =$ ________

5. How many digits are in the number 2,040?

____

6. $9 \div \square = 3$

7. Calculate the perimeter of the rectangle.

____

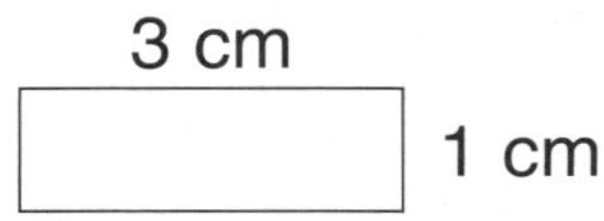

8. ________ quarts = 6 pints

9. **Sports Played Each Year**

	1st Trimester	2nd Trimester	3rd Trimester
Troy	soccer	basketball	baseball
Jessica	golf	basketball	track
Allison	soccer	diving	Swimming

Which children play the same sport the 1st trimester?

____

10. I drink 500 mL of milk each day. How much do I drink in 6 days?

____

NAME: ____________________

DIRECTIONS Solve each problem.

1.

$$\begin{array}{r} 37 \\ +\ 33 \\ \hline \end{array}$$

2. Is $\frac{1}{4}$ less than or greater than $\frac{1}{8}$?

____

3. $7\overline{)57}$

4. Divide 30 by 7. ________

5. Is 2,497 closer to 2,400 or 2,500?

____

6. 7 + 7 + 7 + ☐ = 28

7. Fill in the blanks for the time shown.

4: ______
____ past 4

8. 4 yards = ________ feet

9. Is this a right angle? Use the corner of a page to test.

____

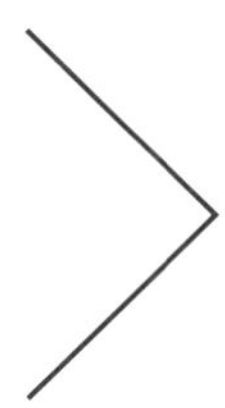

10. Ice cream treats at a carnival are \$2.50 each or 3 for \$6.00. Which is the better value?

____

SCORE

1. Ⓨ Ⓝ
2. Ⓨ Ⓝ
3. Ⓨ Ⓝ
4. Ⓨ Ⓝ
5. Ⓨ Ⓝ
6. Ⓨ Ⓝ
7. Ⓨ Ⓝ
8. Ⓨ Ⓝ
9. Ⓨ Ⓝ
10. Ⓨ Ⓝ

___ / 10
Total

DAY 84

NAME: ____________________

DIRECTIONS Solve each problem.

SCORE

1. Ⓨ Ⓝ
2. Ⓨ Ⓝ
3. Ⓨ Ⓝ
4. Ⓨ Ⓝ
5. Ⓨ Ⓝ
6. Ⓨ Ⓝ
7. Ⓨ Ⓝ
8. Ⓨ Ⓝ
9. Ⓨ Ⓝ
10. Ⓨ Ⓝ

___ / 10 Total

1. $\begin{array}{r} 36 \\ -\ 19 \\ \hline \end{array}$

2. Which is greater: $\frac{3}{10}$ or $\frac{3}{100}$?

____

3. $24 \div 7 =$ ________

4. $10\overline{)57}$

5. What is 100 more than 1,706?

____

6. $25 \div \square = 5$

7. Would you use kilograms or grams to measure the mass of a slice of cheese?

____

8. How many days are in December?

____

9. How many angles are in a triangle?

____

10. Complete the chart by rounding 2,176 to the specified places.

Ten	
Hundred	
Thousand	

NAME: ______________________________

DIRECTIONS Solve each problem.

1. 42 + 28 = ________

2. 8 x 7 = ____

3. What is the quotient of 15 and 7?

______________________________.

4. 37 ÷ 7 = ________

5. What is the place value of 6 in 3,698?

____

6. 82 – 15 = 73 – ☐

7. Is the area of a room measured in cm^2 or m^2?

____

8. Write the length in inches.

________ inches

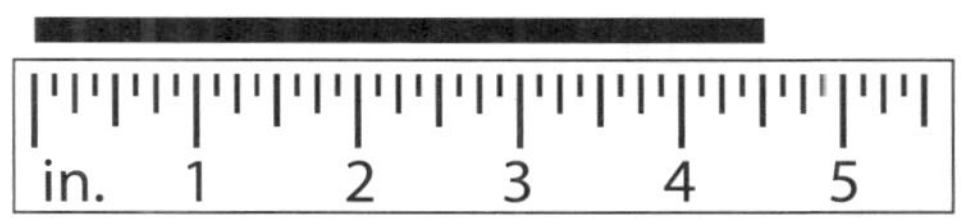

9. What shape forms the base of this pyramid?

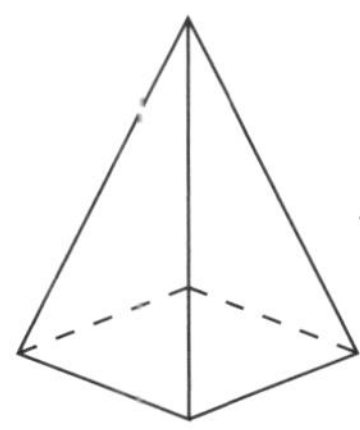

____

10. Color the multiples of 3.

1	2	3	4	5	6	7	8	9	10
11	12	13	14	15	16	17	18	19	20
21	22	23	24	25	26	27	28	29	30
31	32	33	34	35	36	37	38	39	40

SCORE

1. Ⓨ Ⓝ
2. Ⓨ Ⓝ
3. Ⓨ Ⓝ
4. Ⓨ Ⓝ
5. Ⓨ Ⓝ
6. Ⓨ Ⓝ
7. Ⓨ Ⓝ
8. Ⓨ Ⓝ
9. Ⓨ Ⓝ
10. Ⓨ Ⓝ

___ / 10 Total

DAY

86

NAME: ____________________

DIRECTIONS Solve each problem.

SCORE

1. Ⓨ Ⓝ
2. Ⓨ Ⓝ
3. Ⓨ Ⓝ
4. Ⓨ Ⓝ
5. Ⓨ Ⓝ
6. Ⓨ Ⓝ
7. Ⓨ Ⓝ
8. Ⓨ Ⓝ
9. Ⓨ Ⓝ
10. Ⓨ Ⓝ

___ / 10
Total

1. $45 - 29 =$ ________

2. What is $\frac{1}{10}$ of 50? ________

3. $7\overline{)65}$

4. $88 \div 9 =$ ________

5. What is the value of the 7 in 2,738?

____

6. Fill in the missing number.

54, ________, 42, 36, 30

7. How many 20-liter containers can be filled from a 90-liter tank?

____

8. What is the most likely mass of a boy?

45 kilograms

45 grams

45 liters

9. Record the data in the pictograph.
Cheryl has been in 4 plays.
Brooke has been in 8 plays

Number of Plays

Cheryl	
Brooke	

 = 2 plays

10. What number means five ten thousands, three thousands, two hundreds, one ten, and no ones?

____

DAY 87

NAME: ______________________

DIRECTIONS Solve each problem.

1. What is the sum of 26 and 7?

____

2. $\frac{6}{10}$ of \$1 is ________.

3. $49 \div 9 =$ ________

4. $24 \div 9 =$ ________

5. Is 316 an even number?

____

6. $8 \times \square = 32$

7. On which day of the week is September 1st?

____

August						
Sun	Mon	Tues	Wed	Thurs	Fri	Sat
				1	2	3
4	5	6	7	8	9	10
11	12	13	14	15	16	17
18	19	20	21	22	23	24
25	26	27	28	29	30	31

8. How many days are in 2 weeks?

____

9. Is a square a regular shape?

____

10. Our product is 132. The difference between us is 1. What numbers are we?

____

SCORE

1. Ⓨ Ⓝ
2. Ⓨ Ⓝ
3. Ⓨ Ⓝ
4. Ⓨ Ⓝ
5. Ⓨ Ⓝ
6. Ⓨ Ⓝ
7. Ⓨ Ⓝ
8. Ⓨ Ⓝ
9. Ⓨ Ⓝ
10. Ⓨ Ⓝ

___ / 10
Total

NAME: ______________________________

DIRECTIONS Solve each problem.

SCORE

1. Ⓨ Ⓝ
2. Ⓨ Ⓝ
3. Ⓨ Ⓝ
4. Ⓨ Ⓝ
5. Ⓨ Ⓝ
6. Ⓨ Ⓝ
7. Ⓨ Ⓝ
8. Ⓨ Ⓝ
9. Ⓨ Ⓝ
10. Ⓨ Ⓝ

___ / 10 Total

1. $\begin{array}{r} 56 \\ -\ 19 \\ \hline \end{array}$

2. $\frac{1}{3}$ of 30 is ________.

3. $9\overline{)30}$

4. 68 ÷ 9 = ________

5. Write 2,064 in words.

____

6. To find 60 ÷ 6, we say

☐ x 6 = 60

7. I put 500 mL of water in the jug. Next, I put a toy in the jug. How much water was displaced by the toy?

________ mL

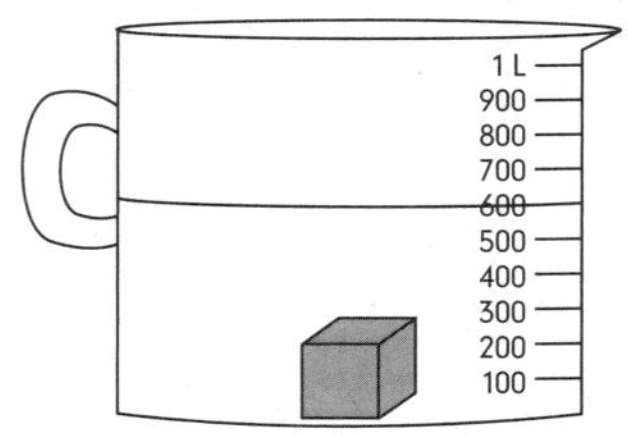

8. What day is 8 days before Saturday?

____

9. Circle the solids that have a rectangular front view.

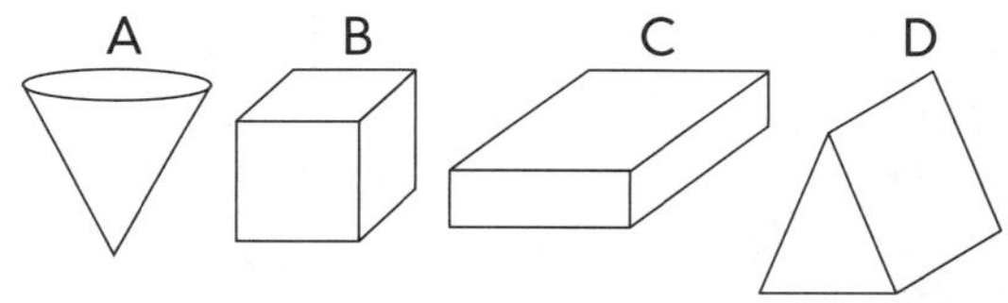

10. Draw the shape that must be added so the pattern is complete.

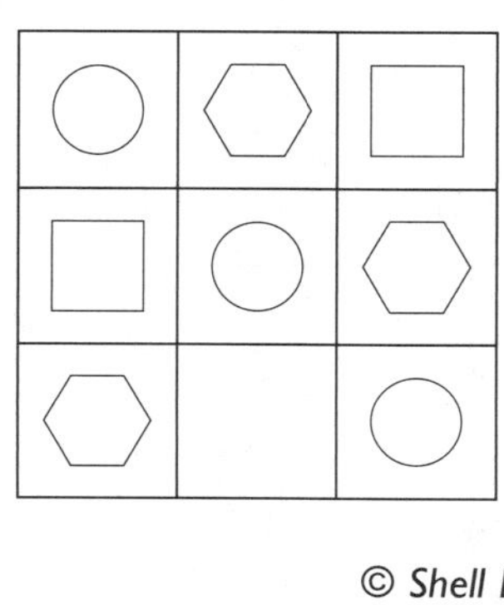

DAY 89

NAME: ____________________

DIRECTIONS Solve each problem.

1.
$$\begin{array}{r} 23 \\ +\ \ 8 \\ \hline \end{array}$$

2. Is 0.6 equal to $\frac{6}{100}$?

____

3. Divide 49 into 7 equal groups.

____

4. $9\overline{)76}$

5. How many digits are in 3,333?

____

6. $\square \div 8 = 3$

7. How many seasons are in a year?

____

8. 2 pints = ________ quart(s)

9. Draw a 180° angle.

10. A pound of ground beef costs $2.00. You have a coupon for 25% off. How much will you pay for a pound of beef?

____

SCORE

1. Ⓨ Ⓝ
2. Ⓨ Ⓝ
3. Ⓨ Ⓝ
4. Ⓨ Ⓝ
5. Ⓨ Ⓝ
6. Ⓨ Ⓝ
7. Ⓨ Ⓝ
8. Ⓨ Ⓝ
9. Ⓨ Ⓝ
10. Ⓨ Ⓝ

___ / 10 Total

NAME: ____________________

DIRECTIONS Solve each problem.

SCORE

1. Ⓨ Ⓝ
2. Ⓨ Ⓝ
3. Ⓨ Ⓝ
4. Ⓨ Ⓝ
5. Ⓨ Ⓝ
6. Ⓨ Ⓝ
7. Ⓨ Ⓝ
8. Ⓨ Ⓝ
9. Ⓨ Ⓝ
10. Ⓨ Ⓝ

___ / 10 Total

1. $33 - 17 =$ ________

2. How many objects are in 4 columns of 7?

____

3. $9 \overline{)60}$

4. $40 \div 9 =$ ________

5. Round 372 to the nearest hundred.

____

6. $6 \times \square = 42$

7. To find the height of a door, is the unit of measure m or m^2?

____

8. You want to see a movie that starts at 3:00. Is it A.M. or P.M.?

____

9. Does this shape tessellate?

____

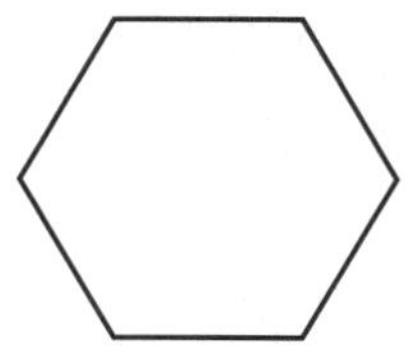

10. $\frac{1}{4}$ of 24 is 6, so $\frac{3}{4}$ of 24 =

____

NAME: ______________________

DIRECTIONS Solve each problem.

1. 24 + 33 = ________

2.

$$\begin{array}{r} \$2.50 \\ - \$1.25 \\ \hline \end{array}$$

3. Divide 30 by 8. ________

4. $4\overline{)36}$

5. 700 + 40 + 6 = ________

6. Fill in the missing number.

56, 49, ________, 35, 28

7. Write the length in centimeters.

____

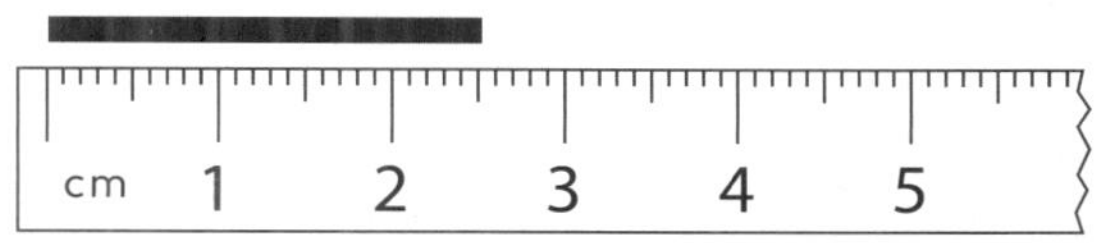

8. What is the temperature?

____

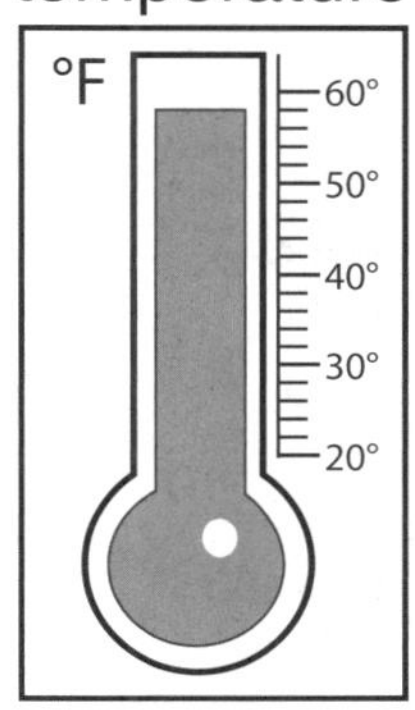

9. What type of prism is shown?

____

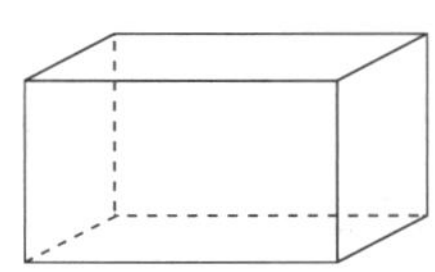

10. Complete the subtraction grid.

–	45	47	56	63	77	82
19						
29						
39						

SCORE

1. Ⓨ Ⓝ
2. Ⓨ Ⓝ
3. Ⓨ Ⓝ
4. Ⓨ Ⓝ
5. Ⓨ Ⓝ
6. Ⓨ Ⓝ
7. Ⓨ Ⓝ
8. Ⓨ Ⓝ
9. Ⓨ Ⓝ
10. Ⓨ Ⓝ

___ / 10 Total

NAME: ______________________________

DIRECTIONS Solve each problem.

SCORE

1. Ⓨ Ⓝ
2. Ⓨ Ⓝ
3. Ⓨ Ⓝ
4. Ⓨ Ⓝ
5. Ⓨ Ⓝ
6. Ⓨ Ⓝ
7. Ⓨ Ⓝ
8. Ⓨ Ⓝ
9. Ⓨ Ⓝ
10. Ⓨ Ⓝ

___ / 10
Total

1. $\begin{array}{r} 45 \\ -\ 26 \\ \hline \end{array}$

2. Write $\frac{5}{100}$ as a decimal.

____

3. $42 \div 8 =$ ________

4. $5 \overline{)\,23}$

5. What is the value of the hundreds place in 1,573?

____

6. Complete the chart to find the value of five 50¢ coins.

1 Coin	2 Coins	3 Coins	4 Coins	5 Coins
50¢				

7. Is area the measurement of mass or surface?

____

8. Each cube has 1-cm sides. What is the volume of the model?

____

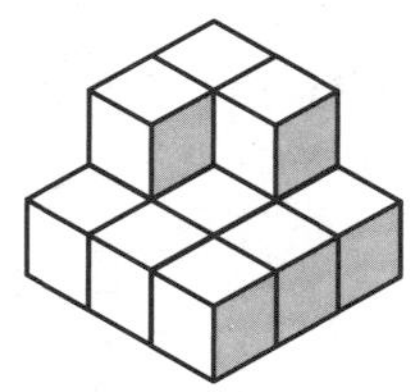

9. Complete around the axis of symmetry.

10. Follow the pattern in the first circle to complete the second circle.

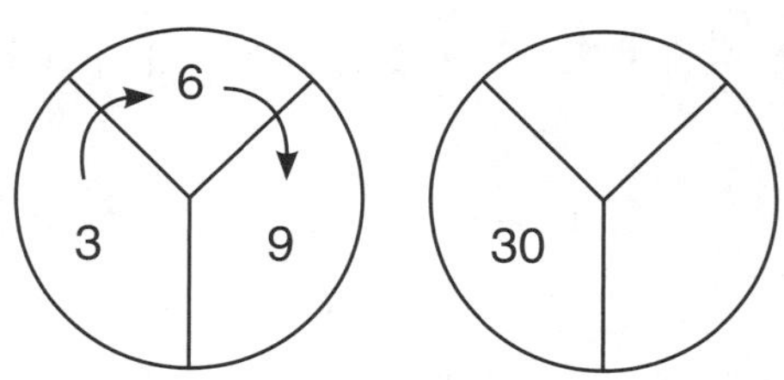

NAME: ____________________

DIRECTIONS Solve each problem.

1.
```
   16
    7
+  14
-----
```

2. Which is larger: $\frac{4}{100}$ or $\frac{4}{10}$?

____

3. 36 ÷ 8 = ________

4. 36 ÷ 9 = ________

5. Write the smallest 3-digit number using 2, 8, 1, and 4.

____

6. 15 + 5 = 18 + ☐

7. Draw the time that is 20 minutes later.

8. 1 ________ = 60 seconds

9. **Dollars Earned in May**

Audrey	$15
Dameon	$23
Jason	$12
Lauren	$18

What was the total amount of money earned in May by the children?

____

10. If one ticket costs $2.50, how many tickets can be bought with $15.00?

____

SCORE

1. Ⓨ Ⓝ
2. Ⓨ Ⓝ
3. Ⓨ Ⓝ
4. Ⓨ Ⓝ
5. Ⓨ Ⓝ
6. Ⓨ Ⓝ
7. Ⓨ Ⓝ
8. Ⓨ Ⓝ
9. Ⓨ Ⓝ
10. Ⓨ Ⓝ

___ / 10 Total

DAY
94

NAME: ____________________

DIRECTIONS Solve each problem.

SCORE

1. Ⓨ Ⓝ
2. Ⓨ Ⓝ
3. Ⓨ Ⓝ
4. Ⓨ Ⓝ
5. Ⓨ Ⓝ
6. Ⓨ Ⓝ
7. Ⓨ Ⓝ
8. Ⓨ Ⓝ
9. Ⓨ Ⓝ
10. Ⓨ Ⓝ

___ / 10
Total

1. $63 - 9 =$ ________

2. What is one-fourth of 12?

____

3. $8\overline{)65}$

4. Divide 5 into 43.

____

5. What is the next even number after 398?

____

6. $10 - x = 2$

$x =$ ________

7. Sam's mass is 8 kg greater than Joe's, whose mass is 34 kg. What is Sam's mass?

____

8. How many gallons make up four quarts?

____

9. Name this shape. ________

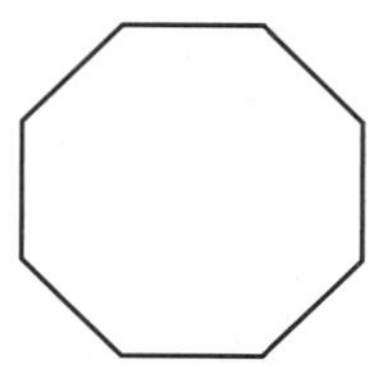

10. Complete the chart. Round the number 4,832.

Tens	
Hundreds	
Thousands	

DAY 95

NAME: ____________________

DIRECTIONS Solve each problem.

1. 25 + 8 = ________

2. 4 x 9 = ________

3. Share 24 equally among 4 groups.

____

4. 77 ÷ 8 = ________

5. What is 300 more than 2,476?

____

6. 9 + 4 = 13 – ☐

7. How many centimeters are in 6 meters?

____

8. What month is 4 months after September?

____

9. Draw the top view of the solid.

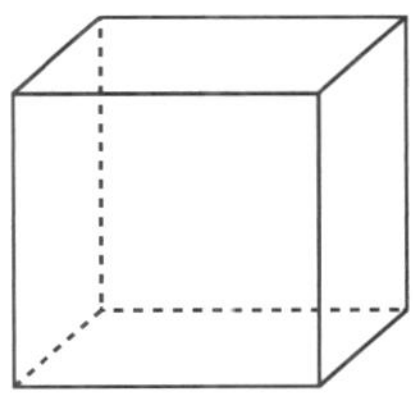

10. Use different colors to color pairs of numbers that equal the product shown in the center.

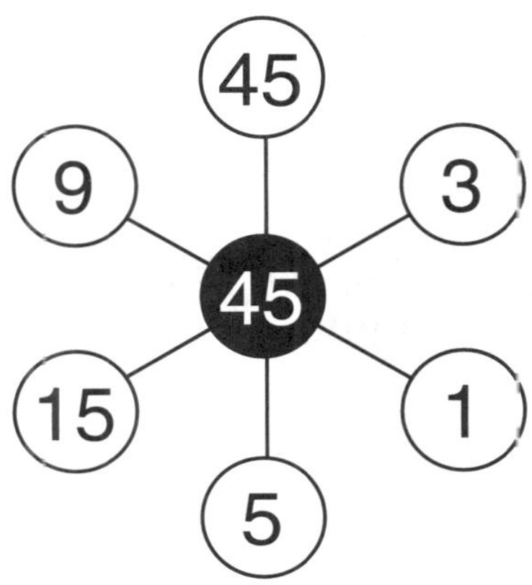

SCORE

1. Ⓨ Ⓝ
2. Ⓨ Ⓝ
3. Ⓨ Ⓝ
4. Ⓨ Ⓝ
5. Ⓨ Ⓝ
6. Ⓨ Ⓝ
7. Ⓨ Ⓝ
8. Ⓨ Ⓝ
9. Ⓨ Ⓝ
10. Ⓨ Ⓝ

___ / 10 Total

DAY
96

NAME: ______________________

DIRECTIONS Solve each problem.

SCORE

1. Ⓨ Ⓝ
2. Ⓨ Ⓝ
3. Ⓨ Ⓝ
4. Ⓨ Ⓝ
5. Ⓨ Ⓝ
6. Ⓨ Ⓝ
7. Ⓨ Ⓝ
8. Ⓨ Ⓝ
9. Ⓨ Ⓝ
10. Ⓨ Ⓝ

___ / 10
Total

1. $\begin{array}{r} 25 \\ -\ \ 6 \\ \hline \end{array}$

2. \$1.20 + \$1.15 = ________

3. $8 \overline{)60}$

4. Calculate the quotient of 56 and 4.

____

5. Write 3,642 in expanded notation.

____

____

6. Fill in the missing number.

28, 35, 42, ________, 56

7. How many liters are in 8,000 milliliters?

____

8. 48 inches = ________ feet

9. Is this a *reflection*, *translation*, or *rotation*?

____

10. A telephone costs \$9.89. A calendar costs \$5.99. A watch costs \$19.50. What is the total cost of the items?

____

NAME: ____________________

DIRECTIONS Solve each problem.

1. 17 + 9 = ______

2. Write $\frac{7}{10}$ as a decimal.

______

3. How many 4s are in 16?

______

4. 52 ÷ 8 = ______

5. What is 10 more than 437?

______

6. Does 6 + 4 = 3 + 7?

______

7. On which day of the week is the last day of August?

______

August						
Sun	Mon	Tues	Wed	Thurs	Fri	Sat
				1	2	3
4	5	6	7	8	9	10
11	12	13	14	15	16	17
18	19	20	21	22	23	24
25	26	27	28	29	30	31

8. Would you use a ruler or a yardstick to measure the height of a drinking glass?

______

9. **Books Read in March**

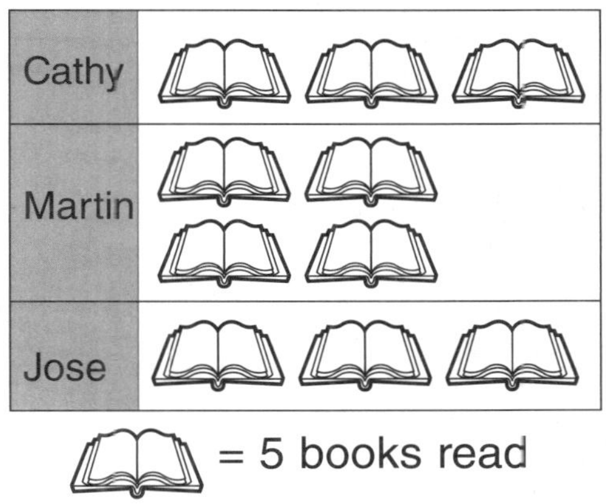

Who read the most books?

______

10. If you subtract me from 1,437, you get 422. What number am I?

______

SCORE

1. Ⓨ Ⓝ
2. Ⓨ Ⓝ
3. Ⓨ Ⓝ
4. Ⓨ Ⓝ
5. Ⓨ Ⓝ
6. Ⓨ Ⓝ
7. Ⓨ Ⓝ
8. Ⓨ Ⓝ
9. Ⓨ Ⓝ
10. Ⓨ Ⓝ

___ / 10
Total

NAME: ____________________

DIRECTIONS Solve each problem.

SCORE

1. Ⓨ Ⓝ
2. Ⓨ Ⓝ
3. Ⓨ Ⓝ
4. Ⓨ Ⓝ
5. Ⓨ Ⓝ
6. Ⓨ Ⓝ
7. Ⓨ Ⓝ
8. Ⓨ Ⓝ
9. Ⓨ Ⓝ
10. Ⓨ Ⓝ

___ / 10 Total

1. $47 - 29 =$ ________

2. Is $\frac{1}{8}$ more than $\frac{1}{4}$?

____

3. $8\overline{)20}$

4. $42 \div 4 =$ ________

5. Write the number for five thousand two hundred fifty-three.

____

6. $6 + 5 = 17 - \square$

7. How many milliliters are in half a liter?

____

8. Circle the most likely time for a 1-mile run.

12 minutes

12 seconds

12 inches

9. Draw the diagonals in the shape.

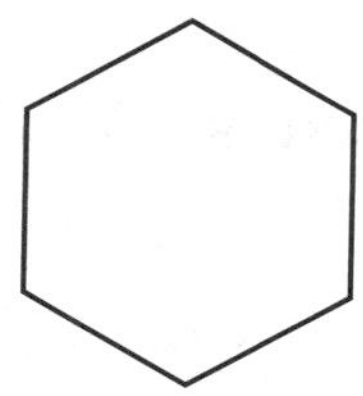

10. Estimate the number of dots in the square. Then check by counting.

Estimate: ________

Actual Number: ________

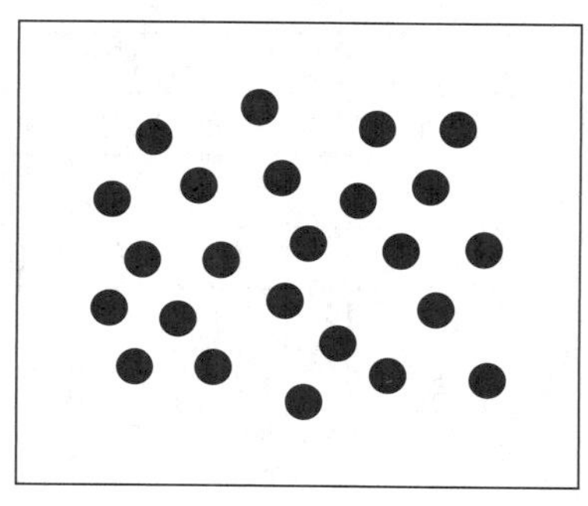

NAME: ____________________

DIRECTIONS Solve each problem.

SCORE

1.
$$\begin{array}{r} 52 \\ +\ \ 9 \\ \hline \end{array}$$

2. Write 0.62 as a fraction.

____

3. List all the factors of 20.

____

4. $12 \div 4 =$ ________

5. Write the ordinal number for forty-two.

____

6. $22 - x = 13$

$x =$ ________

7. Which months are in the second quarter of the year?

____

____

8. Each cube has 1-cm sides. What is the volume of the model?

____

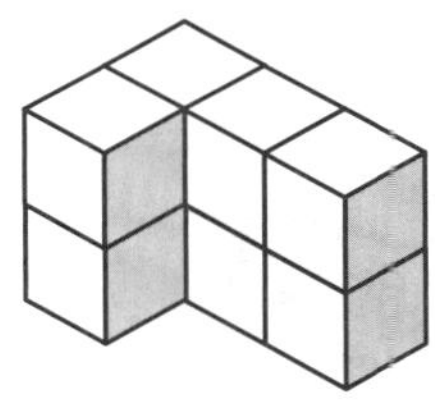

9. A cone has:

________ surfaces

________ edges

10. There are 5 toys in a bag. Shelly buys 8 bags of toys. She then divides the toys evenly among 4 friends. How many toys did each friend get?

____

1. Ⓨ Ⓝ
2. Ⓨ Ⓝ
3. Ⓨ Ⓝ
4. Ⓨ Ⓝ
5. Ⓨ Ⓝ
6. Ⓨ Ⓝ
7. Ⓨ Ⓝ
8. Ⓨ Ⓝ
9. Ⓨ Ⓝ
10. Ⓨ Ⓝ

___ / 10
Total

NAME: ____________________

DIRECTIONS Solve each problem.

SCORE

1. Ⓨ Ⓝ
2. Ⓨ Ⓝ
3. Ⓨ Ⓝ
4. Ⓨ Ⓝ
5. Ⓨ Ⓝ
6. Ⓨ Ⓝ
7. Ⓨ Ⓝ
8. Ⓨ Ⓝ
9. Ⓨ Ⓝ
10. Ⓨ Ⓝ

___ / 10 Total

1. $\begin{array}{r} 27 \\ -\ 19 \\ \hline \end{array}$

2. $7 \times 6 =$ ________

3. $4 \overline{)28}$

4. List all the factors of 36.

____

5. What is the value of the 7 in 374?

____

6. $15 - 6 = \square - 9$

7. My garden bed has an area of 18 m^2. I planted 10 m^2 with peas. What area is left?

____

8. How many weekdays are there?

____

9.

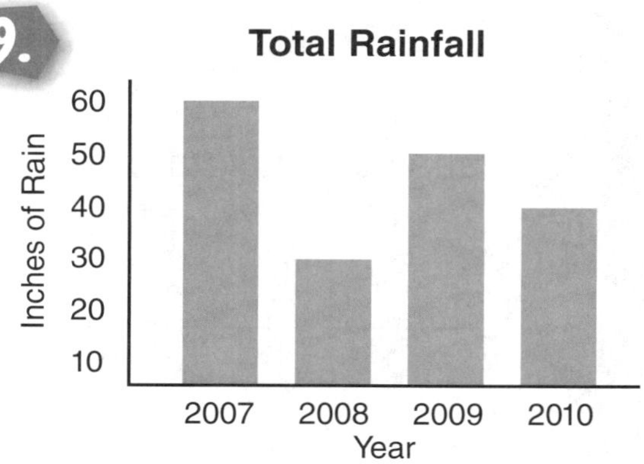

How much did it rain in all the years combined?

____

10. Circle the card that shows the same fraction as the example.

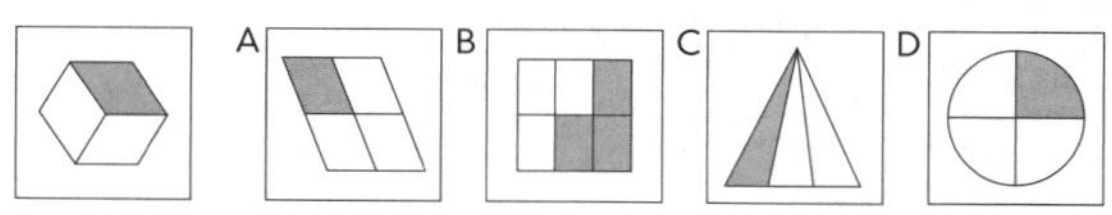

NAME: ______________________________

DIRECTIONS Solve each problem.

1. 45 + 7 = ________

2. $\frac{1}{8}$ of 48 is ________.

3. 32 ÷ 4 = ________

4. $7\overline{)56}$

5. Round 756 to the nearest hundred.

____

6. Fill in the missing number.

42, ________, 28, 21, 14

7. Write the length in millimeters.

____

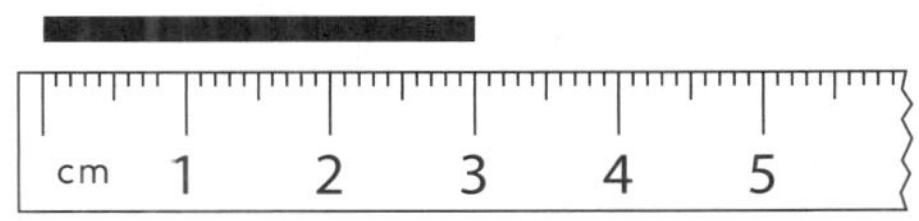

8. Maggie works on her homework from 2:35 P.M. until 3:15 P.M. How long does she spend on homework?

____

9. Circle the sets of parallel lines.

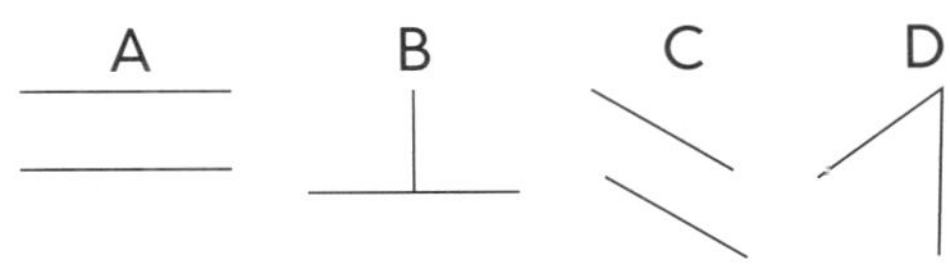

10. Use each of the 5 numbers once and any operations to solve the problem below. You may also add parentheses.

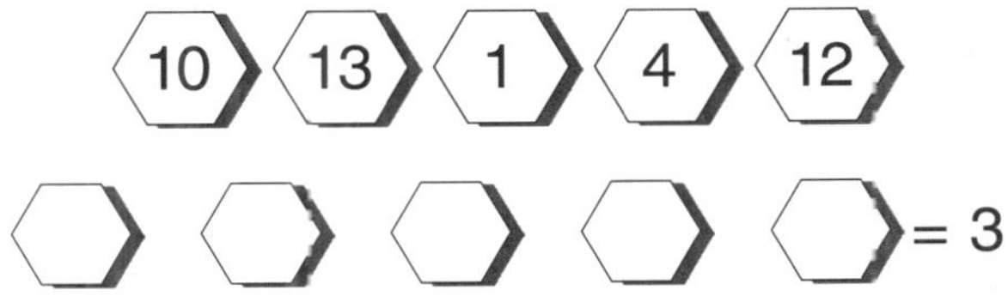

SCORE

1. Ⓨ Ⓝ
2. Ⓨ Ⓝ
3. Ⓨ Ⓝ
4. Ⓨ Ⓝ
5. Ⓨ Ⓝ
6. Ⓨ Ⓝ
7. Ⓨ Ⓝ
8. Ⓨ Ⓝ
9. Ⓨ Ⓝ
10. Ⓨ Ⓝ

___ / 10

Total

DAY
102

NAME: ____________________

DIRECTIONS Solve each problem.

SCORE

1. Ⓨ Ⓝ
2. Ⓨ Ⓝ
3. Ⓨ Ⓝ
4. Ⓨ Ⓝ
5. Ⓨ Ⓝ
6. Ⓨ Ⓝ
7. Ⓨ Ⓝ
8. Ⓨ Ⓝ
9. Ⓨ Ⓝ
10. Ⓨ Ⓝ

___ / 10
Total

1. $63 - 9 =$ ________

2. Is 0.4 greater than 0.29?

____

3. $43 \div 8 =$ ________

4. How many groups of eight are in sixteen?

____

5. Write 8,091 in words.

____

____

6. $32 + 8 = \square - 8$

7. Calculate the area of a square with 5-cm sides.

____

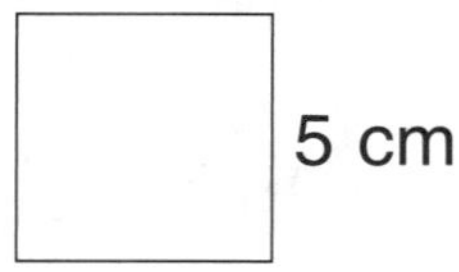

8. If the temperature were 53 degrees Fahrenheit, would you be more likely to wear a bathing suit or a jacket?

____

9. Draw the shape made if you fold along the axis of symmetry.

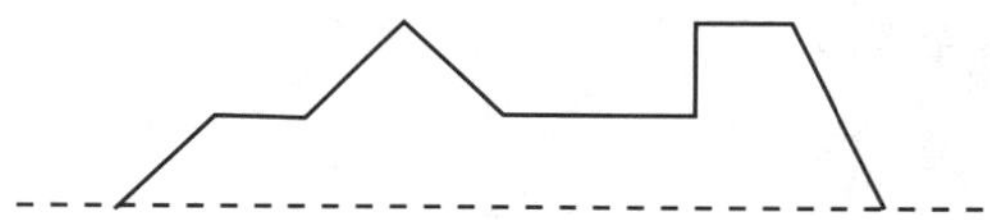

10. A box has 72 pencils in it. Evelyn wants to give an equal number of pencils to each of her 12 friends. How many pencils will each friend get?

____

NAME: ______________________________

DAY 103

DIRECTIONS Solve each problem.

1.
$$\begin{array}{r} 43 \\ +\ 18 \\ \hline \end{array}$$

2. Which is smaller:

$\frac{9}{10}$ or $\frac{9}{100}$?

____

3. Divide 48 into 8 equal groups.

____

4. $8 \overline{)72}$

5. Write 386 in expanded notation.

____

6. Is 7 x 9 equal to 9 x 7?

____

7. Fill in the blanks for the time shown.

5: ______
____ past 5

8. 1 ________ = 24 hours

9. What does the arrow show?

____

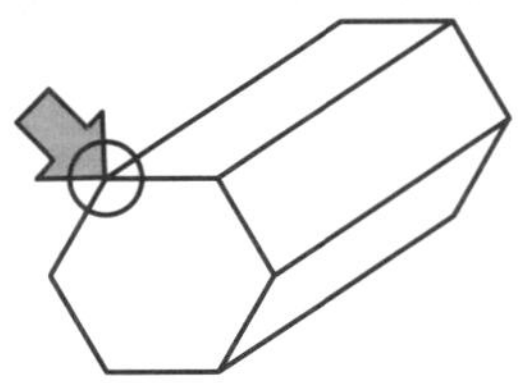

10. Hiro gets $3.00 each week for allowance. He saves $\frac{1}{3}$ of the money and spends the rest. How much does he save each week?

____

SCORE

1. Ⓨ Ⓝ
2. Ⓨ Ⓝ
3. Ⓨ Ⓝ
4. Ⓨ Ⓝ
5. Ⓨ Ⓝ
6. Ⓨ Ⓝ
7. Ⓨ Ⓝ
8. Ⓨ Ⓝ
9. Ⓨ Ⓝ
10. Ⓨ Ⓝ

___ / 10 Total

NAME: ____________________

DIRECTIONS Solve each problem.

SCORE

1. Ⓨ Ⓝ
2. Ⓨ Ⓝ
3. Ⓨ Ⓝ
4. Ⓨ Ⓝ
5. Ⓨ Ⓝ
6. Ⓨ Ⓝ
7. Ⓨ Ⓝ
8. Ⓨ Ⓝ
9. Ⓨ Ⓝ
10. Ⓨ Ⓝ

___ / 10 Total

1. 24 – 8 = ________

2. $1.50 + $1.75 = ________

3. 72 ÷ 9 = ________

4. Calculate the quotient of 32 and 8.

____

5. What is the next number after 809?

____

6. Complete the chart to find the cost of 6 bags at $20 each.

1 Bag	2 Bags	3 Bags	4 Bags	5 Bags	6 Bags
$20					

7. Does a shoe have a mass less than 1 kilogram?

____

8. 6 pints = ________ quart(s)

9.

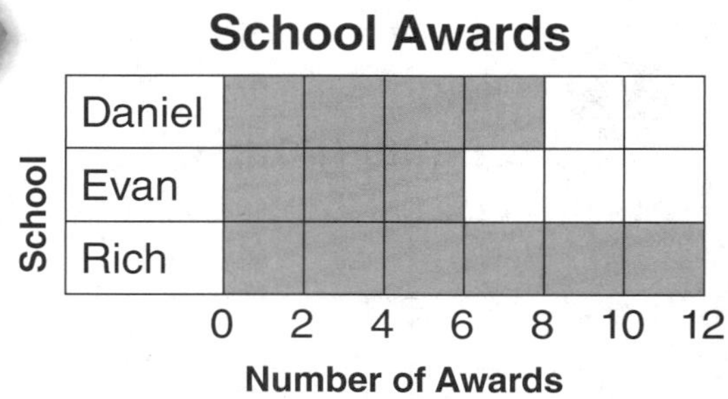

How many more awards did Rich win than Evan?

____

10. Complete the chart for the hundred grid to represent the shaded region.

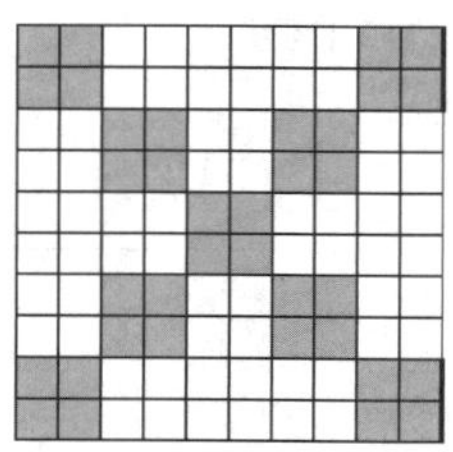

$\overline{100}$	0.	%

NAME: ____________________

DIRECTIONS Solve each problem.

1. 19 + 17 = ______

2. Calculate the product of 5 and 10.

____

3. 56 ÷ 8 = ______

4. $6\overline{)54}$

5. How many digits are in 6,427?

____

6. 24 – 14 = 10, so

24 – ☐ = 14

7. What is the abbreviation for centimeter squared?

____

8. 3 feet = ______ yard(s)

9. Circle the solids that have a triangular front view.

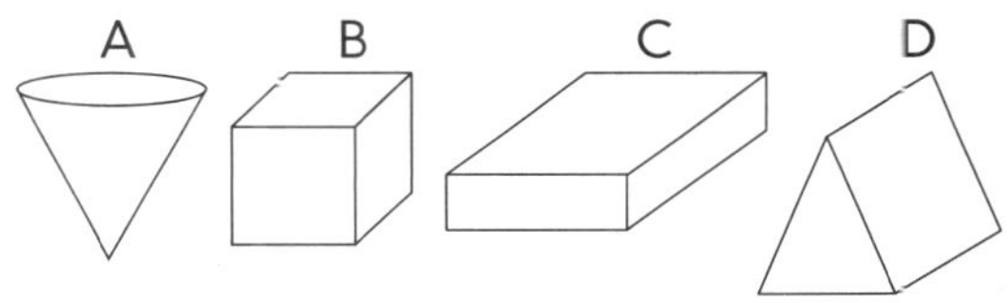

10. Use different colors to color pairs of numbers that equal the product shown in the center.

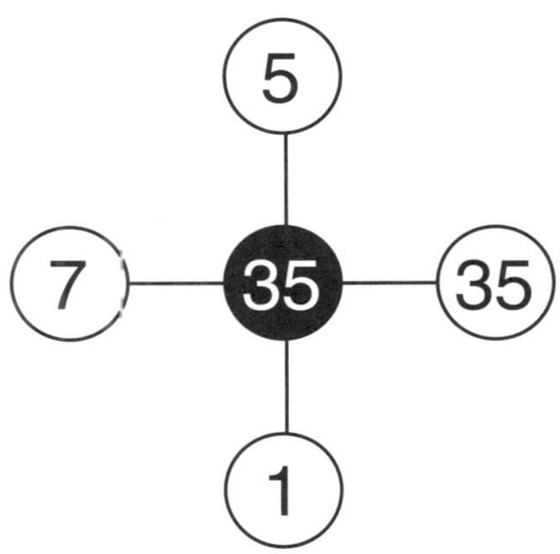

SCORE

1. Ⓨ Ⓝ
2. Ⓨ Ⓝ
3. Ⓨ Ⓝ
4. Ⓨ Ⓝ
5. Ⓨ Ⓝ
6. Ⓨ Ⓝ
7. Ⓨ Ⓝ
8. Ⓨ Ⓝ
9. Ⓨ Ⓝ
10. Ⓨ Ⓝ

___ / 10

Total

DAY
106

NAME: ______________________________

DIRECTIONS Solve each problem.

SCORE

1. Ⓨ Ⓝ
2. Ⓨ Ⓝ
3. Ⓨ Ⓝ
4. Ⓨ Ⓝ
5. Ⓨ Ⓝ
6. Ⓨ Ⓝ
7. Ⓨ Ⓝ
8. Ⓨ Ⓝ
9. Ⓨ Ⓝ
10. Ⓨ Ⓝ

___ / 10
Total

1.

$$\begin{array}{r} 16 \\ -\ \ 7 \\ \hline \end{array}$$

2. Is 0.7 equal to $\frac{7}{10}$?

____

3. Divide 40 into 5 equal groups.

____

4. $28 \div 7 =$ ________

5. What is 400 more than 1,609?

____

6. Fill in the missing number.

________, 45, 54, 63, 72

7. If 7  fill a  and 5  fill a , then ____  fill a .

8. Write the length in inches.

__________________ inches

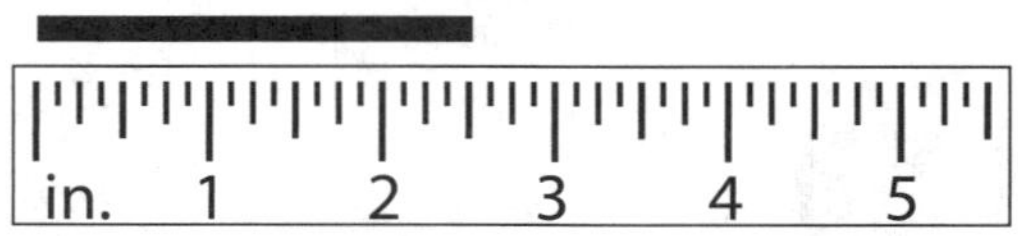

9. **Sports Played Each Year**

	1st Trimester	2nd Trimester	3rd Trimester
Troy	soccer	basketball	baseball
Jessica	golf	basketball	track
Allison	soccer	diving	swimming

Who does not play basketball?

____

10. I am a number. If you divide me by 10 and add 4, the answer is 7. What number am I?

____

NAME: ____________________

DIRECTIONS Solve each problem.

SCORE

1. Add 45 and 16. ________

2. Is 0.6 less than 0.58?

   ____

3. $9 \overline{)45}$

4. Divide 18 into 6 equal groups.

   ____

5. What is the next even number after 137?

   ____

6. 80 – 37 = ☐ – 22

7. School is scheduled to begin the first weekday in September. What date will school begin?

   ____

August						
Sun	Mon	Tues	Wed	Thurs	Fri	Sat
				1	2	3
4	5	6	7	8	9	10
11	12	13	14	15	16	17
18	19	20	21	22	23	24
25	26	27	28	29	30	31

8. Circle the most likely capacity of a large bucket.

   15 liters

   15 cups

   15 inches

9. This prism has:

   ________ faces

   ________ edges

   ________ vertices

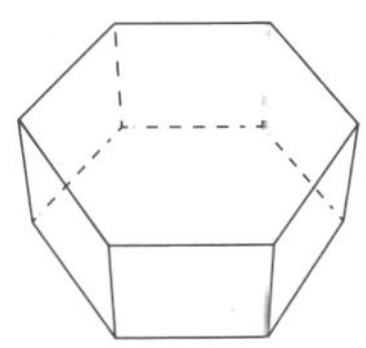

10. Double 32, then subtract 12.

    ____

1. Ⓨ Ⓝ
2. Ⓨ Ⓝ
3. Ⓨ Ⓝ
4. Ⓨ Ⓝ
5. Ⓨ Ⓝ
6. Ⓨ Ⓝ
7. Ⓨ Ⓝ
8. Ⓨ Ⓝ
9. Ⓨ Ⓝ
10. Ⓨ Ⓝ

___ / 10 Total

DAY 108

NAME: ____________________

DIRECTIONS Solve each problem.

SCORE

1. Ⓨ Ⓝ
2. Ⓨ Ⓝ
3. Ⓨ Ⓝ
4. Ⓨ Ⓝ
5. Ⓨ Ⓝ
6. Ⓨ Ⓝ
7. Ⓨ Ⓝ
8. Ⓨ Ⓝ
9. Ⓨ Ⓝ
10. Ⓨ Ⓝ

___ / 10 Total

1. $32 - 9 =$ ______

2. Write $\frac{3}{4}$ as a decimal.

____

3. List all the factors of 30.

____

4. $12 \div 6 =$ ______

5. $8000 + 40 + 7 =$ ______

6. $6 + 6 + 6 + \square = 4 \times 6$

7. Record in milliliters.

______ mL

8. How many months are in two and a half years?

____

9. Which triangle has only 2 equal sides?

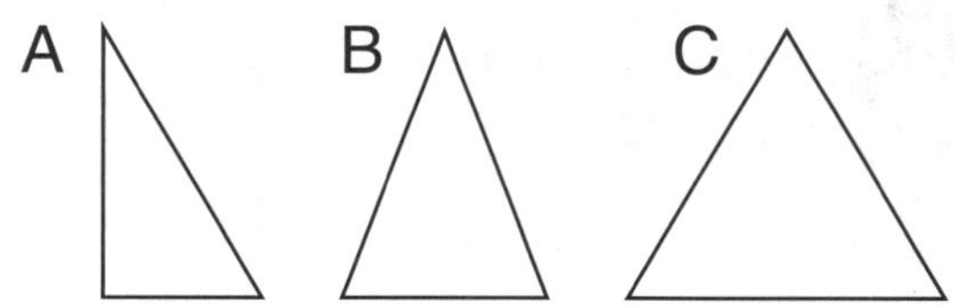

10. Draw a circle on the coordinate (C,7).

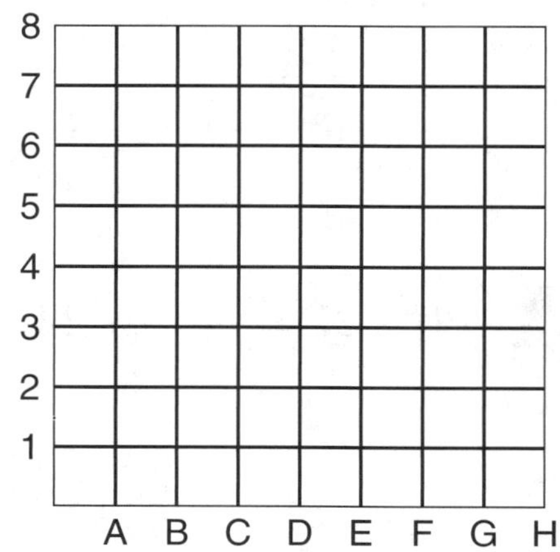

NAME: ________________________________

DIRECTIONS Solve each problem.

1.

$$\begin{array}{r} 36 \\ +\ 15 \\ \hline \end{array}$$

2. \$10.00 – \$6.50 = ________

3. Share 56 equally among 7.

____

4. $7\overline{)21}$

5. What is the value of the 9 in 5,439?

____

6. 4 x 5 = 20 ÷ ☐

7. What is the first month of the year?

____

What is the last month of the year?

____

8. Each cube has 1 cm sides. What is the volume of the model?

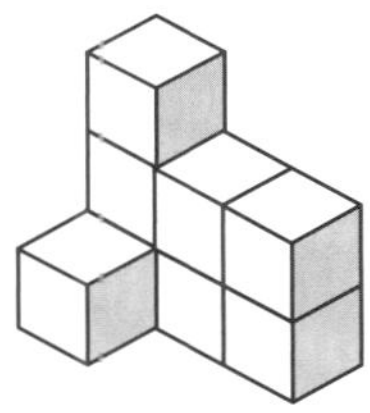

____

9. Name this shape.

____

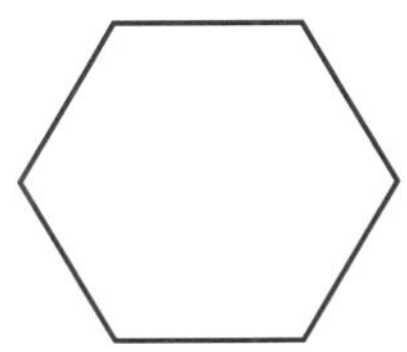

10. There are 12 squares. Half of them are green and 25% are blue. The rest are orange. How many squares are orange?

____

SCORE

1. Ⓨ Ⓝ
2. Ⓨ Ⓝ
3. Ⓨ Ⓝ
4. Ⓨ Ⓝ
5. Ⓨ Ⓝ
6. Ⓨ Ⓝ
7. Ⓨ Ⓝ
8. Ⓨ Ⓝ
9. Ⓨ Ⓝ
10. Ⓨ Ⓝ

___ / 10 Total

NAME: ____________________

DIRECTIONS Solve each problem.

SCORE

1. Ⓨ Ⓝ
2. Ⓨ Ⓝ
3. Ⓨ Ⓝ
4. Ⓨ Ⓝ
5. Ⓨ Ⓝ
6. Ⓨ Ⓝ
7. Ⓨ Ⓝ
8. Ⓨ Ⓝ
9. Ⓨ Ⓝ
10. Ⓨ Ⓝ

___ / 10 Total

1. $\begin{array}{r} 43 \\ -\ 8 \\ \hline \end{array}$

2. 7 x 9 = ________

3. How many groups of 8 are in 48?

____

4. 28 ÷ 4 = ________

5. What ordinal number is after thirtieth?

____

6. 50 – 32 = 60 – n

n = ________

7. One side of a square is 9 cm. What is the area?

____

8. You set your alarm clock to wake up at 6:30 A.M. If you sleep in until 7:28 A.M., how long did you oversleep?

____

9. Record the data in the bar graph.

Home Runs Hit

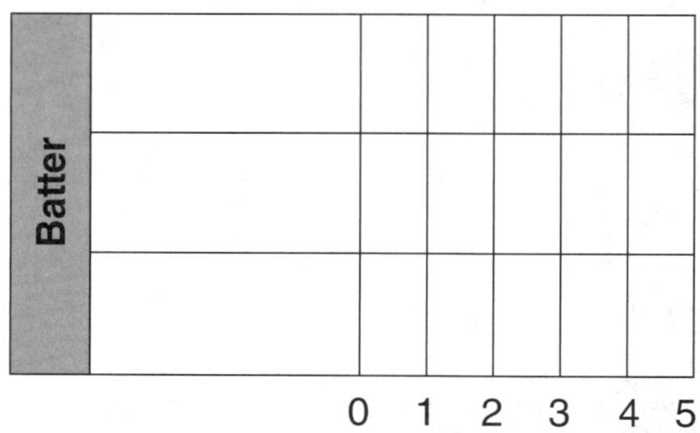

Harry has hit 4 home runs.

Dean has hit 5 home runs.

Dale has hit 2 home runs.

10. $\frac{1}{8}$ of 48 = 6, so $\frac{5}{8}$ of 48 =

____

NAME: ______________________________

DIRECTIONS Solve each problem.

1. 27 + 14 = ________

2. $\frac{3}{10}$ of 70 = ________

3. $7\overline{)63}$

4. 35 ÷ 7 = ________

5. Write 7,903 in expanded notation.

____

____

6. Fill in the missing number.

30, 36, ________, 48, 54

7. Write the length in centimeters.

____

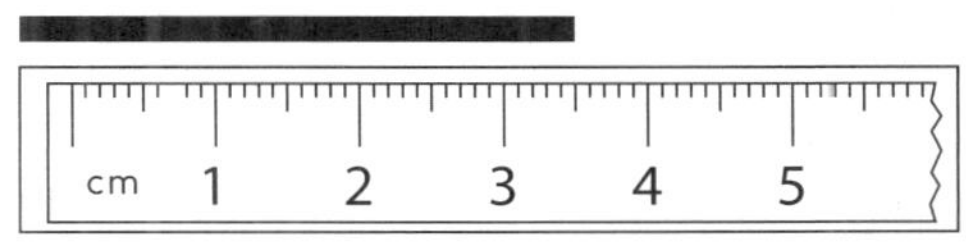

8. What is the temperature?

____

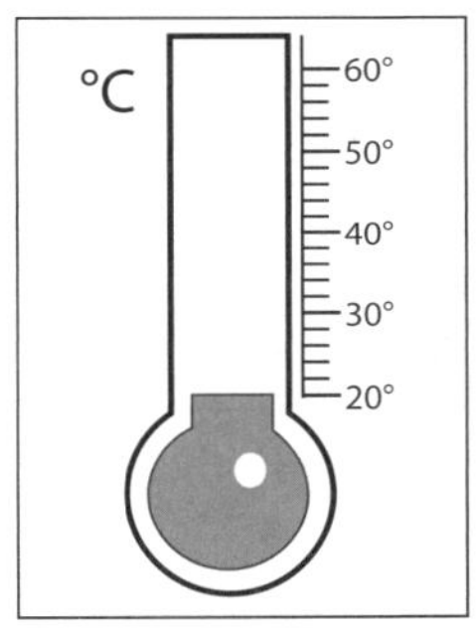

9. What type of prism is shown?

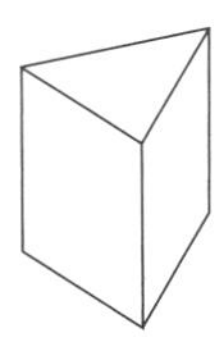

____

10. Write two odd numbers that total the even number 42.

____

SCORE

1. Ⓨ Ⓝ
2. Ⓨ Ⓝ
3. Ⓨ Ⓝ
4. Ⓨ Ⓝ
5. Ⓨ Ⓝ
6. Ⓨ Ⓝ
7. Ⓨ Ⓝ
8. Ⓨ Ⓝ
9. Ⓨ Ⓝ
10. Ⓨ Ⓝ

___ / 10
Total

DAY
112

NAME: ____________________________________

DIRECTIONS Solve each problem.

SCORE

1. Ⓨ Ⓝ
2. Ⓨ Ⓝ
3. Ⓨ Ⓝ
4. Ⓨ Ⓝ
5. Ⓨ Ⓝ
6. Ⓨ Ⓝ
7. Ⓨ Ⓝ
8. Ⓨ Ⓝ
9. Ⓨ Ⓝ
10. Ⓨ Ⓝ

___ / 10
Total

1. 52 – 6 = ________

2. Write 0.25 as a fraction.

____

3. 14 ÷ 7 = ________

4. Calculate the quotient of 72 and 9.

____

5. What is the place value of 7 in 7,891?

____

6. Is 5 x 4 equal to 5 x 3 + 5?

____

7. Calculate the perimeter of the rectangle.

____

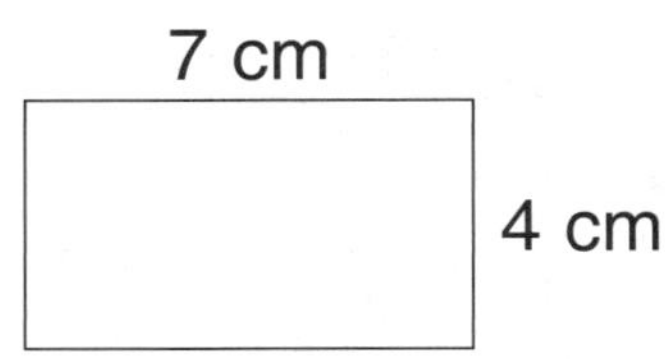

8. 7 ________ = 1 week

9. An equilateral triangle has:

________ angles

________ sides

________ axes of symmetry

10. One bag of peas has a mass of 175 grams. What is the mass of 4 bags?

____

NAME: ______________________________

DIRECTIONS Solve each problem.

1.
$$\begin{array}{r} 18 \\ +\ 13 \\ \hline \end{array}$$

2. What percent is shaded?

____

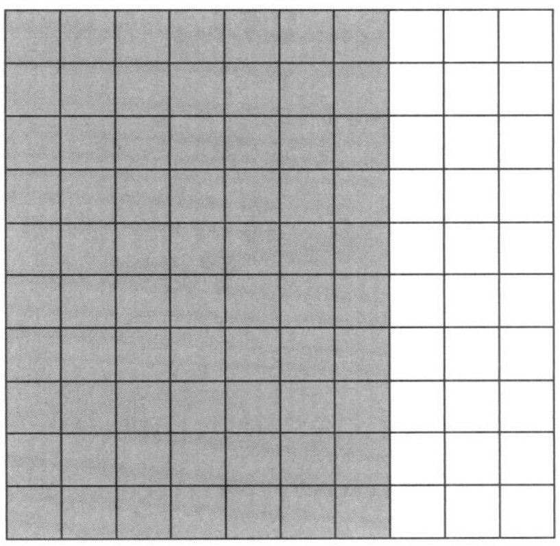

3. $9\overline{)25}$

4. 18 ÷ 9 = ________

5. Is 357 greater than 375?

____

6. 7 x 8 = 56, so

56 ÷ ☐ = 8

7. Draw the time that is 8 minutes later.

8. 8 pints = ________ gallon(s)

9. Find the perimeter of a regular pentagon with 3-inch sides.

____

10. Cheryl has $25.00 in her piggy bank. She saves $6.00 more and then spends $15.00. How much does she have in her piggy bank now?

____

SCORE

1. Ⓨ Ⓝ
2. Ⓨ Ⓝ
3. Ⓨ Ⓝ
4. Ⓨ Ⓝ
5. Ⓨ Ⓝ
6. Ⓨ Ⓝ
7. Ⓨ Ⓝ
8. Ⓨ Ⓝ
9. Ⓨ Ⓝ
10. Ⓨ Ⓝ

___ / 10
Total

DAY 114

NAME: ______________________

DIRECTIONS Solve each problem.

SCORE

1. Ⓨ Ⓝ
2. Ⓨ Ⓝ
3. Ⓨ Ⓝ
4. Ⓨ Ⓝ
5. Ⓨ Ⓝ
6. Ⓨ Ⓝ
7. Ⓨ Ⓝ
8. Ⓨ Ⓝ
9. Ⓨ Ⓝ
10. Ⓨ Ⓝ

___ / 10 Total

1. What is the difference between 32 and 19?

______________________.

2. Is $\frac{7}{10}$ greater than $\frac{7}{100}$?

____

3. Divide 54 by 9. ________

4. $63 \div 6 =$ ________

5. Is 4,736 even or odd?

____

6. $8 + 8 + 8 + 8 = \square \times 8$

7. Circle the best estimate for the weight of the object.

100 g   20 kg   5 kg   1 kg

8. 36 inches equals how many yards?

____

9. Draw the front view.

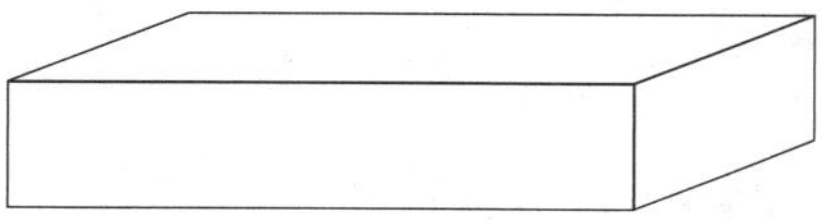

10. Add 9 tens and 5 ones to the number 43.

____

NAME: ____________________

DIRECTIONS Solve each problem.

1. 24 + 18 = ______

2.
```
   7
 x 8
```

3. 63 ÷ 9 = ______

4. 6)48

5. Is 946 closer to 900 or 1,000?

____

6. 5 x 8 = ☐ x 10

7. How many cm are in 50 mm?

____

8. How many days are in July?

____

9. Draw 1 line of symmetry.

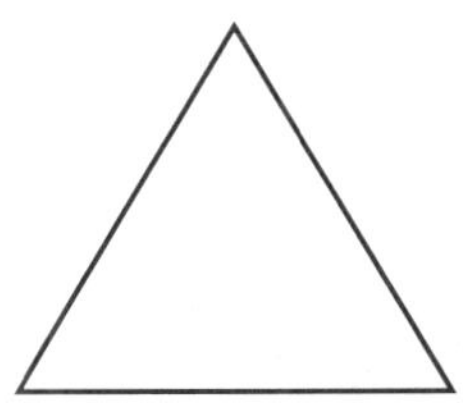

10. Complete the chart with the missing factors.

Product	24	25	28	30
Factor	3	5	4	10
Factor				

SCORE

1. Ⓨ Ⓝ
2. Ⓨ Ⓝ
3. Ⓨ Ⓝ
4. Ⓨ Ⓝ
5. Ⓨ Ⓝ
6. Ⓨ Ⓝ
7. Ⓨ Ⓝ
8. Ⓨ Ⓝ
9. Ⓨ Ⓝ
10. Ⓨ Ⓝ

___ / 10 Total

NAME: ____________________

DIRECTIONS Solve each problem.

SCORE

1. Ⓨ Ⓝ
2. Ⓨ Ⓝ
3. Ⓨ Ⓝ
4. Ⓨ Ⓝ
5. Ⓨ Ⓝ
6. Ⓨ Ⓝ
7. Ⓨ Ⓝ
8. Ⓨ Ⓝ
9. Ⓨ Ⓝ
10. Ⓨ Ⓝ

___ / 10 Total

1. $\begin{array}{r} 24 \\ -\ \ 9 \\ \hline \end{array}$

2. What fraction is shaded?

____

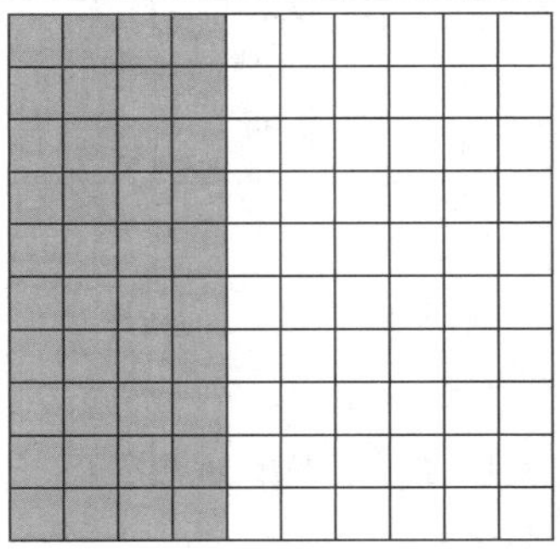

3. Calculate 39 divided by 9.

____

4. $6\overline{)36}$

5. Write the number for four thousand six hundred twenty.

____

6. Fill in the missing number.

32, 40, 48, 56, ________

7. What is the difference in capacity between the cartons of milk and cream?

____

8. Would you use square inches or square feet to measure the area of a bedroom?

____

9. Name the shape of the solid's base.

____

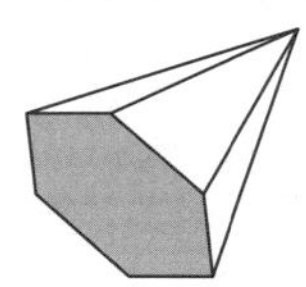

10. Yi Min's school is six miles from her home. Yi Min traveled back and forth to school on the bus all five days last week. How many total miles did Yi Min ride on the school bus during the week?

____

NAME: ______________________

DIRECTIONS Solve each problem.

1.
$$\begin{array}{r} 15 \\ +\ 19 \\ \hline \end{array}$$

2. Is $\frac{4}{10}$ equal to $\frac{4}{100}$?

____

3. $45 \div 9 =$ ________

4. Calculate the quotient of 91 and 10.

____

5. Round 436 to the nearest ten.

____

6. 12 seeds are in a packet. Complete the chart to show how many are in 4 packets.

1 Packet	2 Packets	3 Packets	4 Packets
12			

7. Molly's birthday is the 3rd Saturday in August. If today is July 31st, how many days are there until Molly's birthday?

____

August						
Sun	Mon	Tues	Wed	Thurs	Fri	Sat
				1	2	3
4	5	6	7	8	9	10
11	12	13	14	15	16	17
18	19	20	21	22	23	24
25	26	27	28	29	30	31

8. Which would be the best measure for the lemonade in a full pitcher: a liter, a cup, or a kilogram?

____

9. What shape is the cross-section?

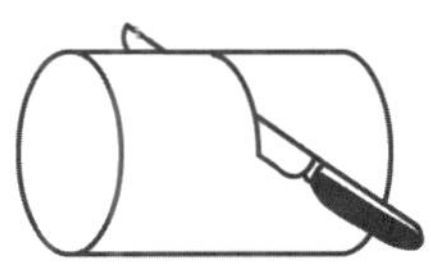

____

10. If you multiply me by 8, the product is 96. What number am I?

____

SCORE

1. Ⓨ Ⓝ
2. Ⓨ Ⓝ
3. Ⓨ Ⓝ
4. Ⓨ Ⓝ
5. Ⓨ Ⓝ
6. Ⓨ Ⓝ
7. Ⓨ Ⓝ
8. Ⓨ Ⓝ
9. Ⓨ Ⓝ
10. Ⓨ Ⓝ

___ / 10 Total

DAY 118

NAME: ____________________

DIRECTIONS Solve each problem.

SCORE

1. Ⓨ Ⓝ
2. Ⓨ Ⓝ
3. Ⓨ Ⓝ
4. Ⓨ Ⓝ
5. Ⓨ Ⓝ
6. Ⓨ Ⓝ
7. Ⓨ Ⓝ
8. Ⓨ Ⓝ
9. Ⓨ Ⓝ
10. Ⓨ Ⓝ

___ / 10 Total

1. 35 – 19 = ________

2. Shade 70%.

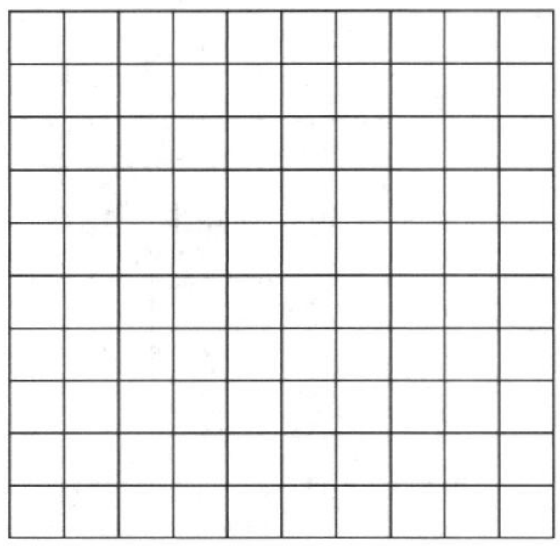

3. 24 ÷ 12 = ________

4. $6\overline{)72}$

5. What is 100 more than 5,634?

____

6. 8 x 4 is equal to ☐ x 8.

7. How many 250 milliliter cups will fill a 1 liter bucket?

____

8. If it is Friday, what day is it 20 days from now?

____

9.

Dollars Earned in May

Audrey	$15
Dameon	$23
Jason	$12
Lauren	$18

If Jason earns an additional $5.00, how much money will he have?

____

10. Do you make this pattern by *reflecting*, *translating*, or *rotating*?

____

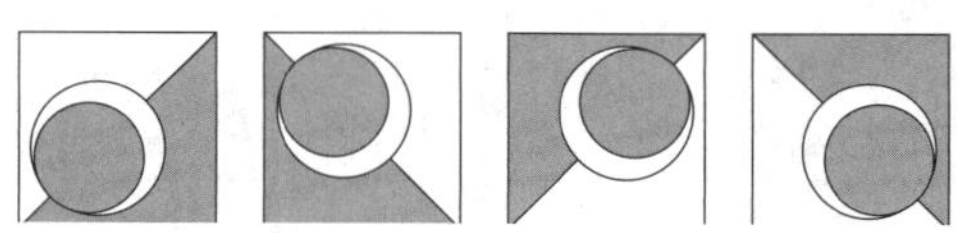

NAME: ______________________

DIRECTIONS Solve each problem.

1. 24 + 29 = ________

2. Write $\frac{50}{100}$ as a percentage.

____

3. $9\overline{)63}$

4. 24 ÷ 6 = ________

5. Write 56 in words.

____

6. 9 + 9 + 9 = ☐ x 9

7. Which month follows:

March? ______________

May? ______________

8. Each cube has 1-cm sides. What is the volume of the model?

____

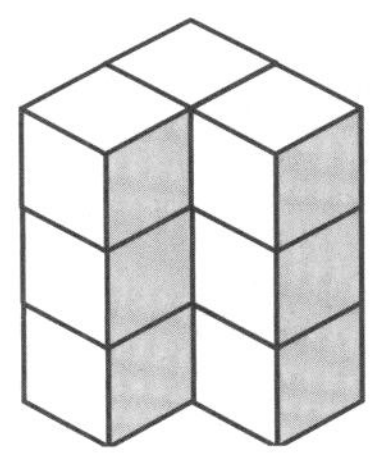

9. Fill in the blank with *rotate*, *reflect*, or *translate*.

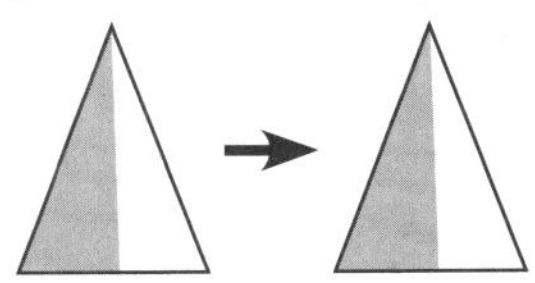

____

10. Patrick has swimming lessons 3 times a week for $\frac{1}{2}$ hour. How much time does he spend in 4 weeks at swimming lessons?

____

SCORE

1. Ⓨ Ⓝ
2. Ⓨ Ⓝ
3. Ⓨ Ⓝ
4. Ⓨ Ⓝ
5. Ⓨ Ⓝ
6. Ⓨ Ⓝ
7. Ⓨ Ⓝ
8. Ⓨ Ⓝ
9. Ⓨ Ⓝ
10. Ⓨ Ⓝ

___ / 10 Total

DAY
120

NAME: ______________________

DIRECTIONS Solve each problem.

SCORE

1. Ⓨ Ⓝ
2. Ⓨ Ⓝ
3. Ⓨ Ⓝ
4. Ⓨ Ⓝ
5. Ⓨ Ⓝ
6. Ⓨ Ⓝ
7. Ⓨ Ⓝ
8. Ⓨ Ⓝ
9. Ⓨ Ⓝ
10. Ⓨ Ⓝ

___ / 10
Total

1. $\begin{array}{r} 46 \\ -\ 29 \\ \hline \end{array}$

2. 6 x 40 = ________

3. 72 ÷ 8 = ________

4. $7\overline{)63}$

5. What is the first odd number before 624?

____

6. 9 x 4 = 36, so

36 ÷ ☐ = 9

7. Is the area of a tennis court measured in cm^2 or m^2?

____

8. It takes you 12 minutes to get to your friend's house. You leave at 8:10. What time will you arrive at your friend's house?

____

9. Does this shape tessellate?

____

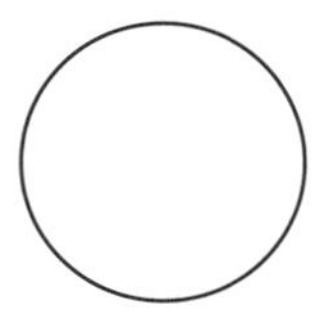

10. Color half of the area so that both the colored and uncolored parts have the same shape.

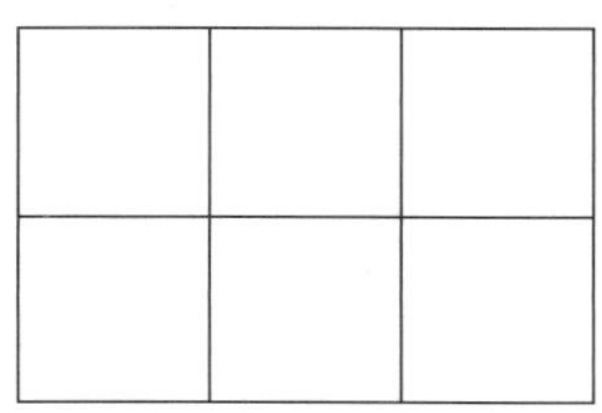

DAY 121

NAME: ____________________________

DIRECTIONS Solve each problem.

1. What is the sum of 27 and 19?

______________________.

2. $\frac{1}{5}$ of 30 = ________

3. 81 ÷ 9 = ________

4. Calculate the quotient of twenty-four and six.

____

5. 5,000 + 40 + 6 = ________

6. Fill in the missing fraction.

$\frac{1}{8}$, $\frac{2}{8}$, $\frac{3}{8}$, ________, $\frac{5}{8}$

7. Write the length in millimeters.

____

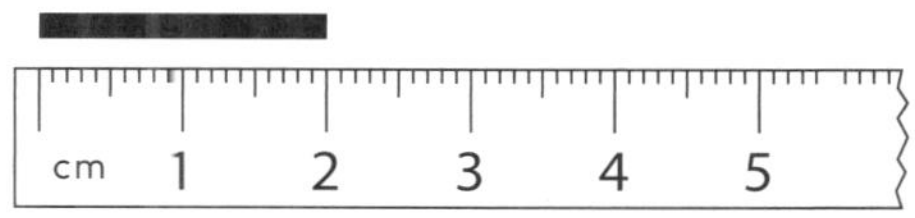

8. Is a 24°F day warm or cold?

____

9. Draw a line from the real-life object to the solid.

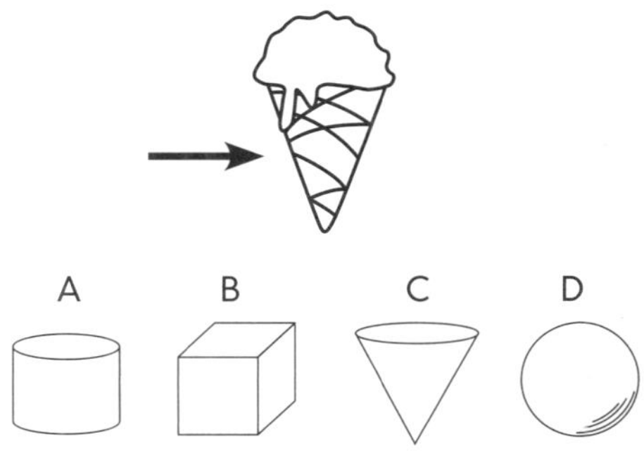

10. Follow the pattern in the first circle to complete the second circle.

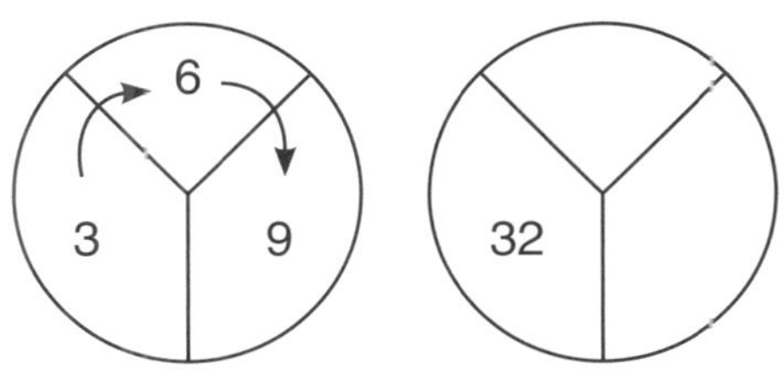

SCORE

1. Ⓨ Ⓝ
2. Ⓨ Ⓝ
3. Ⓨ Ⓝ
4. Ⓨ Ⓝ
5. Ⓨ Ⓝ
6. Ⓨ Ⓝ
7. Ⓨ Ⓝ
8. Ⓨ Ⓝ
9. Ⓨ Ⓝ
10. Ⓨ Ⓝ

___ / 10 Total

DAY
122

NAME: ____________________

DIRECTIONS Solve each problem.

SCORE

1. Ⓨ Ⓝ
2. Ⓨ Ⓝ
3. Ⓨ Ⓝ
4. Ⓨ Ⓝ
5. Ⓨ Ⓝ
6. Ⓨ Ⓝ
7. Ⓨ Ⓝ
8. Ⓨ Ⓝ
9. Ⓨ Ⓝ
10. Ⓨ Ⓝ

___ / 10 Total

1. 69 – 26 = ________

2. Write 45% as a decimal.

____

3. 121 ÷ 11 = ________

4. Divide 45 into 9 equal groups.

____

5. Write 6,802 in expanded notation.

____

6. 7 + 7 + 7 + 7 = ☐ x 7

7. Calculate the area of a square with 7-cm sides.

____

8. ________ months = 1 year

9. **Books Read in March**

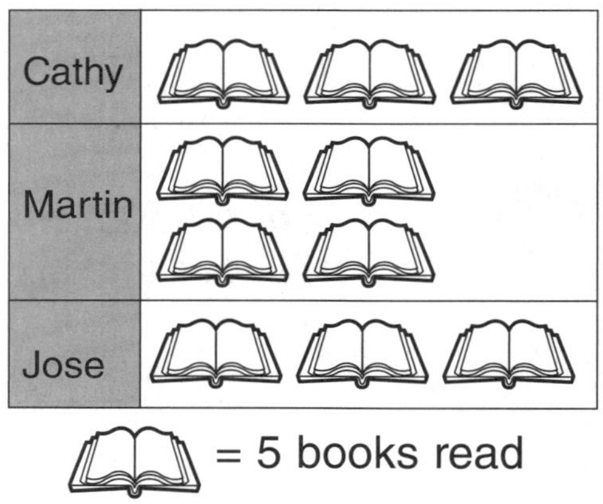

Jose's goal was to read 25 books in March. Did he reach his goal?

____

10. Mick's fishing line was 73 m. He cut off 42 m. How long is it now?

____

NAME: ____________________

DIRECTIONS Solve each problem.

1. $\begin{array}{r} 25 \\ +\ 8 \\ \hline \end{array}$

2. Is $\frac{9}{10}$ equal to $\frac{9}{100}$?

____

3. $7\overline{)56}$

4. $43 \div 8 =$ ______

5. Write the ordinal number for 463.

____

6. 25 + ☐ + 12 = 57

7. Fill in the blanks for the time shown.

6: ______
______ to 7

8. 4 pints = ______ gallon(s)

9. Circle the prism and put an X on the pyramid.

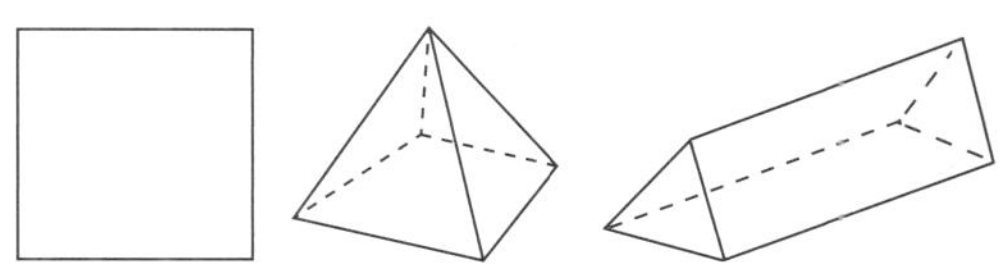

10. Jarome buys some school supplies. The total is $8.52. He pays with a $10 bill. How much change will he get?

____

SCORE

1. Ⓨ Ⓝ
2. Ⓨ Ⓝ
3. Ⓨ Ⓝ
4. Ⓨ Ⓝ
5. Ⓨ Ⓝ
6. Ⓨ Ⓝ
7. Ⓨ Ⓝ
8. Ⓨ Ⓝ
9. Ⓨ Ⓝ
10. Ⓨ Ⓝ

___ / 10
Total

NAME: ______________________________

DIRECTIONS Solve each problem.

SCORE

1. Ⓨ Ⓝ
2. Ⓨ Ⓝ
3. Ⓨ Ⓝ
4. Ⓨ Ⓝ
5. Ⓨ Ⓝ
6. Ⓨ Ⓝ
7. Ⓨ Ⓝ
8. Ⓨ Ⓝ
9. Ⓨ Ⓝ
10. Ⓨ Ⓝ

___ / 10
Total

1.
$$\begin{array}{r} 19 \\ -\ 15 \\ \hline \end{array}$$

2. \$10.00 – \$7.25 = ________

3. $8\overline{)40}$

4. Calculate the quotient of 45 and 5.

____

5. What is the place value of 8 in 2,836?

____

6. 10 x 3 = 60 – ☐

7. Would you use kilograms or grams to measure the mass of a pen?

____

8. 48 inches = ________ feet

9. Do perpendicular lines meet at right angles?

____

10. Complete the chart for the hundred grid to represent the shaded region.

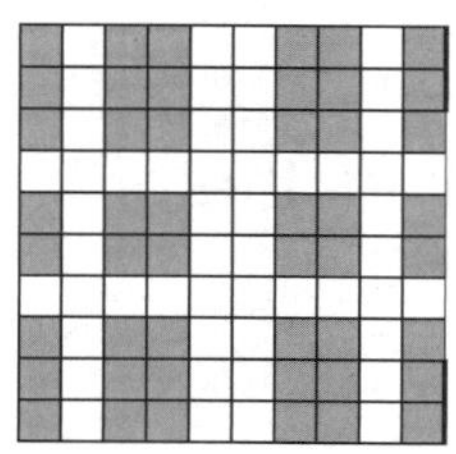

$\frac{\quad}{100}$	0.	%

NAME: ______________________________

DIRECTIONS Solve each problem.

1. 59 + 5 = ________

2. What is the total number of apples if there are 8 bags of 4 apples?

____

3. Divide 8 into 48.

____

4. $6\overline{)54}$

5. Is 7,323 even or odd?

____

6. 7 x 4 = 28, so

28 ÷ ☐ = 7

7. Circle the best estimate for the area of a CD case.

150 cm^2 150 m^2

8. Write the length in inches.

______________ inches

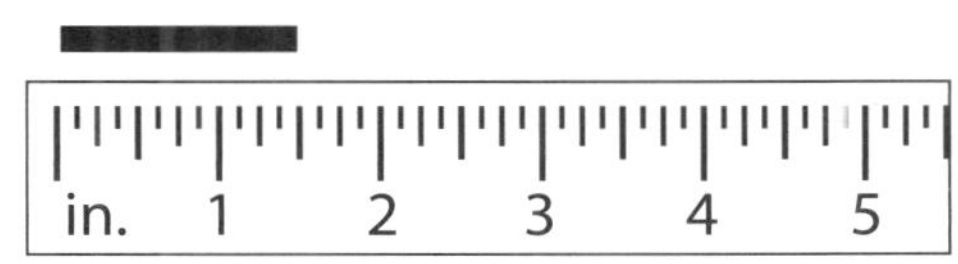

9. Circle the solids that have a triangle as their base. Each base is shown in grey.

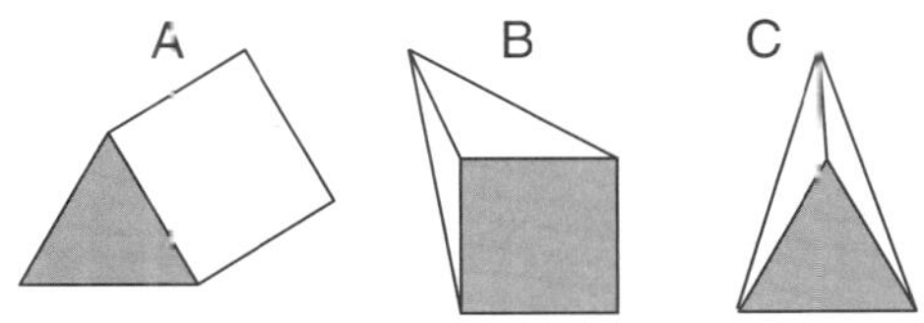

10. Complete the multiplication wheel.

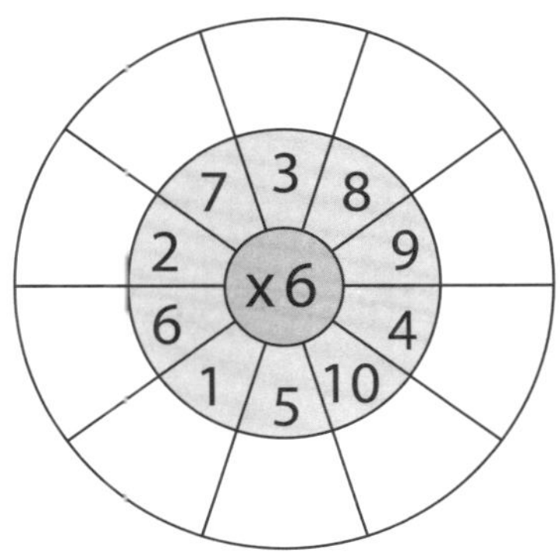

SCORE

1. Ⓨ Ⓝ
2. Ⓨ Ⓝ
3. Ⓨ Ⓝ
4. Ⓨ Ⓝ
5. Ⓨ Ⓝ
6. Ⓨ Ⓝ
7. Ⓨ Ⓝ
8. Ⓨ Ⓝ
9. Ⓨ Ⓝ
10. Ⓨ Ⓝ

___ / 10
Total

NAME: ____________________

DIRECTIONS Solve each problem.

SCORE

1. Ⓨ Ⓝ
2. Ⓨ Ⓝ
3. Ⓨ Ⓝ
4. Ⓨ Ⓝ
5. Ⓨ Ⓝ
6. Ⓨ Ⓝ
7. Ⓨ Ⓝ
8. Ⓨ Ⓝ
9. Ⓨ Ⓝ
10. Ⓨ Ⓝ

___ / 10
Total

1. 27 – 16 = ________

2. What percentage is shaded?

____

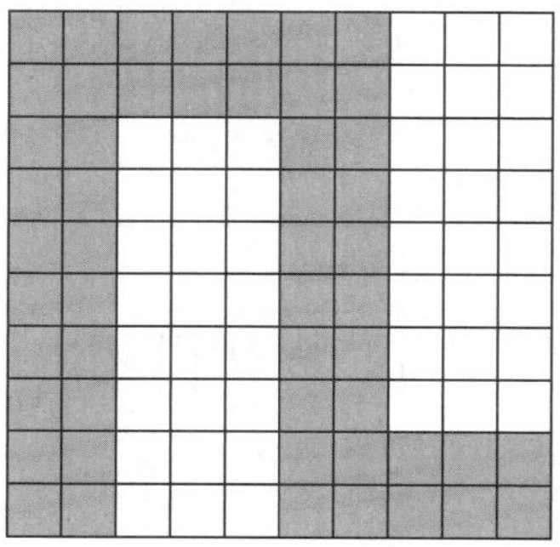

3. 81 ÷ 9 = ________

4. 45 ÷ 5 = ________

5. Write the number for three thousand fifty-eight.

____

6. Fill in the missing number.

150, 160, ________, 180, 190

7. How many times can a 1-L container of oil be filled from a 4-L jug?

____

8. What is the most likely width of a book?

8 inches

8 feet

8 minutes

9.

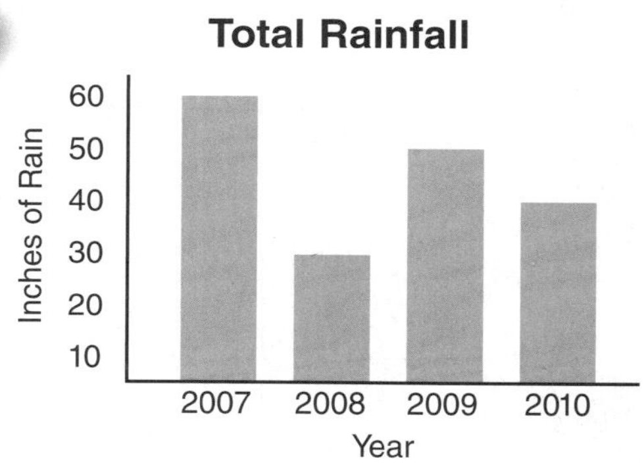

How much more did it rain in 2009 than in 2010?

____

10. What is the area of a square that is 12 inches on each side?

____

NAME: ____________________

DIRECTIONS Solve each problem.

SCORE

1.
$$\begin{array}{r} 24 \\ +\ 19 \\ \hline \end{array}$$

2. Is $\frac{70}{100}$ equal to $\frac{7}{10}$?

____

3. $72 \div 9 =$ ________

4. Calculate the quotient of 35 and 7.

____

5. What is 10 more than 479?

____

6. Is 6 x 7 equal to 6 x 6 + 6?

____

7. What day of the week was July 31st?

____

August						
Sun	Mon	Tues	Wed	Thurs	Fri	Sat
				1	2	3
4	5	6	7	8	9	10
11	12	13	14	15	16	17
18	19	20	21	22	23	24
25	26	27	28	29	30	31

8. How many days are there in 4 years? (Remember leap year!)

____

9. What type of prism is shown?

____

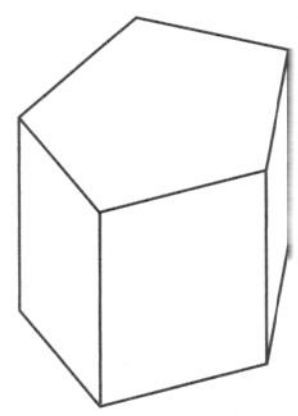

10. Triple 16, then add 100.

____

1. Ⓨ Ⓝ
2. Ⓨ Ⓝ
3. Ⓨ Ⓝ
4. Ⓨ Ⓝ
5. Ⓨ Ⓝ
6. Ⓨ Ⓝ
7. Ⓨ Ⓝ
8. Ⓨ Ⓝ
9. Ⓨ Ⓝ
10. Ⓨ Ⓝ

___ / 10
Total

DAY
128

NAME: ______________________________

DIRECTIONS Solve each problem.

SCORE

1. Ⓨ Ⓝ
2. Ⓨ Ⓝ
3. Ⓨ Ⓝ
4. Ⓨ Ⓝ
5. Ⓨ Ⓝ
6. Ⓨ Ⓝ
7. Ⓨ Ⓝ
8. Ⓨ Ⓝ
9. Ⓨ Ⓝ
10. Ⓨ Ⓝ

___ / 10
Total

1. Subtract 21 from 34.

____

2. Write $\frac{9}{10}$ as a percentage.

____

3. $24 \div 5 =$ ________

4. $7 \overline{)\,28}$

5. Round 789 to the nearest hundred.

____

6. $7 \times 8 = 56 \times \square$

7. I put 700 mL of water in the cup. Next I put a toy in the cup. How much water was displaced by the toy?

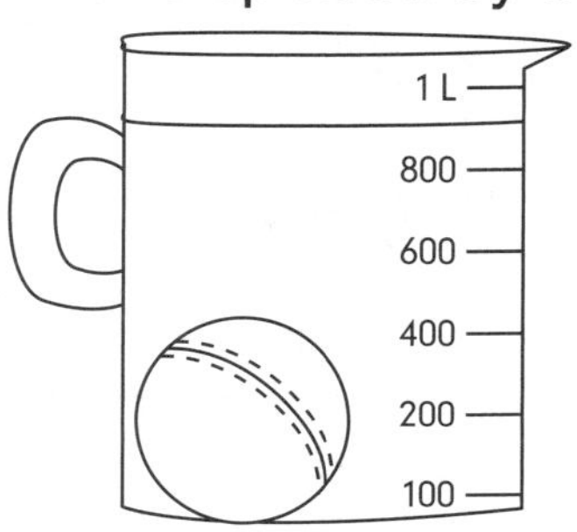

________ mL

8. Calculate the perimeter.

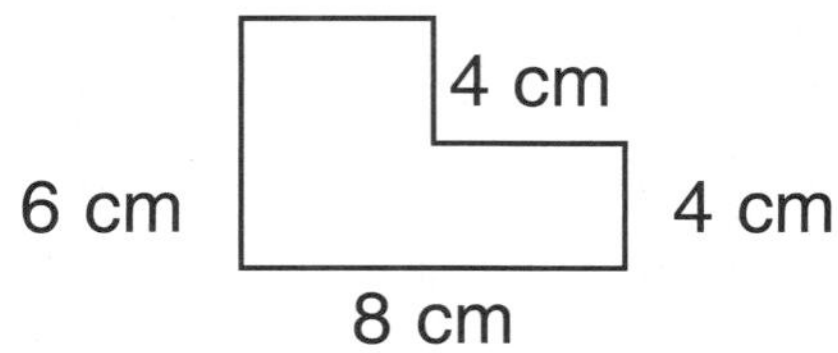

9. Which numbers are inside the rectangle, circle, and triangle?

____

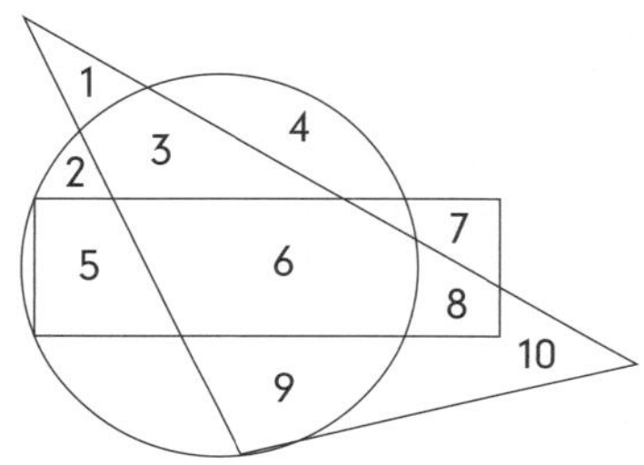

10. Plot each set of coordinates to make a triangle. (D, 7); (B, 3); (G, 3)

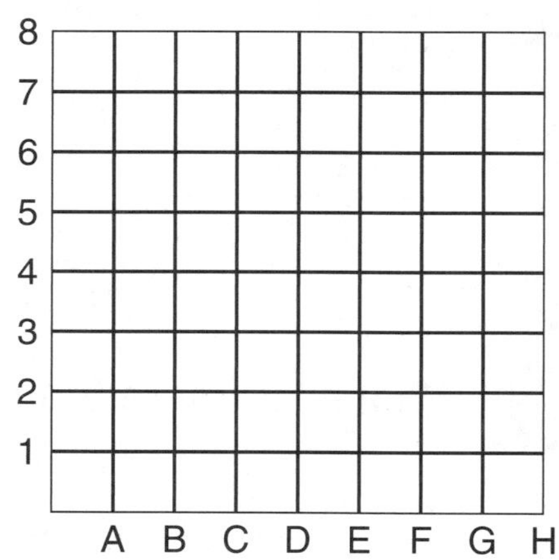

NAME: ____________________

DIRECTIONS Solve each problem.

1. 28 + 29 = ________

2. Shade 90%.

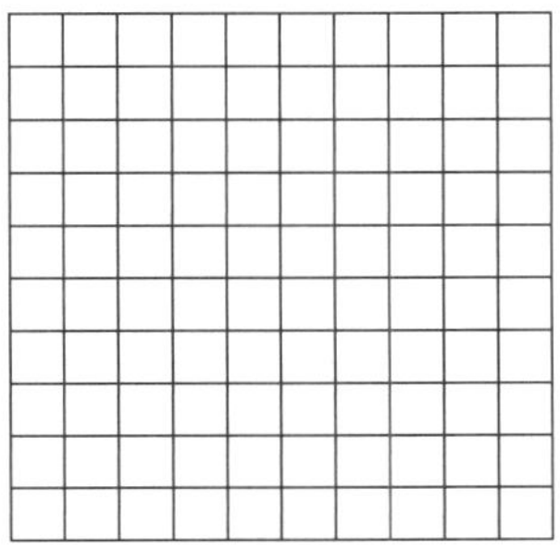

3. 7 ⟌ 36

4. 24 ÷ 6 = ________

5. How many digits are in the number 1,079?

____

6. Complete the chart. There are 9 nails in a bag. You need 45 nails. How many bags will you buy?

____

1 Bag	2 Bags	3 Bags	4 Bags	5 Bags	6 Bags
9					

7. Which months are in the first quarter of the year?

____

____

____

8. Calculate the volume of a cube with 2-cm sides.

____

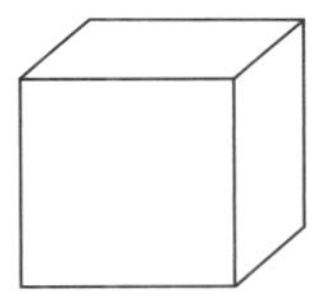

9. Draw the top view.

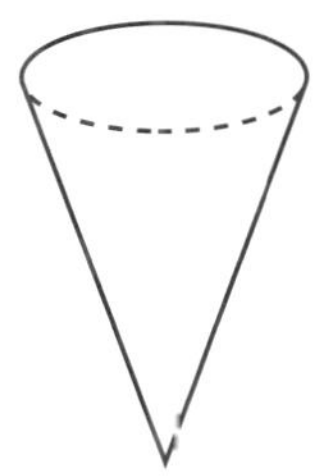

10. Kelly's mom pays her $4.00 an hour to babysit her baby sister. How much money will she make in 4 weeks if she watches her sister 3 hours every week?

____

SCORE

1. Ⓨ Ⓝ
2. Ⓨ Ⓝ
3. Ⓨ Ⓝ
4. Ⓨ Ⓝ
5. Ⓨ Ⓝ
6. Ⓨ Ⓝ
7. Ⓨ Ⓝ
8. Ⓨ Ⓝ
9. Ⓨ Ⓝ
10. Ⓨ Ⓝ

___ / 10 Total

DAY 130

NAME: ____________________

DIRECTIONS Solve each problem.

SCORE

1. Ⓨ Ⓝ
2. Ⓨ Ⓝ
3. Ⓨ Ⓝ
4. Ⓨ Ⓝ
5. Ⓨ Ⓝ
6. Ⓨ Ⓝ
7. Ⓨ Ⓝ
8. Ⓨ Ⓝ
9. Ⓨ Ⓝ
10. Ⓨ Ⓝ

___ / 10 Total

1. $\begin{array}{r} 28 \\ -\ 17 \\ \hline \end{array}$

2. $3 \times 8 =$ ________

3. 41 divided by 4 is

________________.

4. $100 \div 10 =$ ________

5. Is 473 greater than 4,073?

____

6. $10 - 2 = 4 \times \square$

7. Our lunchroom floor is 50 m^2. The tables cover 14 m^2. What area is free?

____

8. You want to go to a 3:15 movie. It takes you 25 minutes to get to the theater. What time should you leave?

____

9.

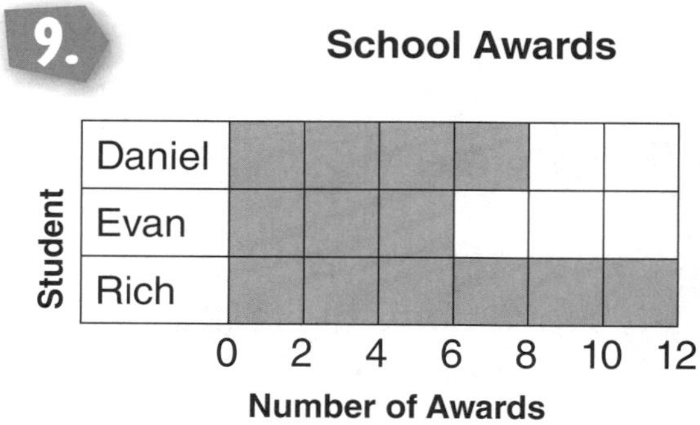

How many more awards does Daniel have to win to tie with Rich?

____

10. $\frac{1}{4}$ of 36 = 9, so $\frac{3}{4}$ of 36 =

____

NAME: ______________________________

DIRECTIONS Solve each problem.

1. Total 35 and 27.

____

2. Is $\frac{9}{10}$ greater than $\frac{9}{100}$?

____

3. 88 ÷ 11 = ________

4. $4\overline{)64}$

5. Is 537 even or odd?

____

6. Fill in the missing number.

930, 920, 910, ________, 890

7. Would you measure the pencil in centimeters or meters?

____

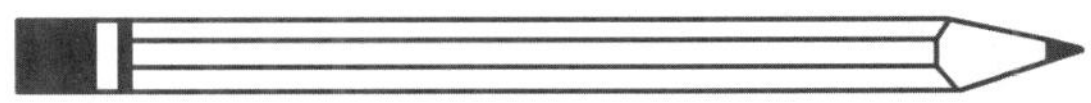

8. What is the temperature?

____

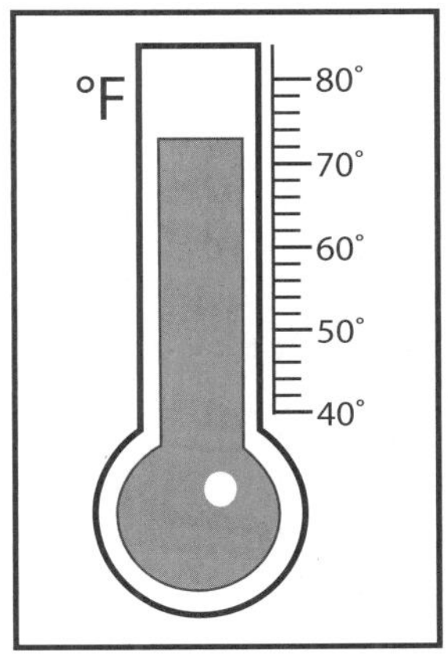

9. Draw 1 line of symmetry.

10. Write two odd numbers that total the even number 58.

____

SCORE

1. Ⓨ Ⓝ
2. Ⓨ Ⓝ
3. Ⓨ Ⓝ
4. Ⓨ Ⓝ
5. Ⓨ Ⓝ
6. Ⓨ Ⓝ
7. Ⓨ Ⓝ
8. Ⓨ Ⓝ
9. Ⓨ Ⓝ
10. Ⓨ Ⓝ

___ / 10
Total

NAME: ____________________

DIRECTIONS Solve each problem.

SCORE

1. Ⓨ Ⓝ
2. Ⓨ Ⓝ
3. Ⓨ Ⓝ
4. Ⓨ Ⓝ
5. Ⓨ Ⓝ
6. Ⓨ Ⓝ
7. Ⓨ Ⓝ
8. Ⓨ Ⓝ
9. Ⓨ Ⓝ
10. Ⓨ Ⓝ

___ / 10 Total

1. 46 – 25 = ______

2. Write 0.5 as a percentage.

____

3. 75 ÷ 5 = ______

4. $8\overline{)40}$

5. Round 4,506 to the nearest hundred.

____

6. 9 + 9 + 9 + ☐ = 4 x 9

7. Calculate the perimeter of a square with 7-cm sides.

____

8. ______ hours = 120 minutes

9. I have one curved surface and no flat surfaces. What solid am I?

____

10. Sheila bought 3 dozen eggs. How many eggs did she buy?

____

NAME: ______________________________

DIRECTIONS Solve each problem.

1.
$$\begin{array}{r} 18 \\ +\ \ 6 \\ \hline \end{array}$$

2. $\frac{1}{10}$ of 20 = ________

3. Divide 15 into 3 equal groups.

____

4. 82 ÷ 6 = ________

5. Write 4,825 in words.

____

____

6. 23 – 15 = ☐ + 8

7. Draw the time that is 16 minutes later.

8. ________ gallon(s) = 2 quarts

9. **Sports Played Each Year**

	1st Trimester	2nd Trimester	3rd Trimester
Troy	soccer	basketball	baseball
Jessica	golf	basketball	track
Allison	soccer	diving	swimming

How many children play soccer?

____

10. Haru gets $2.50 each week for allowance. How much does he get in 4 weeks?

____

SCORE

1. Ⓨ Ⓝ
2. Ⓨ Ⓝ
3. Ⓨ Ⓝ
4. Ⓨ Ⓝ
5. Ⓨ Ⓝ
6. Ⓨ Ⓝ
7. Ⓨ Ⓝ
8. Ⓨ Ⓝ
9. Ⓨ Ⓝ
10. Ⓨ Ⓝ

___ / 10
Total

DAY
134

NAME: ____________________________

DIRECTIONS Solve each problem.

SCORE

1. Ⓨ Ⓝ
2. Ⓨ Ⓝ
3. Ⓨ Ⓝ
4. Ⓨ Ⓝ
5. Ⓨ Ⓝ
6. Ⓨ Ⓝ
7. Ⓨ Ⓝ
8. Ⓨ Ⓝ
9. Ⓨ Ⓝ
10. Ⓨ Ⓝ

___ / 10
Total

1. $\begin{array}{r} 53 \\ -\ 22 \\ \hline \end{array}$

2. $\frac{3}{4}$ of 16 = ________

3. 25 ÷ 5 = ________

4. $2\overline{)17}$

5. Write 624 in expanded notation.

____

____

6. 218 + 12 = 240 − ☐

7. Joe's mass is half the mass of Sam, whose mass is 46 kg. What is Joe's mass?

____

8. 6 inches = ________ foot

9. A rectangle has:

________ angles

________ sides

________ axes of symmetry

10. Subtract 7 tens and 0 ones from the number 83.

____

NAME: ____________________

DIRECTIONS Solve each problem.

1. 37 + 24 = ______

2. 8 x 6 = ______

3. 40 ÷ 4 = ______

4. 19 ÷ 3 = ______

5. 600 + 70 = ______

6. Is 4 x 3 equal to 6 x 2?

____

7. How many meters are in 600 centimeters?

____

8. What month comes before August?

____

9. Is a square a rectangle?

____

10. Complete the chart with the missing factors.

Product	32	36	40	42
Factor	4	6	5	6
Factor				

SCORE

1. Ⓨ Ⓝ
2. Ⓨ Ⓝ
3. Ⓨ Ⓝ
4. Ⓨ Ⓝ
5. Ⓨ Ⓝ
6. Ⓨ Ⓝ
7. Ⓨ Ⓝ
8. Ⓨ Ⓝ
9. Ⓨ Ⓝ
10. Ⓨ Ⓝ

___ / 10 Total

DAY
136

NAME: ____________________

DIRECTIONS Solve each problem.

SCORE

1. Ⓨ Ⓝ
2. Ⓨ Ⓝ
3. Ⓨ Ⓝ
4. Ⓨ Ⓝ
5. Ⓨ Ⓝ
6. Ⓨ Ⓝ
7. Ⓨ Ⓝ
8. Ⓨ Ⓝ
9. Ⓨ Ⓝ
10. Ⓨ Ⓝ

___ / 10
Total

1. 68 – 34 = ________

2. 10% of 30 = ________

3. $9\overline{)45}$

4. Divide 37 by 3. ________

5. What is the value of the hundreds place in 1,743?

____

6. Fill in the missing number.

0.85, 0.80, ________, 0.70

7. I drink 250 mL of milk each day. How much milk do I drink in 5 days?

____

8. How many minutes are there between 5:38 A.M. and 9:42 P.M.?

____

9. This prism has:

________ faces

________ edges

A ____________ for a base

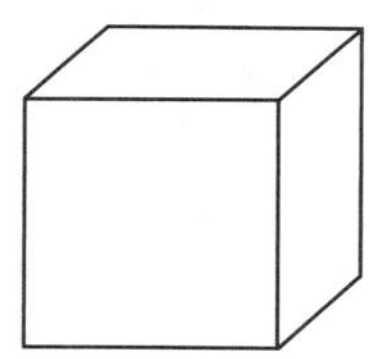

10. You have 57 cents. You want to buy new pencils. Each pencil costs 10 cents. What is the greatest number of pencils you can buy?

____

NAME: ______________________

DIRECTIONS Solve each problem.

SCORE

1. $\begin{array}{r} 24 \\ +\ 14 \\ \hline \end{array}$

2. Is $\frac{1}{8}$ less than $\frac{1}{4}$?

____

3. Calculate the quotient of 26 and 13.

____

4. $65 \div 10 =$ ________

5. What is the place value of 6 in 216?

____

6. $27 \div n = 9$

$n =$ ________

7. What day of the week is the first day in December?

____

December						
Sun	Mon	Tues	Wed	Thurs	Fri	Sat
	1	2	3	4	5	6
7	8	9	10	11	12	13
14	15	16	17	18	19	20
21	22	23	24	25	26	27
28	29	30	31			

8. Would you use a thermometer or a ruler to measure distance?

____

9. Name a two-dimensional shape that has two equal acute angles and two equal obtuse angles.

____

10. If you divide me by 8, you get 6. What number am I?

____

1. Ⓨ Ⓝ
2. Ⓨ Ⓝ
3. Ⓨ Ⓝ
4. Ⓨ Ⓝ
5. Ⓨ Ⓝ
6. Ⓨ Ⓝ
7. Ⓨ Ⓝ
8. Ⓨ Ⓝ
9. Ⓨ Ⓝ
10. Ⓨ Ⓝ

___ / 10

Total

DAY 138

NAME: ____________________

DIRECTIONS Solve each problem.

SCORE

1. Ⓨ Ⓝ
2. Ⓨ Ⓝ
3. Ⓨ Ⓝ
4. Ⓨ Ⓝ
5. Ⓨ Ⓝ
6. Ⓨ Ⓝ
7. Ⓨ Ⓝ
8. Ⓨ Ⓝ
9. Ⓨ Ⓝ
10. Ⓨ Ⓝ

___ / 10 Total

1. $\begin{array}{r} 28 \\ -\ 13 \\ \hline \end{array}$

2. Calculate 50 percent of 40.

____

3. $76 \div 8 =$ ________

4. $6\overline{)89}$

5. How many digits are in 9,092?

____

6. $100 \div 2 = \square \times 5$

7. How many 250-milliliter scoops of ice cream are in a 6-liter carton?

____

8. 48 hours = ________ days

9. Is this a right angle?

____

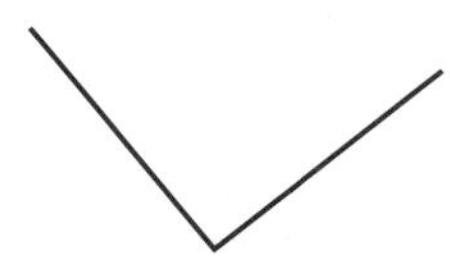

10. Write the directions for the path the counter moved.

____

____

____

____

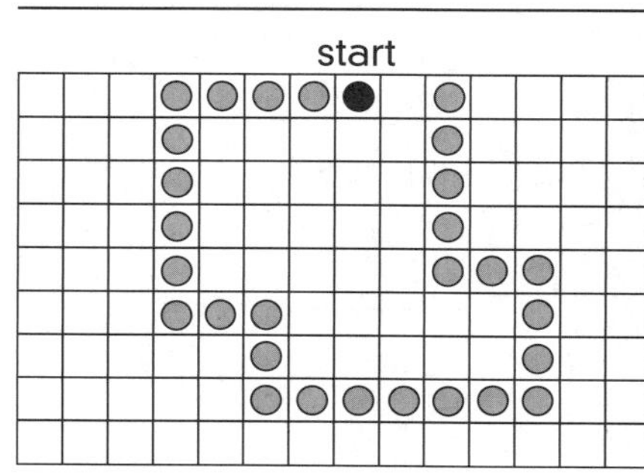

NAME: ______________________

DIRECTIONS Solve each problem.

1. 27 + 15 = ________

2. $\frac{1}{8}$ of 40 is ________.

3. 50 ÷ 10 = ________

4. $9\overline{)38}$

5. Round 4,737 to the nearest thousand.

____

6. 7 + 7 + 7 + 7 + ☐ = 5 x 7

7. How many days are in

January? ________

May? ________

August? ________

8. 10 mm = ________ cm

9. Label with *reflection*, *rotation*, or *translation*.

____

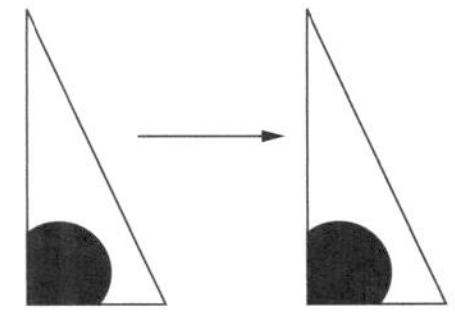

10. Draw 9 triangles. Color $\frac{2}{3}$ of them yellow. Color the rest blue. How many are blue?

____

SCORE

1. Ⓨ Ⓝ
2. Ⓨ Ⓝ
3. Ⓨ Ⓝ
4. Ⓨ Ⓝ
5. Ⓨ Ⓝ
6. Ⓨ Ⓝ
7. Ⓨ Ⓝ
8. Ⓨ Ⓝ
9. Ⓨ Ⓝ
10. Ⓨ Ⓝ

___ / 10

Total

NAME: ____________________

DIRECTIONS Solve each problem.

SCORE

1. Ⓨ Ⓝ
2. Ⓨ Ⓝ
3. Ⓨ Ⓝ
4. Ⓨ Ⓝ
5. Ⓨ Ⓝ
6. Ⓨ Ⓝ
7. Ⓨ Ⓝ
8. Ⓨ Ⓝ
9. Ⓨ Ⓝ
10. Ⓨ Ⓝ

___ / 10 Total

1. 28 – 16 = ________

2. List the first 3 multiples of 7.

________ ________ ________

3. 43 ÷ 7 = ________

4. $6\overline{)27}$

5. Is 421 even or odd?

____

6. 7 x 6 = 42, so

42 ÷ ☐ = 6

7. Is the area of a computer screen measured in cm^2 or m^2?

____

8. ________ seconds = 14 minutes

9. Draw the top view.

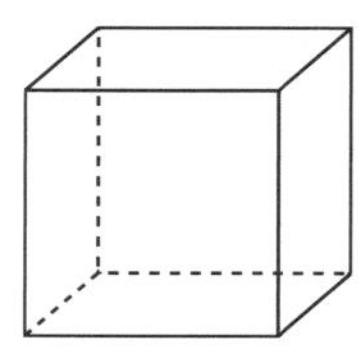

10. Color half of the area so that both the colored and uncolored parts have the same shape.

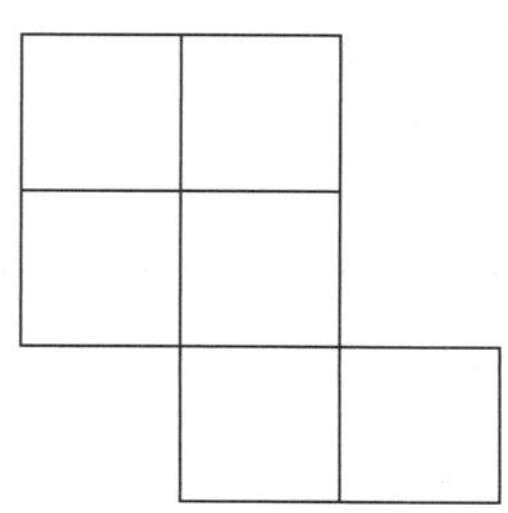

NAME: ____________________

DIRECTIONS Solve each problem.

1.

$$\begin{array}{r} 33 \\ +\ 25 \\ \hline \end{array}$$

2. 10% of 20 is ________.

3. 77 ÷ 11 = ________

4. Divide 4 into 90. ________

5. Write 8,931 in words.

____

____

____

6. Fill in the missing fraction.

$\frac{6}{10}$, $\frac{7}{10}$, ________, $\frac{9}{10}$

7. Write the length in millimeters. ________

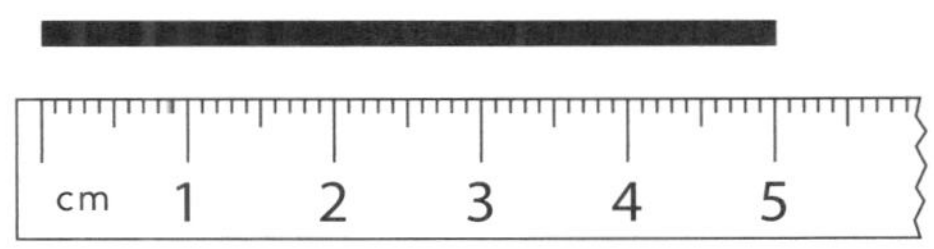

8. ________ yards = 12 feet

9. Name the polygon that has five vertices.

____

10. Use each of the five numbers once and any operations to solve the problem below.

10	13	1	4	12

☐ ☐ ☐ ☐ ☐ = 20

SCORE

1. Ⓨ Ⓝ
2. Ⓨ Ⓝ
3. Ⓨ Ⓝ
4. Ⓨ Ⓝ
5. Ⓨ Ⓝ
6. Ⓨ Ⓝ
7. Ⓨ Ⓝ
8. Ⓨ Ⓝ
9. Ⓨ Ⓝ
10. Ⓨ Ⓝ

___ / 10 Total

NAME: ____________________

DIRECTIONS Solve each problem.

SCORE

1. Ⓨ Ⓝ
2. Ⓨ Ⓝ
3. Ⓨ Ⓝ
4. Ⓨ Ⓝ
5. Ⓨ Ⓝ
6. Ⓨ Ⓝ
7. Ⓨ Ⓝ
8. Ⓨ Ⓝ
9. Ⓨ Ⓝ
10. Ⓨ Ⓝ

___ / 10
Total

1.
$$\begin{array}{r} 36 \\ -\ 24 \\ \hline \end{array}$$

2. \$10 – \$4.50 = ________

3. 55 ÷ 11 = ________

4. $7\overline{)66}$

5. What is the next odd number after 893?

____

6. Complete the chart. There are six sides on a cube. How many sides are on 6 cubes?

____

1 Cube	2 Cubes	3 Cubes
6		

4 Cubes	5 Cubes	6 Cubes

7. Calculate the perimeter of the rectangle.

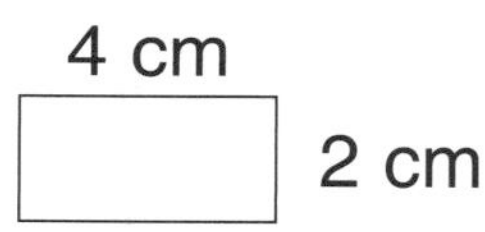

____

8. 104 weeks = ________ years

9. How many lines of symmetry does a pentagon have?

____

10. Beth can jump rope twice as many times as Veronica. Veronica can jump 132 times. How many times can Beth jump?

____

NAME: ____________________

DIRECTIONS Solve each problem.

1. 34 + 28 =

____

2. Is 50% equal to $\frac{1}{2}$?

____

3. 12 ÷ 3 = ________

4. 44 ÷ 5 = ________

5. Is 928 greater than 982?

____

6. 36 + ☐ = 72 − 14

7. Show 5 past 6 on both clocks.

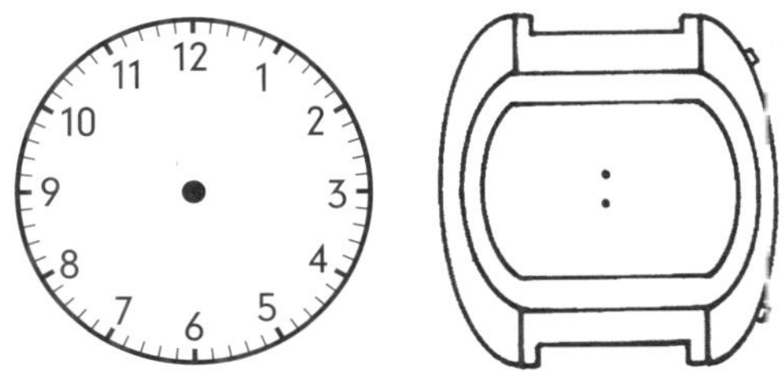

8. What month comes after June?

____

9. True or false? All plane shapes are polygons.

____

10. Tickets for a movie are $\frac{1}{2}$ off if you buy the tickets early. If the full-price ticket costs $12.00, how much will you save by buying a ticket early?

____

SCORE

1. Ⓨ Ⓝ
2. Ⓨ Ⓝ
3. Ⓨ Ⓝ
4. Ⓨ Ⓝ
5. Ⓨ Ⓝ
6. Ⓨ Ⓝ
7. Ⓨ Ⓝ
8. Ⓨ Ⓝ
9. Ⓨ Ⓝ
10. Ⓨ Ⓝ

___ / 10
Total

NAME: ____________________

DIRECTIONS Solve each problem.

SCORE

1. Ⓨ Ⓝ
2. Ⓨ Ⓝ
3. Ⓨ Ⓝ
4. Ⓨ Ⓝ
5. Ⓨ Ⓝ
6. Ⓨ Ⓝ
7. Ⓨ Ⓝ
8. Ⓨ Ⓝ
9. Ⓨ Ⓝ
10. Ⓨ Ⓝ

___ / 10
Total

1. 54 – 23 = ________

2. 50% of 20 is ________.

3. 78 ÷ 12 = ________

4. $8 \overline{)53}$

5. Write the number for seven thousand, five hundred one.

____

6. 6 x ☐ = 8 x 3

7. One pack of nails has a mass of 250 grams. What is the mass of 3 packs?

____

8. Write the length in inches.

________ inches

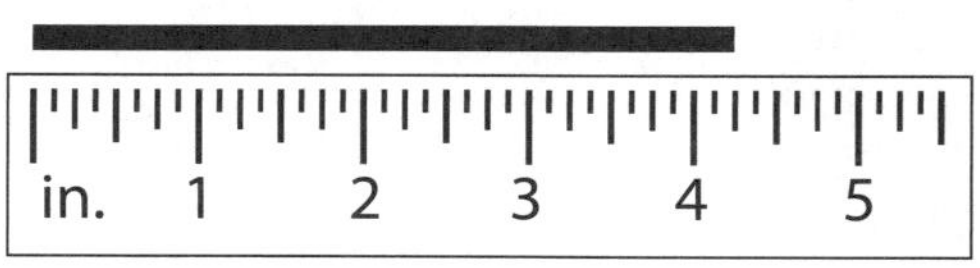

9. Name the shape of the solid's base.

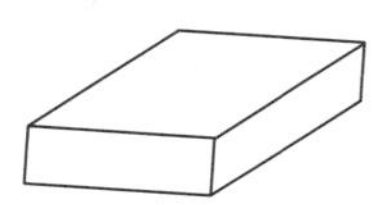

____

10. Subtract 5 tens and 2 ones from the number 97.

____

NAME: ______________________

DIRECTIONS Solve each problem.

1.

$$\begin{array}{r} 37 \\ +\ 26 \\ \hline \end{array}$$

2. 5 x 60 = ________

3. Divide 5 into 52. ________

4. 67 ÷ 10 = ________

5. Write 1,857 in expanded notation.

____

____

6. 7 x 6 = 42 ÷ ☐

7. What is the abbreviation for cubic meter?

____

8. Which would be the best tool for measuring the width of a book: a ruler, a clock, or a meter stick?

____

9.

Dollars Earned in May

Audrey	$15
Dameon	$23
Jason	$12
Lauren	$18

Audrey wants to buy a new CD that costs $13.99. Did she earn enough money in May to buy the CD?

____

10. Use different colors to color pairs of numbers that equal the product shown in the center.

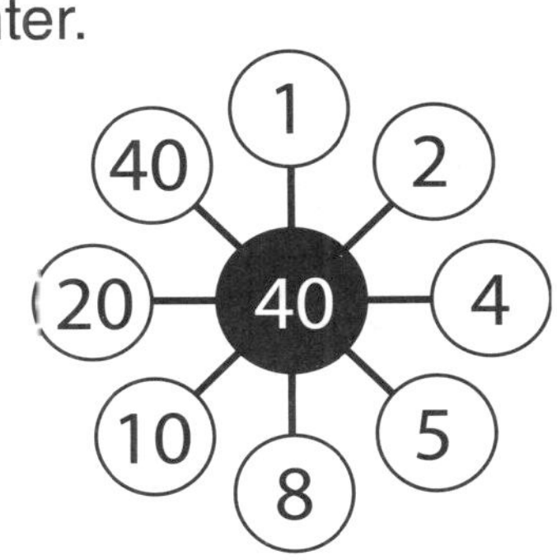

SCORE

1. Ⓨ Ⓝ
2. Ⓨ Ⓝ
3. Ⓨ Ⓝ
4. Ⓨ Ⓝ
5. Ⓨ Ⓝ
6. Ⓨ Ⓝ
7. Ⓨ Ⓝ
8. Ⓨ Ⓝ
9. Ⓨ Ⓝ
10. Ⓨ Ⓝ

___ / 10 Total

DAY
146

NAME: ______________________________

DIRECTIONS Solve each problem.

SCORE

1. Ⓨ Ⓝ
2. Ⓨ Ⓝ
3. Ⓨ Ⓝ
4. Ⓨ Ⓝ
5. Ⓨ Ⓝ
6. Ⓨ Ⓝ
7. Ⓨ Ⓝ
8. Ⓨ Ⓝ
9. Ⓨ Ⓝ
10. Ⓨ Ⓝ

___ / 10
Total

1. $\begin{array}{r} 68 \\ -\ 27 \\ \hline \end{array}$

2. Is $\frac{1}{2}$ more than $\frac{1}{8}$?

____

3. $9\overline{)39}$

4. $91 \div 7 =$ ________

5. What is the value in the tens place in 3,827?

____

6. Fill in the missing number.

749, 742, ________, 728, 721

7. How many liters are in 6,000 milliliters?

____

8. ____ minutes = 360 seconds

9. Draw a line that is parallel to the line below.

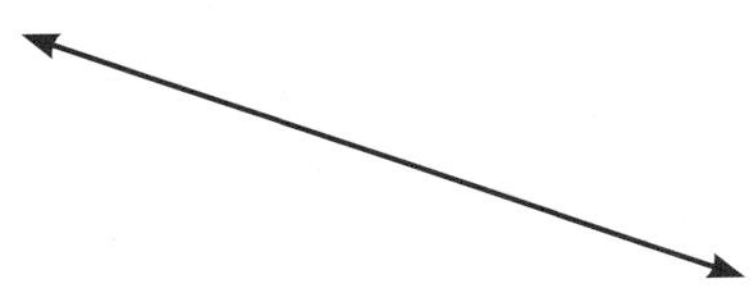

10. A large can of green beans weighs 500 grams. How many cans of green beans weigh 2 kilograms?

____

NAME: ______________________________

DIRECTIONS Solve each problem.

1. 43 + 28 = ________

2. 50% of 10 is ________.

3. 60 ÷ 6 = ________

4. Divide 40 into 10 equal groups.

____

5. Is 432 closer to 400 or 500?

____

6. 245 = 200 + ________ + 5

7. What is the date of the 3rd Sunday in December?

____

December						
Sun	Mon	Tues	Wed	Thurs	Fri	Sat
	1	2	3	4	5	6
7	8	9	10	11	12	13
14	15	16	17	18	19	20
21	22	23	24	25	26	27
28	29	30	31			

8. How many days are in August?

____

9. Does this shape tessellate?

____

10. Halve 64, then add 12.

____

SCORE

1. Ⓨ Ⓝ
2. Ⓨ Ⓝ
3. Ⓨ Ⓝ
4. Ⓨ Ⓝ
5. Ⓨ Ⓝ
6. Ⓨ Ⓝ
7. Ⓨ Ⓝ
8. Ⓨ Ⓝ
9. Ⓨ Ⓝ
10. Ⓨ Ⓝ

___ / 10 Total

DAY
148

NAME: ____________________

DIRECTIONS Solve each problem.

SCORE

1. Ⓨ Ⓝ
2. Ⓨ Ⓝ
3. Ⓨ Ⓝ
4. Ⓨ Ⓝ
5. Ⓨ Ⓝ
6. Ⓨ Ⓝ
7. Ⓨ Ⓝ
8. Ⓨ Ⓝ
9. Ⓨ Ⓝ
10. Ⓨ Ⓝ

___ / 10
Total

1. 25 – 14 = ________

2. $\frac{1}{2}$ of 20 = ________

3. $6 \overline{)54}$

4. How many 5s are in 15?

____

5. 1,000 + 600 + 30 + 2 =

____

6. 10 x 6 = 6 x ☐

7. Record in liters: ________ L

8. ________ weeks = 2 years

9. I have 2 circular bases and my other face is curved. What solid am I?

____

10. Richard can bounce a basketball 36 times in 2 minutes. How many times would you expect him to bounce the ball in 1 minute?

____

NAME: ____________________

DIRECTIONS Solve each problem.

1.
$$\begin{array}{r} 18 \\ +\ 9 \\ \hline \end{array}$$

2. Is 0.6 greater than 0.59?

____

3. $8 \overline{)16}$

4. 68 ÷ 9 = ________

5. Write 7,490 in expanded notation.

____

6. Is 5 x 9 equal to 9 + 9 + 9 + 9 + 9 + 9?

____

7. Which months are in the last quarter of the year?

____

____

____

8. Record the volume if the side of each cube is 5 cm.

____

9.

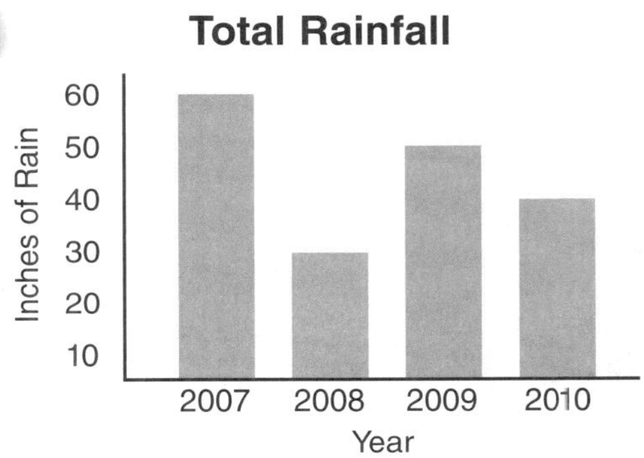

Half of the rain in 2008 fell in the month of January. How much did it rain in January?

____

10. Estimate the number of dots in the square. Then check by counting.

Estimate: ________

Actual Number: ________

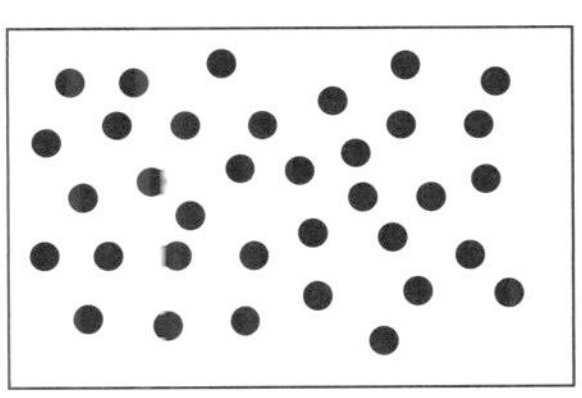

SCORE

1. Ⓨ Ⓝ

2. Ⓨ Ⓝ

3. Ⓨ Ⓝ

4. Ⓨ Ⓝ

5. Ⓨ Ⓝ

6. Ⓨ Ⓝ

7. Ⓨ Ⓝ

8. Ⓨ Ⓝ

9. Ⓨ Ⓝ

10. Ⓨ Ⓝ

___ / 10 Total

DAY 150

NAME: ______________________

DIRECTIONS Solve each problem.

SCORE
1. Ⓨ Ⓝ
2. Ⓨ Ⓝ
3. Ⓨ Ⓝ
4. Ⓨ Ⓝ
5. Ⓨ Ⓝ
6. Ⓨ Ⓝ
7. Ⓨ Ⓝ
8. Ⓨ Ⓝ
9. Ⓨ Ⓝ
10. Ⓨ Ⓝ
___ / 10 Total

1.

$$\begin{array}{r} 28 \\ -\ 15 \\ \hline \end{array}$$

2. Calculate the product of 5 and 70.

____

3. $12 \div 4 =$ ________

4. $55 \div 5 =$ ________

5. What is the place value of 1 in 8,126?

____

6. $45 + 45 = 90 \times \square$

7. Would the unit of measure for the area of a hand be cm^2 or m^2?

80 __________

8. $\frac{1}{2}$ yard = ________ inches

9. A regular hexagon has:

________ angles

________ sides

________ axes of symmetry

10. $\frac{1}{10}$ of 40 = 4, so $\frac{3}{10}$ of 40 =

____

NAME: ____________________

DIRECTIONS Solve each problem.

1. 25 + 13 = ________

2. $1.50 + $2.25 = ________

3. 5 ⟌ 20

4. 41 ÷ 9 = ________

5. Round 2,747 to the nearest hundred.

____

6. Fill in the missing number.

318, 321, ________, 327, 330

7. Write the length in centimeters.

____

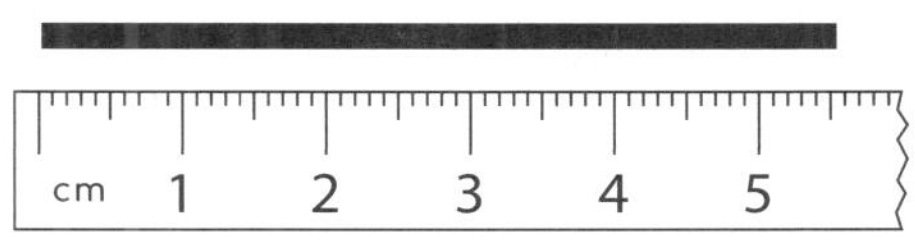

8. Would you be more likely to use a ruler or a yardstick to measure the length of a room?

____

9. A square has:

________ axes of symmetry

and ________ right angles.

10. Follow the pattern in the first circle to complete the second circle.

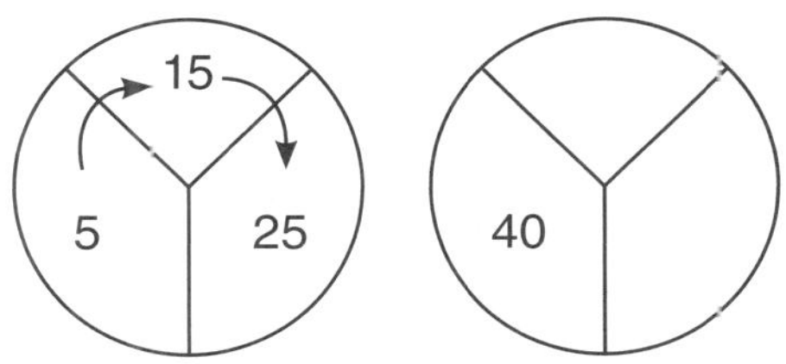

SCORE

1. Ⓨ Ⓝ

2. Ⓨ Ⓝ

3. Ⓨ Ⓝ

4. Ⓨ Ⓝ

5. Ⓨ Ⓝ

6. Ⓨ Ⓝ

7. Ⓨ Ⓝ

8. Ⓨ Ⓝ

9. Ⓨ Ⓝ

10. Ⓨ Ⓝ

___ / 10 Total

DAY
152

NAME: ____________________

DIRECTIONS Solve each problem.

SCORE

1. Ⓨ Ⓝ
2. Ⓨ Ⓝ
3. Ⓨ Ⓝ
4. Ⓨ Ⓝ
5. Ⓨ Ⓝ
6. Ⓨ Ⓝ
7. Ⓨ Ⓝ
8. Ⓨ Ⓝ
9. Ⓨ Ⓝ
10. Ⓨ Ⓝ

___ / 10
Total

1. Subtract 29 from 68.

____

2. Write 81% as a fraction.

____

3. $80 \div 8 =$ ________

4. Divide 6 into 92. ________

5. How many digits are in the number 237?

____

6. $20 \div 1 = \square \times 5$

7. Calculate the perimeter of a square with 4-cm sides.

____

8. 4 days = ________ hours

9. Circle the solids that have a triangular top view.

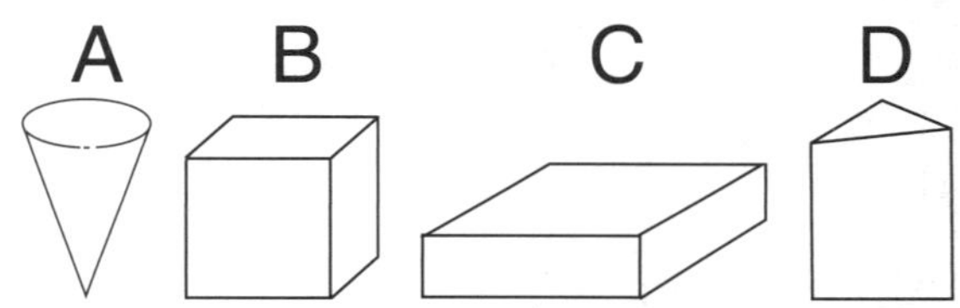

10. A post was 189 cm tall. Alan cut off 36 cm. How tall is it now?

____

DAY
153

NAME: ____________________

DIRECTIONS Solve each problem.

1.
$$\begin{array}{r} 26 \\ +\ 18 \\ \hline \end{array}$$

2. 50% of 30 is ________

3. $16 \div 8 =$ ________

4. $7 \overline{)69}$

5. Write 9,058 in words.

____

____

6. $29 - 17 = \square \times 4$

7. Complete the clocks for the time 15 past 9.

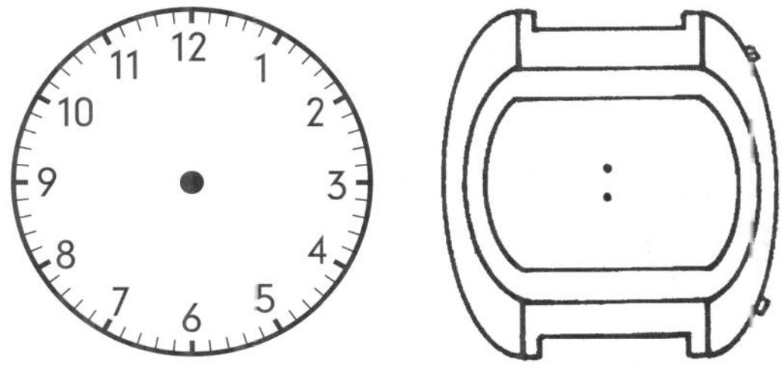

8. What month comes before February?

____

9.

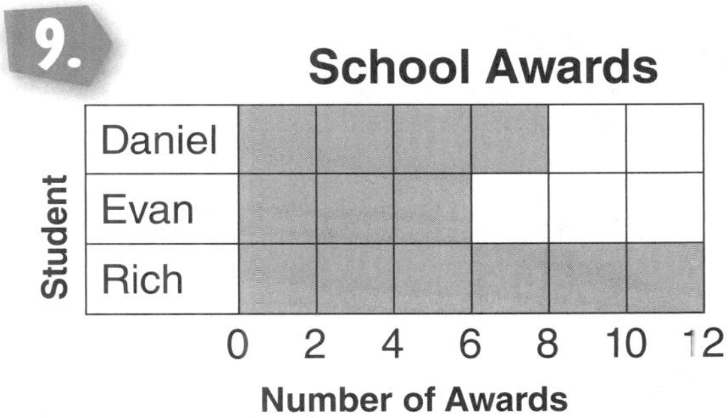

If Evan wins 2 more awards, how many awards will he have won?

____

10. Hiro gets $3.00 each week for allowance. He saves $\frac{1}{3}$ of the money and spends the rest. How much does he save each month?

____

SCORE

1. Ⓨ Ⓝ
2. Ⓨ Ⓝ
3. Ⓨ Ⓝ
4. Ⓨ Ⓝ
5. Ⓨ Ⓝ
6. Ⓨ Ⓝ
7. Ⓨ Ⓝ
8. Ⓨ Ⓝ
9. Ⓨ Ⓝ
10. Ⓨ Ⓝ

___ / 10
Total

DAY
154

NAME: ____________________

DIRECTIONS Solve each problem.

SCORE

1. Ⓨ Ⓝ
2. Ⓨ Ⓝ
3. Ⓨ Ⓝ
4. Ⓨ Ⓝ
5. Ⓨ Ⓝ
6. Ⓨ Ⓝ
7. Ⓨ Ⓝ
8. Ⓨ Ⓝ
9. Ⓨ Ⓝ
10. Ⓨ Ⓝ

___ / 10
Total

1.

$$\begin{array}{r} 17 \\ -\ 15 \\ \hline \end{array}$$

2. What percentage is shaded?

____

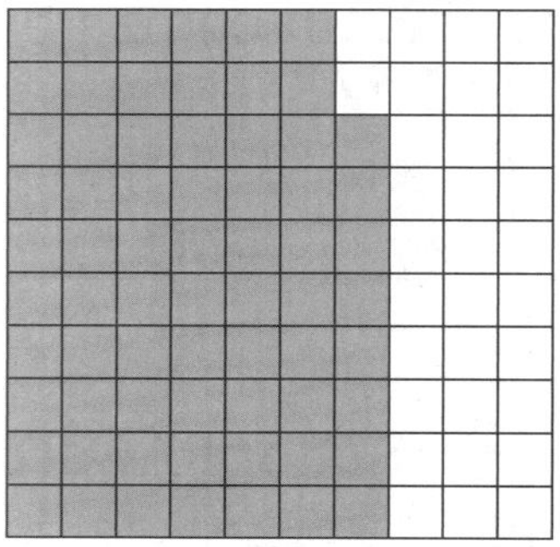

3. Divide 18 into 2 equal groups.

____

4. 93 ÷ 10 = ________

5. Write 2,573 in expanded notation.

____

____

6. 46 + 14 = 20 x ☐

7. Circle the best estimate for the weight of the object.

100 g   2 kg   5 kg   10 kg

8. ________ months = 10 years

9. Draw 1 line of symmetry.

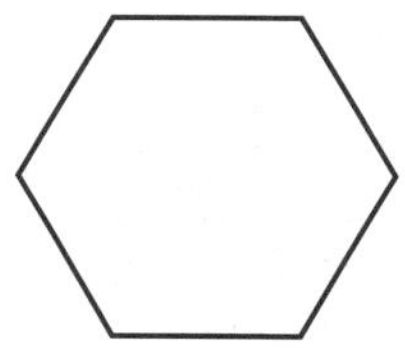

10. Complete the chart by rounding 1,326 to the specified place.

Ten	
Hundred	
Thousand	

NAME: ____________________

DIRECTIONS Solve each problem.

1. Add 34 and 37.

____

2. 6 x 7 = ________

3. 81 ÷ 9 = ________

4. $7\overline{)56}$

5. 4,000 + 50 + 3 = ________

6. $\frac{1}{4}$ of 36 = 4 + ☐

7. Is 10 mm equal to 1 cm?

____

8. 4 pints = ________ quart(s)

9. How many angles are in this shape?

____

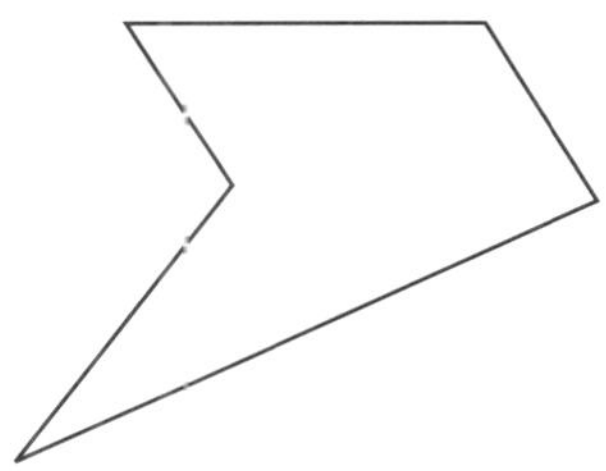

10. Complete the chart with the missing factors.

Product	48	56	60	81
Factor	8	7	6	9
Factor				

SCORE

1. Ⓨ Ⓝ
2. Ⓨ Ⓝ
3. Ⓨ Ⓝ
4. Ⓨ Ⓝ
5. Ⓨ Ⓝ
6. Ⓨ Ⓝ
7. Ⓨ Ⓝ
8. Ⓨ Ⓝ
9. Ⓨ Ⓝ
10. Ⓨ Ⓝ

___ / 10 Total

NAME: ____________________

DIRECTIONS Solve each problem.

SCORE

1. Ⓨ Ⓝ
2. Ⓨ Ⓝ
3. Ⓨ Ⓝ
4. Ⓨ Ⓝ
5. Ⓨ Ⓝ
6. Ⓨ Ⓝ
7. Ⓨ Ⓝ
8. Ⓨ Ⓝ
9. Ⓨ Ⓝ
10. Ⓨ Ⓝ

___ / 10
Total

1. 28 – 17 = ______

2. Is 0.7 less than 0.59?

____

3. 42 ÷ 2 = ______

4. 21 ÷ 4 = ______

5. What is the even number before 1,802?

____

6. Write the next two numbers in the pattern.

0.6, 0.7, 0.8, _____, _____

7. How many buckets will it take to empty the tank?

____

8. How many days are in November?

____

9. This pyramid has:

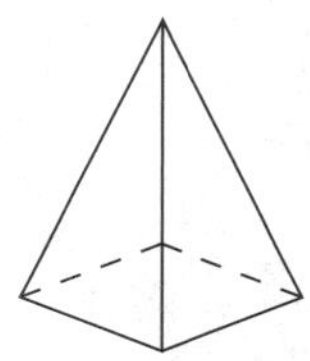

________ faces

________ vertices

A __________ for a base

10. Joel's pencil was 13.2 cm long. Ming's pencil was 15.45 cm long. How much longer was Ming's pencil?

____

NAME: ______________________

DIRECTIONS Solve each problem.

1.
```
  46
+ 25
```

2. Write $\frac{1}{4}$ as a decimal.

____

3. 70 ÷ 7 = ________

4. 46 ÷ 6 = ________

5. What is the value of the tens place in 2,504?

____

6. When Amy walks, she covers 58 cm with each step. Complete the chart to find the distance she covers in 5 steps.

____

Step 1	Step 2	Step 3	Step 4	Step 5
58				

7. Which day of the week is New Year's Eve?

____

December						
Sun	Mon	Tues	Wed	Thurs	Fri	Sat
	1	2	3	4	5	6
7	8	9	10	11	12	13
14	15	16	17	18	19	20
21	22	23	24	25	26	27
28	29	30	31			

8. 24 months = ________ years

9. What is another name for a right angle?

____

10. If you multiply me by 13, you get 52. What number am I?

____

SCORE

1. Ⓨ Ⓝ
2. Ⓨ Ⓝ
3. Ⓨ Ⓝ
4. Ⓨ Ⓝ
5. Ⓨ Ⓝ
6. Ⓨ Ⓝ
7. Ⓨ Ⓝ
8. Ⓨ Ⓝ
9. Ⓨ Ⓝ
10. Ⓨ Ⓝ

___ / 10
Total

DAY
158

NAME: ____________________

DIRECTIONS Solve each problem.

SCORE

1. Ⓨ Ⓝ
2. Ⓨ Ⓝ
3. Ⓨ Ⓝ
4. Ⓨ Ⓝ
5. Ⓨ Ⓝ
6. Ⓨ Ⓝ
7. Ⓨ Ⓝ
8. Ⓨ Ⓝ
9. Ⓨ Ⓝ
10. Ⓨ Ⓝ

___ / 10
Total

1.

$$\begin{array}{r} 36 \\ -\ 25 \\ \hline \end{array}$$

2. Write 0.71 as a fraction.

____

3. $24 \div 8 =$ ________

4. $8\overline{)82}$

5. Is 2,567 greater than or less than 2,675?

____

6. 1,467 =
1,000 + ________ + 60 + 7

7. How many 4 liter bottles can be filled with 36 liters of juice?

____

8. Circle the most likely length of a vacation.

7 days

7 months

7 meters

9. Draw in the diagonals for the shape.

10. Draw a square on the coordinates (G,5).

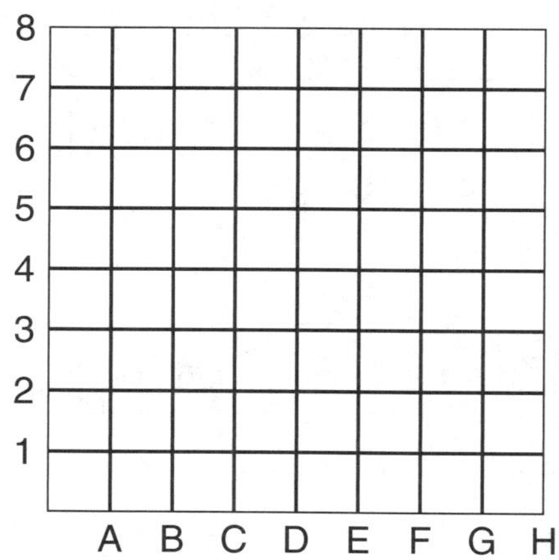

NAME: ____________________________________

DIRECTIONS Solve each problem.

1. 38 + 23 = ________

2. Shade 85%.

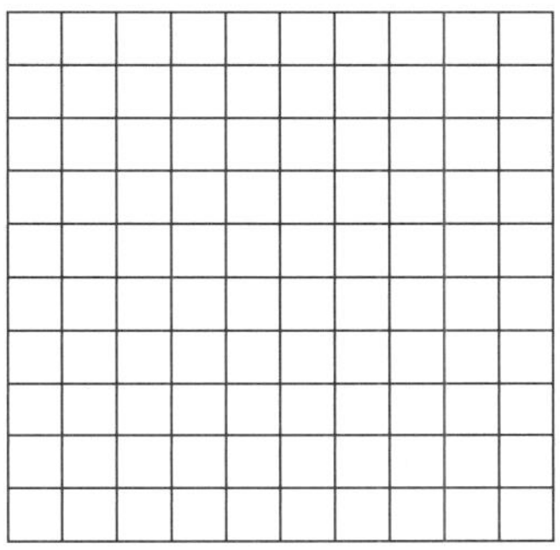

3. 6 ⟌ 94

4. 43 ÷ 7 = ________

5. 1,000 + 50 + 6 = ________

6. 10 – 2 = ☐ x 4

7. How many days are in a year?

____

8. ________ m = 1 km

9. Fill in the blank with *rotation*, *reflection*, or *translation*.

____

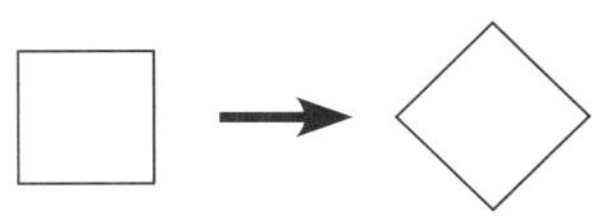

10. There are 8 circles. 25% are blue. 50% are red. The rest are orange. What fraction of the circles are orange?

____

SCORE

1. Ⓨ Ⓝ
2. Ⓨ Ⓝ
3. Ⓨ Ⓝ
4. Ⓨ Ⓝ
5. Ⓨ Ⓝ
6. Ⓨ Ⓝ
7. Ⓨ Ⓝ
8. Ⓨ Ⓝ
9. Ⓨ Ⓝ
10. Ⓨ Ⓝ

___ / 10
Total

DAY 160

NAME: ____________________

DIRECTIONS Solve each problem.

SCORE

1. Ⓨ Ⓝ
2. Ⓨ Ⓝ
3. Ⓨ Ⓝ
4. Ⓨ Ⓝ
5. Ⓨ Ⓝ
6. Ⓨ Ⓝ
7. Ⓨ Ⓝ
8. Ⓨ Ⓝ
9. Ⓨ Ⓝ
10. Ⓨ Ⓝ

___ / 10 Total

1. 47 – 8 = ________

2. 50% of 60 = ________

3. Calculate the quotient of 525 and 7.

____

4. 57 ÷ 5 = ________

5. What is the number after 4,989?

____

6. 81 ÷ 9 = 9 x ☐

7. The floor has an area of 16 m^2. It is covered with a mat of 9 m^2. What area is uncovered?

____

8. 1 ________ = 60 minutes

9. What type of prism is shown?

____

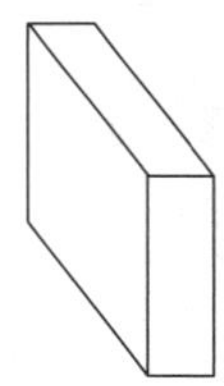

10. If the shaded area is one, what is the area of the crossed region?

____

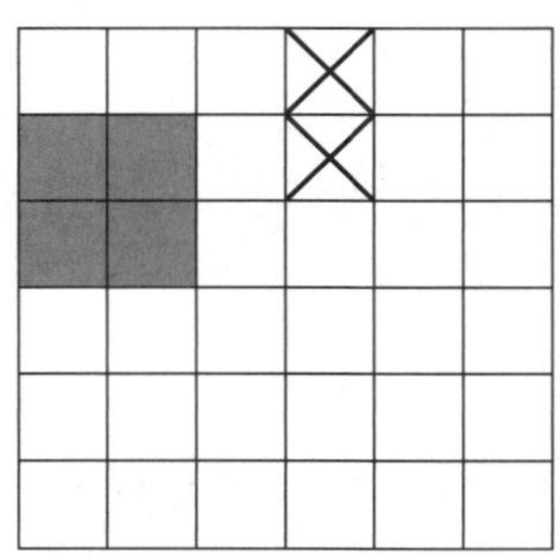

NAME: ____________________

DIRECTIONS Solve each problem.

1.

$$\begin{array}{r} 29 \\ +\ 14 \\ \hline \end{array}$$

2. Write 25% as a fraction.

____

3. Calculate 71 divided by 10.

____

4. 24 ÷ 6 = ________

5. Write 1,414 in expanded notation.

____

6. Fill in the missing fraction.

$\frac{1}{100}$, $\frac{2}{100}$, $\frac{3}{100}$, ________, $\frac{5}{100}$

7. Write the length in millimeters.

____

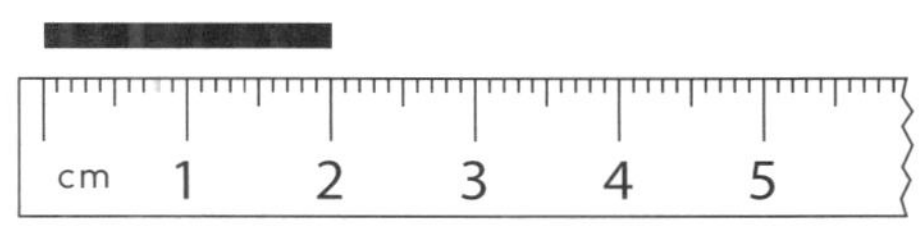

8. 16 pints = ________ gallons

9. How many faces does a square pyramid have?

____

10. Use each of the five numbers once and any operations to solve the problem below.

____

10	13	1	4	12	
☐	☐	☐	☐	☐	= 10

SCORE

1. Ⓨ Ⓝ
2. Ⓨ Ⓝ
3. Ⓨ Ⓝ
4. Ⓨ Ⓝ
5. Ⓨ Ⓝ
6. Ⓨ Ⓝ
7. Ⓨ Ⓝ
8. Ⓨ Ⓝ
9. Ⓨ Ⓝ
10. Ⓨ Ⓝ

___ / 10 Total

DAY 162

NAME: ____________________

DIRECTIONS Solve each problem.

SCORE

1. Ⓨ Ⓝ
2. Ⓨ Ⓝ
3. Ⓨ Ⓝ
4. Ⓨ Ⓝ
5. Ⓨ Ⓝ
6. Ⓨ Ⓝ
7. Ⓨ Ⓝ
8. Ⓨ Ⓝ
9. Ⓨ Ⓝ
10. Ⓨ Ⓝ

___ / 10
Total

1. $\begin{array}{r} 26 \\ -\ 13 \\ \hline \end{array}$

2. Write $\frac{73}{100}$ as a percentage.

____

3. 95 ÷ 5 = ________

4. Divide 8 into 44.

5. What is the place value of 2 in 2,647?

____

6. $3 \times 3 = \frac{1}{3}$ of ☐

7. Calculate the perimeter of a square with 6-cm sides.

____

8. 2 yards = ________ inches

9. Is a hexagon a plane shape or a solid?

____

10. Mom bakes 24 cookies for the soccer team. One-half of the cookies are eaten. How many are not eaten?

____

NAME: ____________________

DIRECTIONS Solve each problem.

SCORE

1. Calculate the sum of 25 and 17.

____

2. Is $\frac{4}{5}$ greater than, less than, or equal to $\frac{4}{50}$?

____

3. $83 \div 6 =$ ________

4. Calculate the quotient of 56 and 7.

____

5. Write four thousand seven hundred with numerals.

____

6. $100 \times 1 = 10 \times$ ☐

7. Show 7:50 on both clocks.

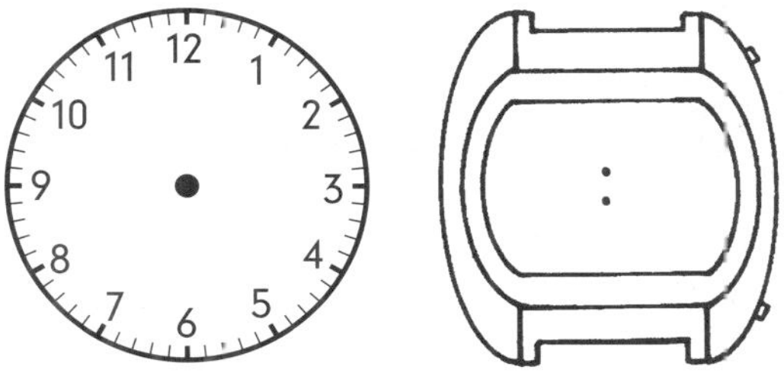

8. Which months are in the last third of the year?

____

____

____

9. Draw the front view.

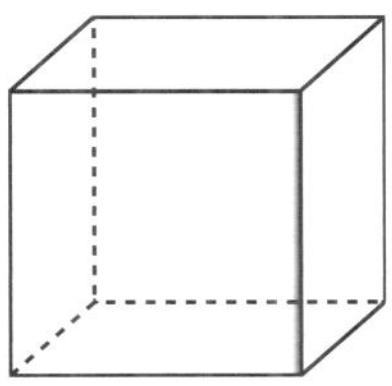

10. You are saving for an mp3 player that costs $75.00. Mom says she will help you by paying for $\frac{1}{3}$ of the cost of the player. How much do you still have to save?

____

1. Ⓨ Ⓝ
2. Ⓨ Ⓝ
3. Ⓨ Ⓝ
4. Ⓨ Ⓝ
5. Ⓨ Ⓝ
6. Ⓨ Ⓝ
7. Ⓨ Ⓝ
8. Ⓨ Ⓝ
9. Ⓨ Ⓝ
10. Ⓨ Ⓝ

___ / 10
Total

DAY **164**

NAME: ____________________

DIRECTIONS Solve each problem.

SCORE

1. Ⓨ Ⓝ
2. Ⓨ Ⓝ
3. Ⓨ Ⓝ
4. Ⓨ Ⓝ
5. Ⓨ Ⓝ
6. Ⓨ Ⓝ
7. Ⓨ Ⓝ
8. Ⓨ Ⓝ
9. Ⓨ Ⓝ
10. Ⓨ Ⓝ

___ / 10 Total

1. 42 – 8 = ________

2. What percent is shaded?

____

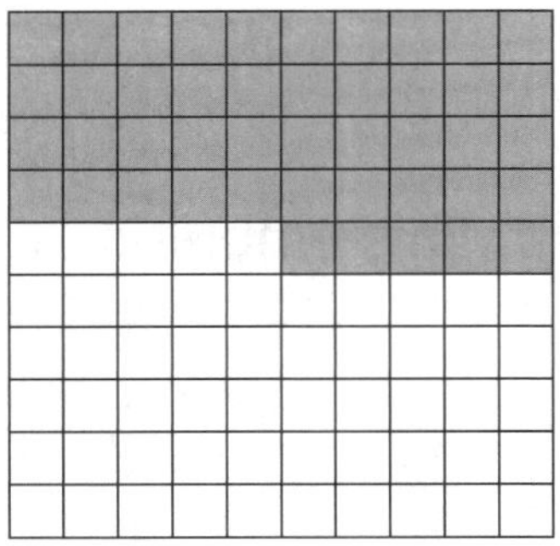

3. Divide 63 into 7 equal groups.

____

4. $5\overline{)25}$

5. What is the number after 4,799?

____

6. $\frac{1}{8}$ of 48 is 2 x ☐

7. An empty wheelbarrow has a mass of 12 kg. How heavy is the load if the full wheelbarrow has a mass of 22 kg?

____

8. How many days are in May?

____

9. **Books Read in March**

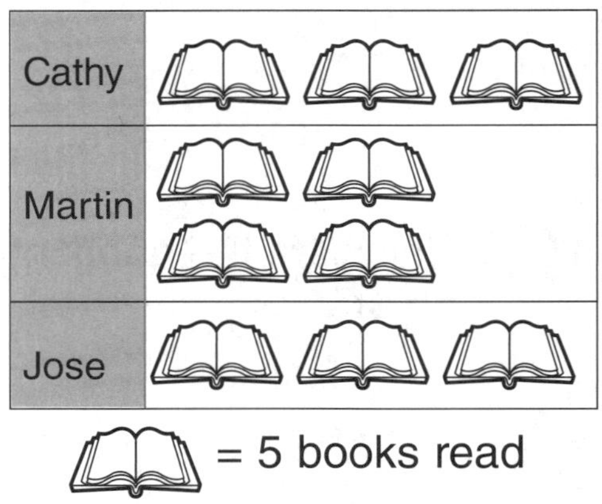

Cathy's goal is to read 10 more books in April than she read in March. What is her new book goal?

____

10. Add 4 hundreds, 3 tens, and 0 ones to 362.

____

NAME: ______________________________

DIRECTIONS Solve each problem.

1.

$$\begin{array}{r} 38 \\ +\ 34 \\ \hline \end{array}$$

2. Is 49 a square number?

____

3. $2\overline{)14}$

4. $45 \div 9 =$ ________

5. What is the value of the hundreds place in 2,604?

____

6. Complete the chart to find the cost of 5 pens at 25¢ each.

____

1 Pen	2 Pens	3 Pens	4 Pens	5 Pens
25¢				

7. How many millimeters are there in 8 centimeters?

____

8. How many times in a year is the date the 31st?

____

9. Draw 1 line of symmetry.

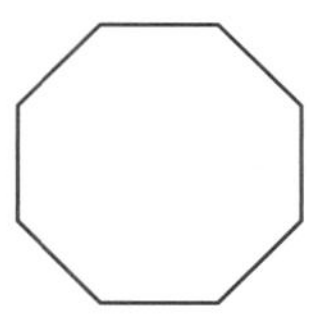

10. A pound of ground beef costs $2.00. You have a coupon for 25% off. How much will you save?

____

SCORE

1. Ⓨ Ⓝ
2. Ⓨ Ⓝ
3. Ⓨ Ⓝ
4. Ⓨ Ⓝ
5. Ⓨ Ⓝ
6. Ⓨ Ⓝ
7. Ⓨ Ⓝ
8. Ⓨ Ⓝ
9. Ⓨ Ⓝ
10. Ⓨ Ⓝ

____ / 10 Total

NAME: ____________________

DIRECTIONS Solve each problem.

SCORE

1. Ⓨ Ⓝ
2. Ⓨ Ⓝ
3. Ⓨ Ⓝ
4. Ⓨ Ⓝ
5. Ⓨ Ⓝ
6. Ⓨ Ⓝ
7. Ⓨ Ⓝ
8. Ⓨ Ⓝ
9. Ⓨ Ⓝ
10. Ⓨ Ⓝ

___ / 10 Total

1.

$$\begin{array}{r} 23 \\ -\ 5 \\ \hline \end{array}$$

2. Write 37% as a decimal.

____

3. Divide 20 into 4 equal groups.

____

4. 59 ÷ 7 = ________

5. Write 3,014 in expanded notation.

____

____

6. Fill in the missing number.

642, 648, 654, ________, 666

7. If 8  fill a  and 5  fill a , then ________  fill a .

8. Which would be the best measure for the length of a commercial on TV: an hour, a minute, or a kilogram?

____

9. What shape is the cross-section?

____

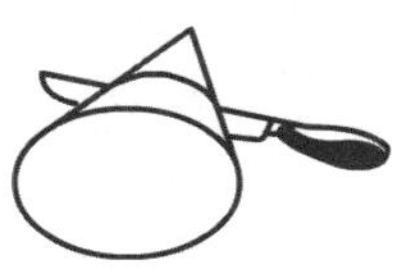

10. What is the next number in the pattern?

1, 5, 9, 13, ________

NAME: ____________________

DIRECTIONS Solve each problem.

1. 44 + 27 = ________

2. 50% of 50 is ________.

3. Calculate the quotient of 72 and 7.

____

4. 96 ÷ 9 = ________

5. Is 1,427 closer to 1,400 or 1,500?

____

6. 27 ÷ 9 = 3 x ☐

7. What date is it one day after December 31st?

____

December						
Sun	Mon	Tues	Wed	Thurs	Fri	Sat
	1	2	3	4	5	6
7	8	9	10	11	12	13
14	15	16	17	18	19	20
21	22	23	24	25	26	27
28	29	30	31			

8. Which would be the best measure for the capacity of a bucket: cup, kilogram, or liter?

____

9. What is the name for lines that intersect to form right angles?

____

10. If you divide me by 12, you get 5. What number am I?

____

SCORE

1. Ⓨ Ⓝ
2. Ⓨ Ⓝ
3. Ⓨ Ⓝ
4. Ⓨ Ⓝ
5. Ⓨ Ⓝ
6. Ⓨ Ⓝ
7. Ⓨ Ⓝ
8. Ⓨ Ⓝ
9. Ⓨ Ⓝ
10. Ⓨ Ⓝ

___ / 10 Total

DAY
168

NAME: ____________________

DIRECTIONS Solve each problem.

SCORE

1. Ⓨ Ⓝ
2. Ⓨ Ⓝ
3. Ⓨ Ⓝ
4. Ⓨ Ⓝ
5. Ⓨ Ⓝ
6. Ⓨ Ⓝ
7. Ⓨ Ⓝ
8. Ⓨ Ⓝ
9. Ⓨ Ⓝ
10. Ⓨ Ⓝ

___ / 10
Total

1. Calculate the difference between 27 and 16.

____

2. Shade 62%.

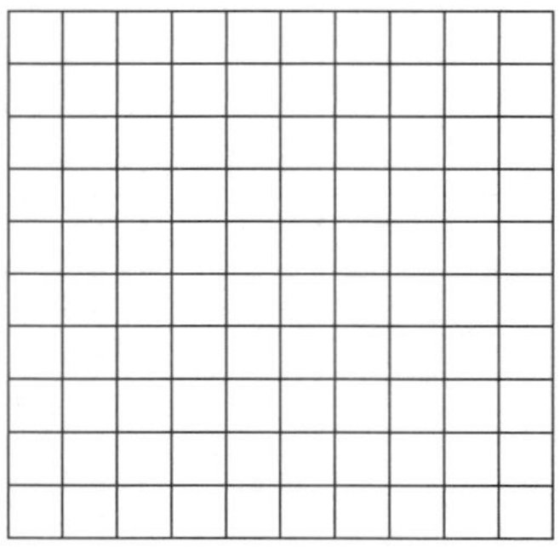

3. $8\overline{)84}$

4. 28 ÷ 7 = ________

5. What is 400 more than 3,570?

____

6. 2,473 =
2,000 + ________ + 70 + 3

7. How many milliliters are in a quarter of a liter?

____

8. ______ seconds = 4 minutes

9. True or false?
Parallel lines never meet.

____

10. Commercials are half a minute long, with 5 commercials every commercial break. How long is each commercial break?

____

NAME: ____________________

DIRECTIONS Solve each problem.

1.

$$\begin{array}{r} 31 \\ 3 \\ +\ 19 \\ \hline \end{array}$$

2. Write $\frac{3}{10}$ as a percentage.

____

3. $8 \overline{)24}$

4. $60 \div 10 =$ ________

5. Is 5,243 less than 5,234?

____

6. Marcia saves $2.50 every week. In what week will she have $8.00?

____

Week 1	Week 2	Week 3	Week 4	Week 5
$2.50				

7. What is the day before January 1?

____

8. Calculate the perimeter of a hexagon with 5-cm sides.

____

9. Draw a line from the real-life object to the matching solid.

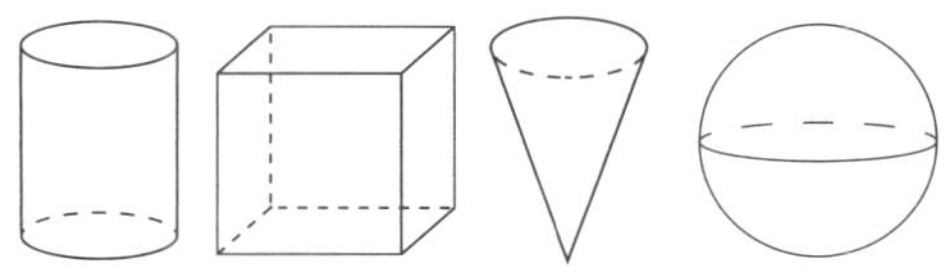

10. Kaylee pays $4.00 for 8 daisies. What is the price of each daisy?

____

SCORE

1. Ⓨ Ⓝ
2. Ⓨ Ⓝ
3. Ⓨ Ⓝ
4. Ⓨ Ⓝ
5. Ⓨ Ⓝ
6. Ⓨ Ⓝ
7. Ⓨ Ⓝ
8. Ⓨ Ⓝ
9. Ⓨ Ⓝ
10. Ⓨ Ⓝ

___ / 10 Total

NAME: ____________________

DIRECTIONS Solve each problem.

SCORE

1. Ⓨ Ⓝ
2. Ⓨ Ⓝ
3. Ⓨ Ⓝ
4. Ⓨ Ⓝ
5. Ⓨ Ⓝ
6. Ⓨ Ⓝ
7. Ⓨ Ⓝ
8. Ⓨ Ⓝ
9. Ⓨ Ⓝ
10. Ⓨ Ⓝ

___ / 10
Total

1. $\begin{array}{r} 32 \\ -\ \ 9 \\ \hline \end{array}$

2. Write 0.35 as a percentage.

____

3. $4 \overline{)23}$

4. $46 \div 12 =$ ________

5. Round 1,276 to the nearest ten.

____

6. $42 \div 6 = 14 \div \square$

7. ____________________ is the amount of surface covered or enclosed by any two-dimensional shape.

8. Matthew wakes up at 7:00 A.M. He got 10 hours sleep. What time did he go to bed?

____

9. Label with *reflection*, *rotation*, or *translation*.

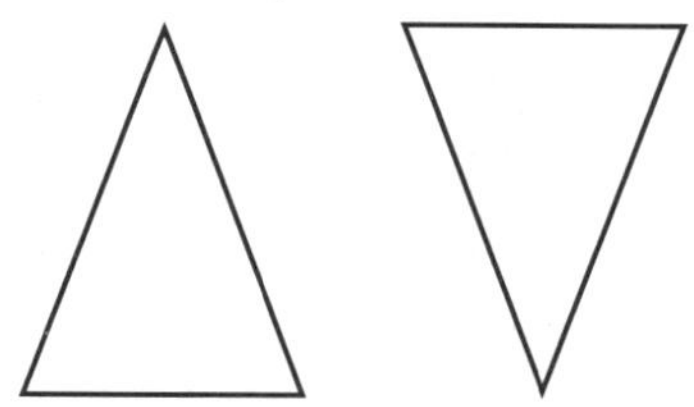

____

10. $\frac{1}{5}$ of 35 = 7, so $\frac{3}{5}$ of 35 =

____

NAME: ______________________________

DIRECTIONS Solve each problem.

1. 35 + 45 = ________

2. Is $\frac{3}{10}$ greater than $\frac{3}{100}$?

____

3. 27 ÷ 12 = ________

4. $5\overline{)85}$

5. Is 9,018 greater than 9,081?

____

6. Fill in the missing number.

854, _______, 840, 833, 826

7. Write the length in centimeters.

____

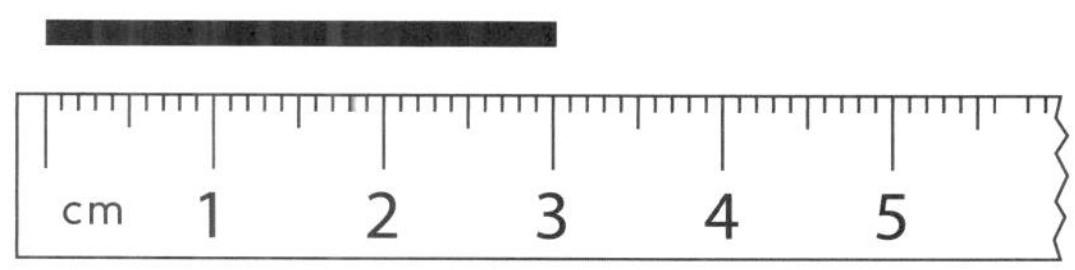

8. What is the temperature?

____

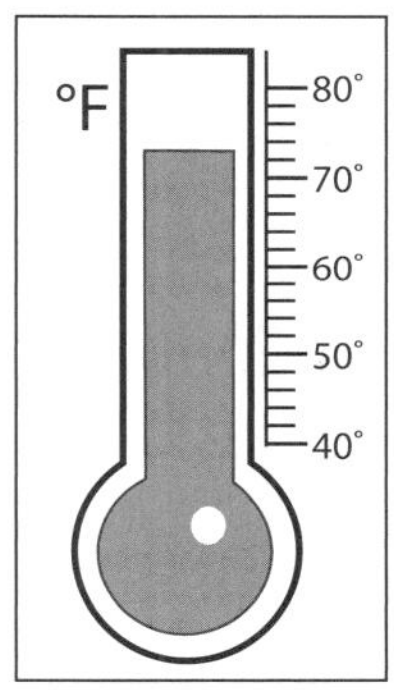

9. *Solid* is a term used to describe any object that is

_____________-dimensional.

10. Use each of the five numbers once and any operations to solve the problem below.

____

10	13	1	4	12

☐ ☐ ☐ ☐ ☐ = 6

SCORE

1. Ⓨ Ⓝ
2. Ⓨ Ⓝ
3. Ⓨ Ⓝ
4. Ⓨ Ⓝ
5. Ⓨ Ⓝ
6. Ⓨ Ⓝ
7. Ⓨ Ⓝ
8. Ⓨ Ⓝ
9. Ⓨ Ⓝ
10. Ⓨ Ⓝ

___ / 10 Total

DAY
172

NAME: ____________________

DIRECTIONS Solve each problem.

SCORE

1. Ⓨ Ⓝ
2. Ⓨ Ⓝ
3. Ⓨ Ⓝ
4. Ⓨ Ⓝ
5. Ⓨ Ⓝ
6. Ⓨ Ⓝ
7. Ⓨ Ⓝ
8. Ⓨ Ⓝ
9. Ⓨ Ⓝ
10. Ⓨ Ⓝ

___ / 10 Total

1. $46 - 34 =$ ________

2. Write 30% as a fraction.

____

3. Calculate the quotient of 97 and 6.

____

4. $73 \div 5 =$ ________

5. What is the value of the digit 4 in the number 2,643?

____

6. $60 \div 10 = \frac{1}{2}$ of ☐

7. A square has a perimeter of 12 cm. What is its area?

____

8. 100 cm = 1 ________

9. Draw the top view.

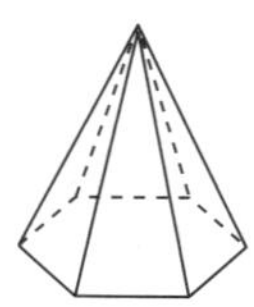

10. Last year my tree was 67 cm tall. It has grown 34 cm. What is its current height?

____

NAME: ____________________

DIRECTIONS Solve each problem.

1.
```
  47
+ 23
```

2. Write 0.84 as a percentage.

____

3. 15)‾45

4. 47 ÷ 10 = ________

5. Write 1,846 in words.

____

____

6. 7 x ☐ is $\frac{1}{4}$ of 56

7. Complete the clocks for the time 25 to 2.

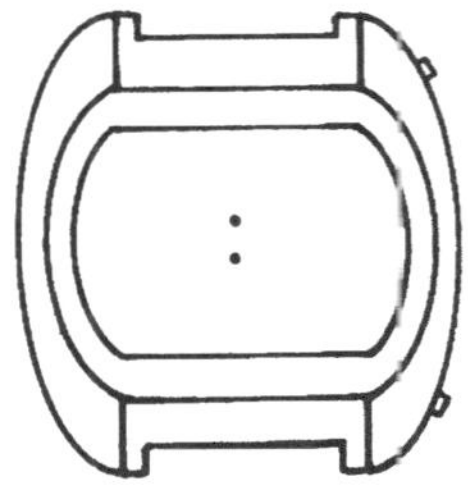

8. 3 quarts = ________ pints

9. How many acute angles are inside this polygon?

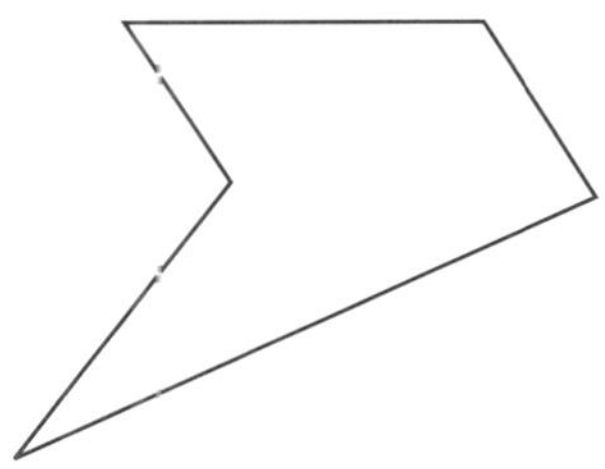

____

10. Dan gets $5.00 each week for allowance. He saves $\frac{1}{2}$ of the money and spends the rest. How much does he spend in 3 weeks?

____

SCORE

1. Ⓨ Ⓝ
2. Ⓨ Ⓝ
3. Ⓨ Ⓝ
4. Ⓨ Ⓝ
5. Ⓨ Ⓝ
6. Ⓨ Ⓝ
7. Ⓨ Ⓝ
8. Ⓨ Ⓝ
9. Ⓨ Ⓝ
10. Ⓨ Ⓝ

___ / 10 Total

DAY 174

NAME: ____________________

DIRECTIONS Solve each problem.

SCORE

1. Ⓨ Ⓝ
2. Ⓨ Ⓝ
3. Ⓨ Ⓝ
4. Ⓨ Ⓝ
5. Ⓨ Ⓝ
6. Ⓨ Ⓝ
7. Ⓨ Ⓝ
8. Ⓨ Ⓝ
9. Ⓨ Ⓝ
10. Ⓨ Ⓝ

___ / 10 Total

1. $\begin{array}{r} 42 \\ -\ 23 \\ \hline \end{array}$

2. 9 x 8 = ________

3. 30 ÷ 5 = ________

4. $6\overline{)61}$

5. 3,000 + 40 + 7 = ________

6. $\frac{1}{5}$ of 45 = 3 x ☐

7. Would you use kilograms or grams to measure the mass of a soccer ball?

____

8. ______ hours = 180 minutes

9. Draw a line perpendicular to the one below.

10. Trish eats one box of cereal every 2 weeks. How many boxes of cereal does she eat in 8 weeks?

____

DAY 175

NAME: ____________________

DIRECTIONS Solve each problem.

1. 32 + 7 + 28 = ________

2. Write 25% as a decimal.

____

3. Calculate the quotient of 32 and 8.

____

4. 98 ÷ 7 = ________

5. What is 400 more than 1,505?

____

6. 23 – 15 = ________ – 48

7. Write the abbreviation for square meter.

____

8. ________ yards = 9 feet

9. Draw the front view.

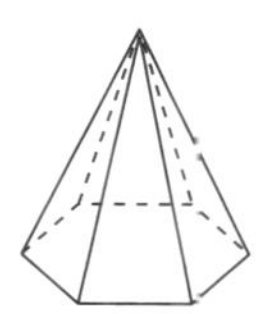

10. Tim has 3 times as many race cars in his collection as Joshua. Joshua has 14 cars. How many does Tim have?

____

SCORE

1. Ⓨ Ⓝ
2. Ⓨ Ⓝ
3. Ⓨ Ⓝ
4. Ⓨ Ⓝ
5. Ⓨ Ⓝ
6. Ⓨ Ⓝ
7. Ⓨ Ⓝ
8. Ⓨ Ⓝ
9. Ⓨ Ⓝ
10. Ⓨ Ⓝ

___ / 10 Total

DAY
176

NAME: ________________________________

DIRECTIONS Solve each problem.

SCORE

1. Ⓨ Ⓝ
2. Ⓨ Ⓝ
3. Ⓨ Ⓝ
4. Ⓨ Ⓝ
5. Ⓨ Ⓝ
6. Ⓨ Ⓝ
7. Ⓨ Ⓝ
8. Ⓨ Ⓝ
9. Ⓨ Ⓝ
10. Ⓨ Ⓝ

___ / 10
Total

1. 33 – 18 = ________

2. 10% of $1 is ________.

3. $7\overline{)56}$

4. 86 ÷ 9 = ________

5. Is 5,237 greater than 5,327?

____

6. Fill in the missing fraction.

$\frac{17}{100}$, $\frac{18}{100}$, $\frac{19}{100}$, ________, $\frac{21}{100}$

7. 6 buckets of water are needed to fill a 30-liter bath. How many liters are in each bucket?

____

8. How many months are in half a year?

____

9. **Sports Played Each Year**

	1st Trimester	2nd Trimester	3rd Trimester
Troy	soccer	basketball	baseball
Jessica	golf	basketball	track
Allison	soccer	diving	swimming

How many different sports are played by these children?

____

10. Mr. Wilson counted 96 spider legs on a nature walk. A spider has 8 legs. How many spiders did Mr. Wilson see?

____

DAY 177

NAME: ______________________

DIRECTIONS Solve each problem.

1. $24 + 8$

2. Is 35% equal to $\frac{35}{100}$?

____

3. $4 \overline{)32}$

4. $62 \div 9 =$ ________

5. Write six thousand forty-two using numerals.

____

6. $\frac{1}{4}$ of 40 is the same as 20 – __________

7. Grandma is coming to visit one week before New Year's Eve. What is the date she will come?

____

December						
Sun	Mon	Tues	Wed	Thurs	Fri	Sat
	1	2	3	4	5	6
7	8	9	10	11	12	13
14	15	16	17	18	19	20
21	22	23	24	25	26	27
28	29	30	31			

8. 1,000 m = 1 ________

9. True or false?
A quadrilateral is a plane shape with more than 4 straight sides.

____

10. Peaches are 89¢ a pound. How much will 3 pounds of peaches cost?

____

SCORE

1. Ⓨ Ⓝ
2. Ⓨ Ⓝ
3. Ⓨ Ⓝ
4. Ⓨ Ⓝ
5. Ⓨ Ⓝ
6. Ⓨ Ⓝ
7. Ⓨ Ⓝ
8. Ⓨ Ⓝ
9. Ⓨ Ⓝ
10. Ⓨ Ⓝ

___ / 10 Total

NAME: ____________________

DIRECTIONS Solve each problem.

SCORE

1. Ⓨ Ⓝ
2. Ⓨ Ⓝ
3. Ⓨ Ⓝ
4. Ⓨ Ⓝ
5. Ⓨ Ⓝ
6. Ⓨ Ⓝ
7. Ⓨ Ⓝ
8. Ⓨ Ⓝ
9. Ⓨ Ⓝ
10. Ⓨ Ⓝ

___ / 10
Total

1.
$$\begin{array}{r} 47 \\ -\ 28 \\ \hline \end{array}$$

2. Write 47% as a fraction.

____

3. 35 ÷ 5 = ________

4. $8\overline{)48}$

5. 2,000 + 500 + 30 + 6 =

____

6. 7 + 8 = 18 − ________

7. How many 250-mL mugs are in 5 L of water?

____

8. Write the length in inches.

________ inches

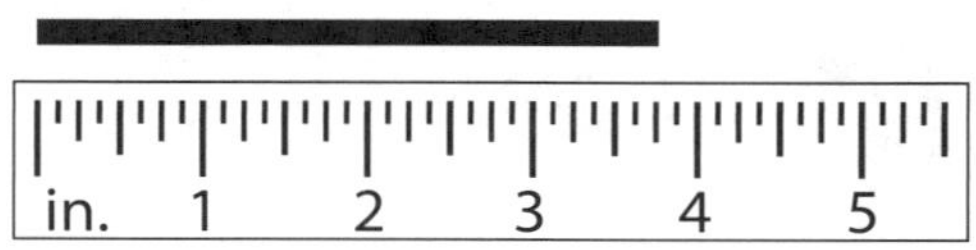

9. Does this shape tessellate?

____

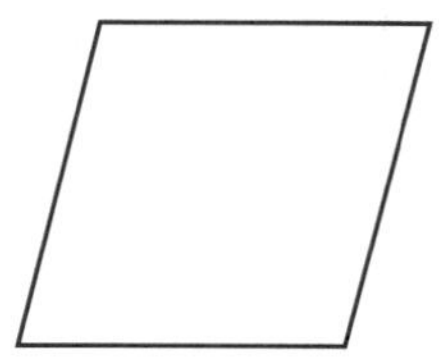

10. A class can sell 150 tickets to their classroom performance. They have already sold 82 tickets. How many more can they sell?

____

NAME: ____________________

DIRECTIONS Solve each problem.

1. 26 + 16 = ______

2. Is 3% equal to $\frac{3}{10}$?

____

3. $10 \overline{)74}$

4. 99 ÷ 11 = ______

5. Is 2,386 closer to 2,300 or 2,400?

____

6. 3,039 = 3,000 + ______

7. Would you use square inches or square feet to measure the area of an area rug?

____

8. What is the volume of a cube with 1-cm sides?

______________.

9. How many obtuse angles are inside this polygon?

____

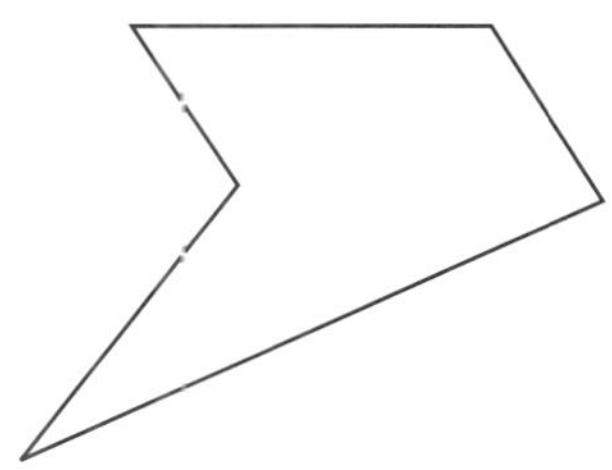

10. Tina practices the piano twice as long as her sister Jenny. Jenny practices the piano 25 minutes every day. How long does Tina practice each day?

____

SCORE

1. Ⓨ Ⓝ
2. Ⓨ Ⓝ
3. Ⓨ Ⓝ
4. Ⓨ Ⓝ
5. Ⓨ Ⓝ
6. Ⓨ Ⓝ
7. Ⓨ Ⓝ
8. Ⓨ Ⓝ
9. Ⓨ Ⓝ
10. Ⓨ Ⓝ

___ / 10 Total

DAY
180

NAME: ____________________

DIRECTIONS Solve each problem.

SCORE

1. Ⓨ Ⓝ
2. Ⓨ Ⓝ
3. Ⓨ Ⓝ
4. Ⓨ Ⓝ
5. Ⓨ Ⓝ
6. Ⓨ Ⓝ
7. Ⓨ Ⓝ
8. Ⓨ Ⓝ
9. Ⓨ Ⓝ
10. Ⓨ Ⓝ

___ / 10
Total

1. 36 – 19 = ________

2. Write 81% as a decimal.

____

3. How many 5s are in 90?

____

4. 87 ÷ 12 = ________

5. What is the place value of 7 in 3,972?

____

6. How much do 6 pens cost if 1 pen costs 30¢?

____

1 Pen	2 Pens	3 Pens	4 Pens	5 Pens	6 Pens
30¢					

7. Are 2,000 milliliters and 2 liters equivalent?

____

8. What is the most likely temperature inside of a house?

7°F   70°F   –70°F

9. I have a square base and all my other faces are triangular. What solid am I?

____

10. Draw the mirror image of this shape so it is symmetrical.

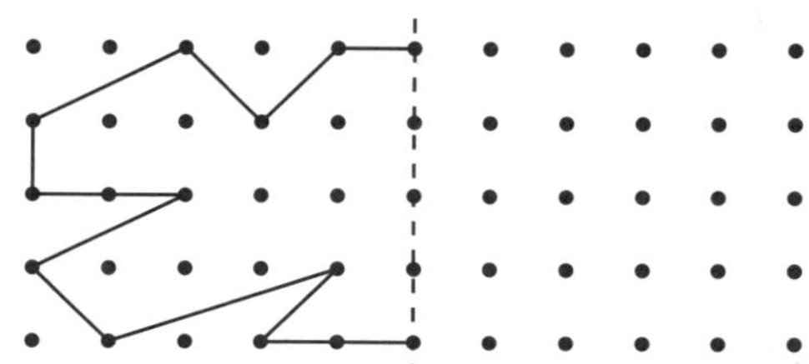

ANSWER KEY

Day 1

1. 23
2. 4 out of 5 boxes should be shaded.
3. 4
4. 2
5. yes
6. 60
7. 4.5 centimeters
8. A.M.
9. 5 sides
10.

+	8	14	17	19	22	36
19	27	33	36	38	41	55
29	37	43	46	48	51	65
39	47	53	56	58	61	75

Day 2

1. 11
2. 24
3. 2
4. 4
5. 4 tens or 40
6. 9
7. 12 cm
8. 92°F
9. face or square
10. 29 kg

Day 3

1. 900
2. 8
3. 2
4. 8
5. 417 should be circled.
6. 2
7. six minutes past seven o'clock
8. 60
9. no
10. $6.00

Day 4

1. 17
2. $3.25
3. 5
4. 8
5. 64
6. 4
7. volume
8. 4
9. pentagon
10. 6

Day 5

1. 100
2. 40
3. 1 R4
4. 4
5. three hundred six
6. 1
7. 2 m^2
8. Monday
9. 3, 6, 0, 2, 3
10. Clockwise, from the top: 8, 24, 40, 12, 28,36, 16, 4, 20, 32

Day 6

1. 11
2. 9
3. 7
4. 7 R7
5. 3 hundreds or 300
6. 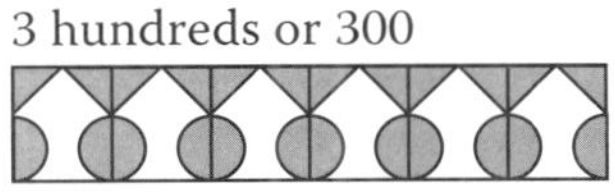
7. 5 buckets
8. 12
9. circle
10. 95 stacks

Day 7

1. 15
2. 3 pentagons should be colored
3. 9
4. 2
5. 200 + 40 + 7
6. 4
7. February 7
8. September
9. yes
10. 34

Day 8

1. 35
2. yes
3. 4
4. 7
5. yes
6. 8
7. 1.1 Liters
8. 4.5 inches
9. rotation
10. Estimate: Answers will vary; Actual Number: 17 dots

Day 9

1. 24
2. 8 eighths
3. 4
4. 9
5. 963 should be circled.
6. 6
7. 10
8. yardstick
9. the square and triangle should be colored.
10. 71 cm

Day 10

1. 19
2. 54
3. 8
4. 3
5. 6 or 6 ones
6. 2
7. perimeter
8. 2
9. a line should be drawn to the sphere.
10. D

ANSWER KEY *(cont.)*

Day 11

1. 25
2. Yes
3. 8
4. 2
5. 47
6. 12
7. 30 mm
8. 25 minutes
9. 
10. Answers may vary: 1 and 11; 3 and 9; 5 and 7

Day 12

1. 29
2. 7
3. 6
4. 7
5. 1 ten or 10
6. 20
7. 16 cm^2
8. scale
9. 48 cm^2
10. 4 boys

Day 13

1. 27
2. no
3. There should be 2 pens in each row.
4. 2
5. tens
6. 4
7. 8 to 10
8. 24
9. parallelogram or quadrilateral
10. $4

Day 14

1. 35
2. no
3. 8
4. 5 fours
5. 33, 43, 73
6. 6
7. grams
8. 2
9. B, C, and D should be circled.
10. Tens: 420; Hundreds: 400

Day 15

1. 31
2. 54
3. 4
4. 9
5. 9 ten thousands or 90,000
6. 6
7. yes
8. 3
9. Triangle A
10. The following pairs should be colored: 1 and 15; 3 and 5

Day 16

1. 25
2. 4
3. 2 sevens
4. 4
5. 500 + 60 + 3
6. 39
7. The brick should be circled.
8. 31 days
9. $18
10. 3 hr. 48 minutes

Day 17

1. 52
2. 4 fourths
3. 2
4. 6
5. 6 tens or 60
6. 2
7. the 21st
8. yardstick
9. yes
10. 46

Day 18

1. 15
2. 0.25
3. 4
4. 10
5. 70
6. 4
7. yes
8. 5 kilograms should be circled.
9. pentagon
10. 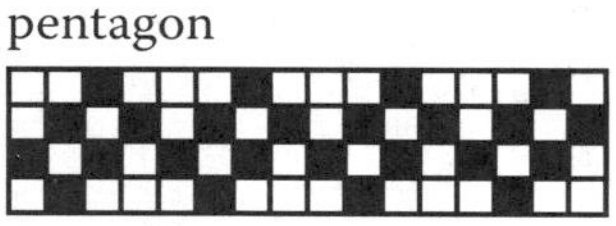

Day 19

1. 35
2. 6
3. 4
4. 12
5. 6
6. 22
7. 9 cm^3
8. A.M.
9. 15 books
10. 40 minutes

Day 20

1. 15
2. 64
3. 10
4. 2
5. 66
6. 2
7. cm^2
8. 1
9. 2 and 4
10. The 3 left or the 3 right squares should be shaded.

Day 21

1. 39
2. 3
3. 4
4. 7
5. hundreds
6. 20
7. 3 cm
8. Cup
9. 
10. Answers will vary: 1 and 7; 3 and 5

ANSWER KEY *(cont.)*

Day 22

1. 6
2. 0.3
3. 7
4. 6
5. no
6. 2
7. 18 cm
8. 32°C
9. a sphere
10. 700 g

Day 23

1. 49
2. 0.35
3. 4
4. 4
5. 34
6. 6
7. 4:01; 1 past 4
8. 1
9. 2007
10. $6.25

Day 24

1. 3
2. $\frac{27}{100}$
3. 9
4. 2
5. 386
6. 16
7. 10 kg
8. 8
9. triangle
10. $\frac{19}{100}$, 0.19, 19%

Day 25

1. 58
2. 12
3. 10 threes
4. 10
5. 1,000 + 60 + 1
6. 10
7. 50 mm
8. 36
9. 4; 0
10. 4, 8, 12, 16, 20, 24, 28, 32, 36, and 40 should be colored.

Day 26

1. 5
2. 0.16
3. 7
4. 5
5. no
6. 92
7. 6
8. February
9. Rich
10. 3,863 ants

Day 27

1. 61
2. 9
3. 3
4. 3
5. 1,568
6. 2
7. Thursday
8. 2
9. A should be circled
10. 5 and 6

Day 28

1. 17
2. 12 fourths
3. 4
4. 2
5. hundreds
6. 5
7. 200 mL
8. ruler
9. yes
10. A triangle should be drawn on the coordinate (G,3).

Day 29

1. 52
2. 0.5
3. 8 twos
4. 4
5. 147
6. 2
7. cubic units or units^3
8. 35 minutes
9. 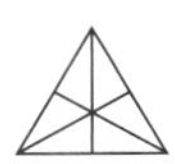
10. no

Day 30

1. 21
2. 35
3. 4
4. 4
5. 60
6. 6
7. 36 m^2
8. no
9. baseball
10. 42

Day 31

1. 26
2. 9
3. 4
4. 5
5. 2,078
6. 80
7. 25 mm
8. bathing suit
9. triangular prism
10.

–	44	48	53	61	72	75
19	25	29	34	42	53	56
29	15	19	24	32	43	46
39	5	9	14	22	33	36

Day 32

1. 26
2. $\frac{3}{10}$
3. 3
4. 6
5. 3,000 + 400 + 20 + 6
6. 11
7. 9 cm^2
8. 52
9. B
10. 50¢

ANSWER KEY *(cont.)*

Day 33
1. 30
2. 6 triangles should be colored.
3. 4
4. 8
5. two thousand, four hundred sixty-seven
6. 27
7. 2:40, analog and digital time
8. 4
9.

	Pizza	Tacos
Sharon		X
Sue	X	X

10. 75¢

Day 34
1. 11
2. 0.60
3. 6
4. 14
5. no
6. 15
7. 78 kg
8. 48
9. reflection
10. 81

Day 35
1. 61
2. 45
3. 3 nines
4. 2
5. 400
6. 4
7. yes
8. June
9. A, B and D should be circled.
10. The following pairs should be colored: 21 and 1, 3 and 7.

Day 36
1. 12
2. 7
3. 10
4. 1, 2, 3, 6
5. 894
6. 750
7. 7 liters
8. ruler
9. A circle should be drawn.
10. 11 inches

Day 37
1. 72
2. 0.75
3. 2
4. 9 nines
5. 800
6. 3
7. Monday
8. 6 feet should be circled.
9. An angle greater than 90°should be drawn.
10. 227

Day 38
1. 12
2. $\frac{1}{10}$
3. 4
4. 6 groups
5. 1,374
6. 20
7. 7,000 millimeters
8. P.M.
9. trapezoid
10. 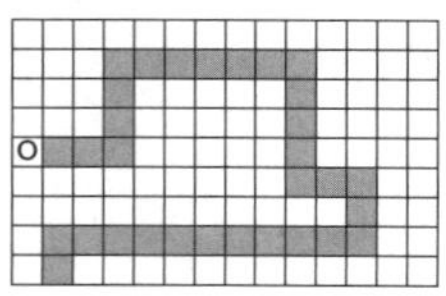

Day 39
1. 41
2. 5
3. 6
4. 1, 2, 4
5. no
6. 6
7. cm
8. warm
9. 4
10. 2 squares should be red.

Day 40
1. 17
2. 42
3. 5
4. 2
5. 1,320
6. 8
7. length
8. 1
9. 3; 2
10. 1

Day 41
1. 53
2. 0.6
3. 1, 3, 9
4. 10
5. 3 digits
6. 56
7. 2 cm
8. 8
9. Dameon
10. Answers will vary: 1 and 19; 3 and 17; 5 and 15; 7 and 13; or 9 and 11.

Day 42
1. 21
2. 30 boxes should be shaded.
3. 2
4. 1, 2, 3, 4, 6, 12
5. 17th
6. 3
7. 20 cm
8. 6
9. false
10. 100 cm or 1 m

Day 43
1. 39
2. 6
3. 1, 2, 4, 8, 16
4. 8
5. 0.3
6. 4
7. 12:09; 9 past 12
8. 30 days
9. 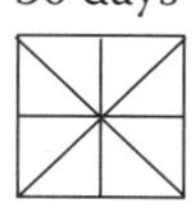
10. $10.00

ANSWER KEY *(cont.)*

Day 44

1. 14
2. 53 boxes should be shaded.
3. 4 sevens
4. 8
5. 6 tens or 60
6. 3
7. no
8. 5
9. rectangle
10. 4

Day 45

1. 38
2. 30
3. 9
4. 1, 2, 3, 6, 9, 18
5. 2,975
6. 9
7. cm^3
8. thermometer
9. Cathy and Jose
10. Clockwise, from the top:
    40 56 16 64 80
    24 48 72 32 0

Day 46

1. 7
2. 9
3. 6 sixes
4. 8
5. 34
6. 159
7. 2
8. 24
9. 8; 8; 8
10. 1/4 pizza

Day 47

1. 17
2. 0.32
3. 7 threes
4. 10
5. No
6. 9
7. March 6
8. 2 hours 15 minutes
9. 2 pairs
10. 8 and 9

Day 48

1. 26
2. 3
3. 7 rows
4. 7
5. no
6. 42
7. 5 liters
8. 34°F
9. 2008
10. Answers will vary.

Day 49

1. 24
2. 9
3. 1, 2, 4, 8
4. 5
5. 4 hundreds or 400
6. 4
7. 8 cm^3
8. 120
9. cube
10. 72 in. or 6 ft. tall

Day 50

1. 19
2. 54
3. 9 twos
4. 1, 2, 3, 4, 6, 8, 12, 24
5. 3,900
6. 6
7. 20 mm
8. 2
9. A and C should be circled.
10. 36

Day 51

1. 38
2. yes
3. 9
4. 6
5. 423
6. 1
7. 55 mm
8. $\frac{1}{2}$ or 0.5
9. 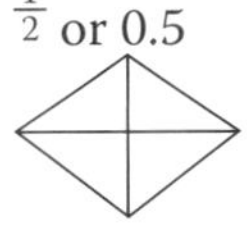
10. Answers will vary: 1 and 15; 3 and 13; 5 and 11; or 7 and 9.

Day 52

1. 33
2. $2.75
3. 5 sixes
4. 8
5. 2,634
6. 6
7. 81 cm^2
8. 12 months
9. 8 awards
10. 2 possible patterns: Add 4 to get 20, 24; Multiply by 2, then by 3 to get 32, 48.

Day 53

1. 33
2. 24
3. 9
4. 4
5. 0
6. 30
7. 11:00, analog and digital time
8. square inches
9. edge
10. $15.00

Day 54

1. 38
2. $\frac{67}{100}$
3. 8
4. 7
5. 36th
6. 6
7. kilograms
8. 1 kilometer should be circled.
9. reflection
10. 870; 900

Day 55

1. 1,280
2. 24
3. 2
4. 9
5. yes
6. 3
7. 1,000 steps
8. 2
9. Soccer, Diving, Swimming
10. 1, 30; 2, 15; and 5, 6 should be colored.

ANSWER KEY *(cont.)*

Day 56

1. 54
2. 3 boxes should be shaded.
3. 7 sixes
4. 10
5. thousands
6. 30
7. B
8. Wednesday
9. 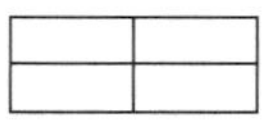
10. 7 with 9 feet remaining

Day 57

1. 68
2. $2.75
3. 9
4. 7
5. 130
6. 7
7. Wednesday
8. P.M.
9. A line should be drawn from the cube to the die.
10. 728

Day 58

1. 46
2. $\frac{99}{100}$
3. 3
4. 10 sevens
5. 128
6. 8
7. 1,100 mL
8. 24°C
9. Jahir: 23
Olivia: 15
Gerald: 35
Mimi: 3
10. 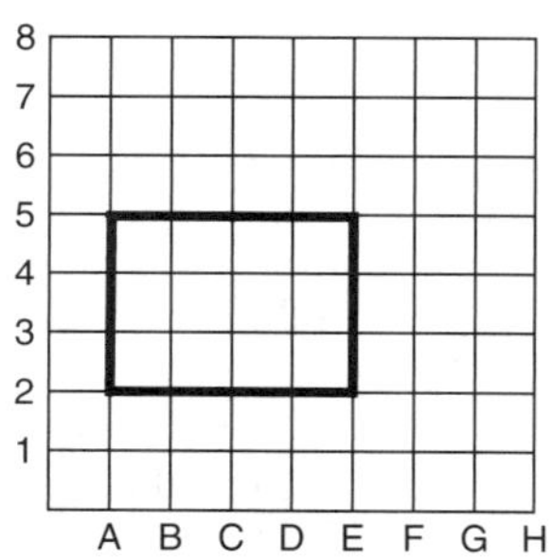

Day 59

1. 43
2. 72
3. 7
4. 6
5. 1,900
6. 39
7. 9 cm^3
8. 2
9. no
10. $1.14

Day 60

1. 9
2. 21
3. 4
4. 9
5. 7 tens or 70
6. 60
7. cm^2
8. 4
9. 1 and 10
10. A

Day 61

1. 64
2. 30 boxes should be shaded.
3. 10
4. 7
5. 79
6. 600
7. 3.5 cm
8. 2
9. circle
10.

+	7	15	18	23	25	28
19	26	34	37	42	44	47
29	36	44	47	52	54	57
39	46	54	57	62	64	67

Day 62

1. 8
2. 0.2
3. 7
4. 6
5. 2,000 + 300 + 60 + 5
6. 27
7. 8 cm
8. 6 faces
9. Answers will vary
10. 4 liters

Day 63

1. 34
2. 56
3. 10
4. 9
5. 5 hundreds or 500
6. 2
7. 7:26; 26 past 7
8. 1.5 or $1\frac{1}{2}$ inches
9. no
10. $4.75

Day 64

1. 17
2. no
3. 9
4. 9
5. 1,264; 1,426; 1,624
6. 8
7. 100 g
8. centimeter
9. no
10. $\frac{46}{100}$; 0.46; 46%

Day 65

1. 31
2. 60
3. 9
4. 8
5. yes
6. 3
7. 75 cm^2
8. 3
9. cube or rectangular
10. Clockwise, from top:
3 15 27 9 24 18
12 30 21 6

Day 66

1. 14
2. 21
3. 5
4. 8
5. 2,003
6. 12
7. 20 bottles
8. 120
9. $3
10. 19 cm

ANSWER KEY *(cont.)*

Day 67

1. 40
2. 7
3. 7
4. 5
5. 4 digits
6. 5
7. 4 Mondays
8. 40 minutes
9. trapezoid
10. 7 and 6

Day 68

1. 9
2. .42
3. 16
4. 5
5. 4 hundreds or 400
6. 7
7. 16 cups of 250 mL each
8. July, August, September
9. 
10. D

Day 69

1. 61
2. 7
3. 4 threes
4. 9 R4
5. 7,532
6. 15
7. yes
8. build a snowman
9. A and C should be colored.
10. 3 times

Day 70

1. 26
2. 81
3. 8
4. 8
5. 1,400
6. 20¢; 30¢; 40¢; 50¢; 60¢; 70¢
7. 60 m^2
8. 60
9. B should be colored.
10. Three cubes on either the right or left should be shaded.

Day 71

1. 55
2. 8
3. 4 sixes
4. 9
5. two thousand, forty-seven
6. 24
7. 5.5 cm
8. 16
9. 5 books
10. Answers will vary: 1 and 23; 3 and 21; or 5 and 19; 7 and 17; 9 and 15; 11 and 13.

Day 72

1. 15
2. $\frac{3}{10}$
3. 8
4. 8
5. 2,907; 2,097; 2,079
6. 7
7. 36 cm^2
8. 9
9. right angle
10. 2 possible answers: Add 4 to get 25, 29; Multiply by 2, then by 3 to get 42, 63

Day 73

1. 40
2. 65 boxes should be shaded.
3. 3 R 5
4. 5
5. 2 hundreds or 200
6. 7
7. The clock should read 1:10.
8. 24 months
9. hexagon
10. $4.50

Day 74

1. 17
2. no
3. 4 sixes
4. 5 R 1
5. 4 digits
6. 6
7. 43 kg
8. 243 cm^3
9. 2007
10. 35

Day 75

1. 50
2. 72
3. 7
4. 9 groups
5. three thousand, fifty-eight
6. 9
7. yes
8. yardstick
9. yes
10. The following pairs should be colored: 8, 4; 16, 2; 32, 1

Day 76

1. 24
2. 6
3. 9
4. 8
5. tens
6. 240
7. 200 mL
8. meter stick
9. 5; 5; 5
10. 2 hr. 50 minutes

Day 77

1. 30
2. $\frac{53}{100}$
3. 7 R3
4. 6
5. 500
6. 45
7. the 19th
8. 4 inches
9. Answers may vary. Possible answers include sphere and egg.
10. 559

Day 78

1. 2
2. yes
3. 6 R4 or 6.8
4. 7
5. yes
6. 9
7. yes
8. 108
9. Evan
10. Answers will vary.

ANSWER KEY *(cont.)*

Day 79

1. 60
2. 0.6
3. 7 R5 or 7.5
4. 8
5. 7 tens or 70
6. 3
7. 72 cm^3
8. 15 hours and 2 minutes
9. rotating
10. 375 beads

Day 80

1. 18
2. 63
3. 5
4. 8 R7 or 8.7
5. 9,710
6. 4
7. cm^2
8. thermometer
9. 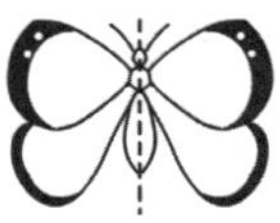
10. 2

Day 81

1. 60
2. No
3. 5
4. 10
5. 289
6. 48
7. 45 mm
8. 120
9. 3, 0, 2
10. Answers will vary. Examples: 1, 49; 25, 25.

Day 82

1. 33
2. 20
3. 6 R2
4. 7
5. 4 digits
6. 3
7. 8 cm
8. 3
9. Troy and Allison
10. 3,000 mL or 3 L

Day 83

1. 70
2. $\frac{1}{4}$ is greater than $\frac{1}{8}$
3. 8 R1
4. 4 R2
5. 2,500
6. 7
7. 4:07; 7 past 4
8. 12
9. yes
10. 3 for $6.00

Day 84

1. 17
2. $\frac{3}{10}$
3. 3 R3
4. 5 R7 or 5.7
5. 1,806
6. 5
7. grams
8. 31 days
9. 3 angles
10. 2,180; 2,200; 2,000

Day 85

1. 70
2. 56
3. 2 R1
4. 5 R2
5. hundreds
6. 6
7. m^2
8. 4.5 or $4\frac{1}{2}$ inches
9. a square
10. 3, 6, 9, 12, 15,18, 21, 24, 27, 30, 33, 36, and 39 should be colored.

Day 86

1. 16
2. 5
3. 9 R2
4. 9 R7
5. 7 hundreds or 700
6. 48
7. 4.5 containers
8. 45 kilograms
9. Cheryl: 2 smiley faces; Brooke: 4 smiley faces
10. 53,210

Day 87

1. 33
2. 60¢
3. 5 R4
4. 2 R6
5. yes
6. 4
7. Sunday
8. 14 days
9. yes
10. 11 and 12

Day 88

1. 37
2. 10
3. 3 R3
4. 7 R5
5. two thousand, sixty-four
6. 10
7. 100 mL
8. Friday
9. B and C
10. a square should be added

Day 89

1. 31
2. no
3. 7
4. 8 R4
5. 4 digits
6. 24
7. 4 seasons
8. 1
9. A straight line should be drawn.
10. $1.50

Day 90

1. 16
2. 28
3. 6 R6
4. 4 R4
5. 400
6. 7
7. m
8. P.M.
9. yes
10. 18

ANSWER KEY *(cont.)*

Day 91

1. 57
2. $1.25
3. 3 R6
4. 9
5. 746
6. 42
7. 2.5 cm
8. 58°F
9. rectangular prism
10.

–	45	47	56	63	77	82
19	26	28	37	44	58	63
29	16	18	27	34	48	53
39	6	8	17	24	38	43

Day 92

1. 19
2. 0.05
3. 5 R2
4. 4 R3
5. 5 hundreds or 500
6. $1.00, $1.50, $2.00, $2.50
7. Area measures surface.
8. 12 cm3
9. 
10. 2 possible answers: Add 3 to get 33, 36; Multiply by 2, then by 3 to get 60, 90

Day 93

1. 37
2. $\frac{4}{10}$
3. 4 R4 or 4.5
4. 4
5. 124
6. 2
7. Clock should show 3:35.
8. minute
9. $68
10. 6 tickets

Day 94

1. 54
2. 3
3. 8 R1
4. 8 R3
5. 400
6. 8
7. 42 kg
8. 1
9. octagon
10. 4,830; 4,800; 5,000

Day 95

1. 33
2. 36
3. 6
4. 9 R5
5. 2,776
6. 0
7. 600 cm
8. January
9. A square should be drawn.
10. The following pairs should be colored: 45, 1; 3, 15; 5, 9

Day 96

1. 19
2. $2.35
3. 7 R4 or 7.5
4. 14
5. 3,000 + 600 + 40 + 2
6. 49
7. 8 liters
8. 4
9. rotation or reflection
10. $35.38

Day 97

1. 26
2. 0.7
3. 4 fours
4. 6 R4 or 6.5
5. 447
6. yes
7. Saturday
8. ruler
9. Martin
10. 1,015

Day 98

1. 18
2. no
3. 2 R4 or 2.5
4. 10 R2 or 10.5
5. 5,253
6. 6
7. 500 milliliters
8. 12 minutes should be circled.
9. 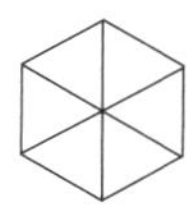
10. Estimate: Answers may vary. Actual Number: 24 dots

Day 99

1. 61
2. $\frac{62}{100}$ or $\frac{31}{50}$
3. 1, 2, 4, 5, 10, 20
4. 3
5. forty-second
6. 9
7. April, May, June
8. 8 cm^3
9. 2 surfaces; 1 edge
10. 10 toys

Day 100

1. 8
2. 42
3. 7
4. 1, 2, 3, 4, 6, 9, 12, 18, 36
5. 7 tens or 70
6. 18
7. 8 m^2
8. 5 weekdays
9. 180 inches
10. C

Day 101

1. 52
2. 6
3. 8
4. 8
5. 800
6. 35
7. 30 mm
8. 40 minutes
9. A and C
10. Answers may vary. Possibilities include (13 + 12 + 4 + 1) ÷ 10 = 3 or 13 – 12 + 10 ÷ (4 + 1) = 3

ANSWER KEY *(cont.)*

Day 102

1. 54
2. yes
3. 5 R3
4. 2 eights
5. eight thousand, ninety-one
6. 48
7. 25 cm^2
8. jacket
9. 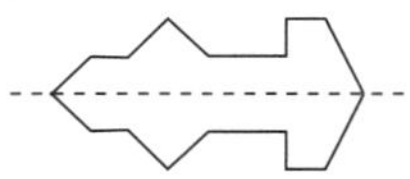
10. 6 pencils

Day 103

1. 61
2. $\frac{9}{100}$
3. 6
4. 9
5. 300 + 80 + 6
6. yes
7. 5:16; 16 past 5
8. day
9. vertex
10. $1.00

Day 104

1. 16
2. $3.25
3. 8
4. 4
5. 810
6. $40; $60; $80; $100; $120
7. yes
8. 3
9. 6 more awards
10. $\frac{36}{100}$; 0.36; 36%

Day 105

1. 36
2. 50
3. 7
4. 9
5. 4 digits
6. 10
7. cm^2
8. 1
9. A and D should be circled.
10. The following pairs should be colored: 35, 1; 7, 5

Day 106

1. 9
2. yes
3. 8
4. 4
5. 2,009
6. 36
7. 35
8. 2.5 or $2\frac{1}{2}$ inches
9. Allison
10. 30

Day 107

1. 61
2. No
3. 5
4. 3
5. 138
6. 65
7. September 2
8. 15 liters should be circled.
9. 8; 18; 12
10. 52

Day 108

1. 23
2. 0.75
3. 1, 2, 3, 5, 6, 10, 15, 30
4. 2
5. 8,047
6. 6
7. 2,500
8. 30 months
9. B
10. A circle should be drawn at coordinate (C,7).

Day 109

1. 51
2. $3.50
3. 8
4. 3
5. 9
6. 1
7. January; December
8. 8 cm^3
9. hexagon
10. 3

Day 110

1. 35
2. 63
3. 6 eights
4. 7
5. thirty-first
6. 42
7. 81 cm^2
8. 58 minutes
9. 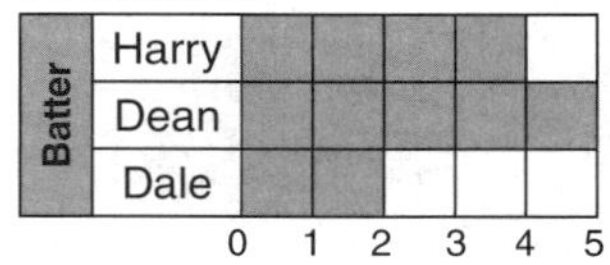

10. 30

Day 111

1. 41
2. 21
3. 9
4. 5
5. 7,000 + 900 + 3
6. 42
7. 3.5 cm
8. 20°C
9. triangular prism
10. Answers will vary. Possibilities include: 1, 41; 3, 39; 5, 37, etc.

Day 112

1. 46
2. $\frac{25}{100}$ or $\frac{1}{4}$
3. 2
4. 8
5. thousands
6. yes
7. 22 cm
8. days
9. 3; 3; 3
10. 700 grams

Day 113

1. 31
2. 70%
3. 2 R7
4. 2
5. no
6. 7
7. The clock should read 6:29.
8. 1
9. 15 inches
10. $16.00

ANSWER KEY *(cont.)*

Day 114
1. 13
2. yes
3. 6
4. 10 R3 or 10.5
5. even
6. 4
7. 5 kg
8. 1
9. A rectangle should be drawn.
10. 138

Day 115
1. 42
2. 56
3. 7
4. 8
5. 900
6. 4
7. 5 cm
8. 31 days
9. A line of symmetry should be drawn from any vertex.
10. 8; 5; 7; 3

Day 116
1. 15
2. $\frac{2}{5}$ or $\frac{4}{10}$ or $\frac{40}{100}$
3. 4 R3
4. 6
5. 4,620
6. 64
7. 700 mL
8. square feet
9. hexagon
10. 60

Day 117
1. 34
2. no
3. 5
4. 9 R1
5. 440
6. 24, 36, 48; 48
7. 17 days
8. liter
9. circle
10. 12

Day 118
1. 16
2. 7 rows or 70 squares should be shaded.
3. 2
4. 12
5. 5,734
6. 4
7. 4 250 mL cups
8. Thursday
9. $17
10. rotating

Day 119
1. 53
2. 50%
3. 7
4. 4
5. fifty-six
6. 3
7. April; June
8. 9 cm^3
9. translate
10. 6 hours

Day 120
1. 17
2. 240
3. 9
4. 9
5. 623
6. 4
7. m^2
8. 8:22
9. no
10. There are 8 possible correct designs involving either a line, a V, or an L shape.

Day 121
1. 46
2. 6
3. 9
4. 4
5. 5,046
6. $\frac{4}{8}$
7. 20 mm
8. cold
9. There should be a line drawn between the ice cream cone and the cone.
10. 2 possible answers: Add 3 to get 35, 38; Multiply by 2, then by 3 to get 64, 96

Day 122
1. 43
2. 0.45
3. 11
4. 5
5. 6,000 + 800 + 2
6. 4
7. 49 cm^2
8. 12
9. no
10. 31 m

Day 123
1. 33
2. no
3. 8
4. 5 R3
5. 463rd
6. 20
7. 6:53; 7 minutes to 7
8. $\frac{1}{2}$
9. The prism (far right) should be circled and pyramid (center) should be crossed out.
10. $1.48

Day 124
1. 4
2. $2.75
3. 5
4. 9
5. hundreds
6. 30
7. grams
8. 4
9. yes
10. $\frac{48}{100}$; 0.48; 48%

Day 125
1. 64
2. 32 apples
3. 6
4. 9
5. odd
6. 4
7. 150 cm^2
8. 1.5 or $1\frac{1}{2}$ inches
9. A and C should be circled.
10. Clockwise, from top:

18	48	54	24	60
30	6	36	12	42

ANSWER KEY *(cont.)*

Day 126
1. 11
2. 52%
3. 9
4. 9
5. 3,058
6. 170
7. 4 times
8. 8 inches should be circled.
9. 10"
10. 144 in²

Day 127
1. 43
2. yes
3. 8
4. 5
5. 489
6. yes
7. Wednesday
8. 1.461 days
9. pentagonal prism
10. 148

Day 128
1. 13
2. 90%
3. 4 R4
4. 4
5. 800
6. 1
7. 200 mL
8. 28 cm
9. 6
10. 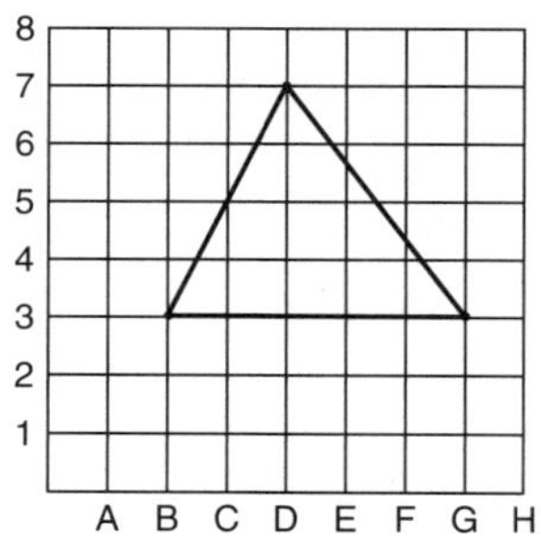

Day 129
1. 57
2. 9 rows or 90 squares should be shaded.
3. 5 R1
4. 4
5. 4 digits
6. 18, 27, 36, 45, 54, 5 bags
7. January, February, March
8. 8 cm^3
9. A circle should be drawn.
10. $48

Day 130
1. 11
2. 24
3. 10 R1
4. 10
5. no
6. 2
7. 36 m^2
8. 2:50
9. 4 awards
10. 27

Day 131
1. 62
2. yes
3. 8
4. 16
5. odd
6. 900
7. centimeters
8. 73°F
9. One of the following lines should be drawn:
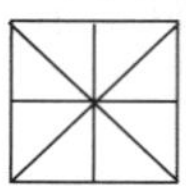
10. Answers will vary. Possibilities include: 1, 57; 3, 55, etc.

Day 132
1. 21
2. 50%
3. 15
4. 5
5. 4,500
6. 9
7. 28 cm
8. 2
9. Answers may vary. Possible answers include sphere and egg.
10. 36 eggs

Day 133
1. 24
2. 2
3. 5
4. 13 R4
5. four thousand, eight hundred twenty-five
6. 0
7. The clock should read 6:37.
8. $\frac{1}{2}$
9. 2 children
10. $10

Day 134
1. 31
2. 12
3. 5
4. 8 R1
5. 600 + 20 + 4
6. 10
7. 23 kg
8. $\frac{1}{2}$
9. 4; 4; 2
10. 13

Day 135
1. 61
2. 48
3. 10
4. 6 R1
5. 670
6. yes
7. 6 meters
8. July
9. yes
10. 8; 6; 8; 7

ANSWER KEY *(cont.)*

Day 136
1. 34
2. 3
3. 5
4. 12 R1
5. 7 hundreds or 700
6. 0.75
7. 1,250 mL
8. 964 minutes
9. 6 faces; 12 edges; a square base
10. 5 pencils

Day 137
1. 38
2. yes
3. 2
4. 6 R5
5. ones
6. 3
7. Monday
8. ruler
9. parallelogram or rhombus
10. 48

Day 138
1. 15
2. 20
3. 9 R4
4. 14 R5
5. 4 digits
6. 10
7. 24
8. 2
9. yes
10. left 4, down 5, right 2, down 2, right 6, up 3, left 2, up 4.

Day 139
1. 42
2. 5
3. 5
4. 4 R2
5. 5,000
6. 7
7. 31; 31; 31
8. 1
9. translation
10. 6 triangles should be colored yellow; 3 triangles should be colored blue.

Day 140
1. 12
2. 7, 14, 21
3. 6 R1
4. 4 R3
5. odd
6. 7
7. cm^2
8. 840
9. A square should be drawn.
10. 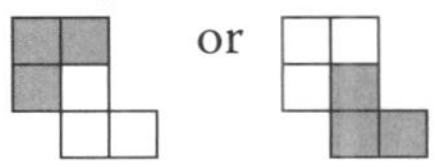

Day 141
1. 58
2. 2
3. 7
4. 22 R2
5. Eight thousand, nine hundred thirty-one
6. $\frac{8}{10}$
7. 50 mm
8. 4
9. pentagon
10. Answers will vary. Possibilities include: 13 −10 + 12 +4 + 1

Day 142
1. 12
2. $5.50
3. 5
4. 9 R3
5. 895
6. 12, 18, 24, 30, 36, 36 sides
7. 12 cm
8. 2
9. 5
10. 264 times

Day 143
1. 62
2. yes
3. 4
4. 8 R4
5. no
6. 22
7. The clocks should read 6:05.
8. July
9. false
10. $6.00

Day 144
1. 31
2. 10
3. 6 R6
4. 6 R5
5. 7,501
6. 4
7. 750 g
8. $4\frac{1}{4}$ inches or 4.25
9. rectangle
10. 45

Day 145
1. 63
2. 300
3. 10 R2
4. 6 R7
5. 1,000 + 800 + 50 + 7
6. 1
7. m^3
8. ruler
9. yes
10. 40,1; 20,2; 8,5; 10,4

Day 146
1. 41
2. yes
3. 4 R3
4. 13
5. 2 tens or 20
6. 735
7. 6 liters
8. 6
9. A parallel line should be drawn.
10. 4

Day 147
1. 71
2. 5
3. 10
4. 4
5. 400
6. 40
7. December 21
8. 31 days
9. yes
10. 44

ANSWER KEY *(cont.)*

Day 148
1. 11
2. 10
3. 9
4. 3 fives
5. 1,632
6. 10
7. 2.5 or $2\frac{1}{2}$ liters
8. 104
9. cylinder
10. 18 times

Day 149
1. 27
2. yes
3. 2
4. 7 R5
5. 7,000 + 400 + 90
6. no
7. October, November, December
8. 1,125 cm^3
9. 15 inches
10. Estimate: Answers will vary. Actual Number: 35 dots

Day 150
1. 13
2. 350
3. 3
4. 11
5. hundreds
6. 1
7. cm^2
8. 18
9. 6; 6; 6
10. 12

Day 151
1. 38
2. $3.75
3. 4
4. 4 R5
5. 2,700
6. 324
7. 5.5 or $5\frac{1}{2}$ cm
8. yardstick
9. 4; 4
10. 2 possible answers: Add 10 to get 50, 60; Multiply by 3, then 5 to get 120, 200

Day 152
1. 39
2. $\frac{81}{100}$
3. 10
4. 15 R2
5. 3 digits
6. 4
7. 16 cm
8. 96
9. D should be circled.
10. 153 cm

Day 153
1. 44
2. 15
3. 2
4. 9 R6
5. nine thousand, fifty-eight
6. 3
7. The clocks should read 9:15.
8. January
9. 8 awards
10. $4.00

Day 154
1. 2
2. 68%
3. 9
4. 9 R3
5. 2000 + 500 + 70 + 3
6. 3
7. 2 kg
8. 120
9. A line of symmetry should be drawn from vertex to vertex or side to side.
10. 1,330; 1,300; 1,000

Day 155
1. 71
2. 42
3. 9
4. 8
5. 4,053
6. 5
7. yes
8. 2
9. 5 angles
10. 6; 8; 10; 9

Day 156
1. 11
2. no
3. 21
4. 5 R1
5. 1,800
6. 0.9, 1.0
7. 6 buckets
8. 30 days
9. 5 faces; 5 vertices; a square base
10. 2.25 cm

Day 157
1. 71
2. 0.25
3. 10
4. 7 R4
5. 0
6. 116, 174, 232, 290; 290 cm
7. Wednesday
8. 2
9. 90° angle
10. 4

Day 158
1. 11
2. $\frac{71}{100}$
3. 3
4. 10 R2
5. 2,567 is less than 2, 675
6. 400
7. 9 bottles
8. 7 days
9. 2 diagonals should be drawn from vertex to vertex.
10. A square should be drawn in (G,5).

Day 159
1. 61
2. 85 squares should be shaded.
3. 15 R4
4. 6 R1
5. 1,056
6. 2
7. 365 days
8. 1,000
9. rotation
10. $\frac{1}{4}$

ANSWER KEY *(cont.)*

Day 160

1. 39
2. 30
3. 75
4. 11 R2
5. 4,990
6. 1
7. 7 m^2
8. hour
9. rectangular prism
10. $\frac{1}{2}$

Day 161

1. 43
2. $\frac{25}{100}$ or $\frac{1}{4}$
3. 7 R1
4. 4
5. 1,000 + 400 + 10 + 4
6. $\frac{4}{100}$
7. 20 mm
8. 2
9. 5
10. Answers will vary. Possibilities include: 12 + 13 – 10 – 4 – 1

Day 162

1. 13
2. 73%
3. 19
4. 5 R4
5. thousands
6. 27
7. 24 cm
8. 72
9. yes
10. 12 cookies

Day 163

1. 42
2. greater than
3. 13 R5
4. 8
5. 4,700
6. 10
7. The clock should read 7:50; 10 to 8
8. September, October, November, December
9. A square should be drawn.
10. $50

Day 164

1. 34
2. 45%
3. 9
4. 5
5. 4,800
6. 3
7. 10 kg
8. 31 days
9. 25 books
10. 792

Day 165

1. 72
2. yes
3. 7
4. 5
5. 6 hundreds or 600
6. 50¢, 75¢, $1.00, $1.25
7. 80 mm
8. 7
9. A line of symmetry should be drawn from vertex to vertex or side to side.
10. 50¢

Day 166

1. 18
2. 0.37
3. 5
4. 8 R3
5. 3,000 + 10 + 4
6. 660
7. 40
8. a minute
9. a circle
10. 17

Day 167

1. 71
2. 25
3. 10 R2
4. 10 R6
5. 1,400
6. 1
7. January 1
8. liter
9. perpendicular lines
10. 60

Day 168

1. 11
2. 62 squares should be shaded.
3. 10 R4
4. 4
5. 3,970
6. 400
7. 250 milliliters
8. 240
9. true
10. $2\frac{1}{2}$ minutes

Day 169

1. 53
2. 30%
3. 3
4. 6
5. no
6. $5.00; $7.50; $10.00; Week 4
7. December 31
8. 30 cm
9. A line should be drawn from the can to the cylinder.
10. 50¢

Day 170

1. 23
2. 35%
3. 5 R3
4. 3 R10
5. 1,280
6. 2
7. area
8. 9:00 P.M.
9. rotation
10. 21

ANSWER KEY *(cont.)*

Day 171

1. 80
2. yes
3. 2 R3
4. 17
5. no
6. 847
7. 3 cm
8. 73°F
9. 3
10. Answers will vary. Possibilities include: 13 – 4 + 10 – 12 – 1

Day 172

1. 12
2. $\frac{30}{100}$ or $\frac{3}{10}$
3. 16 R1
4. 14 R3
5. 4 tens or 40
6. 12
7. 9 cm^2
8. meter
9. 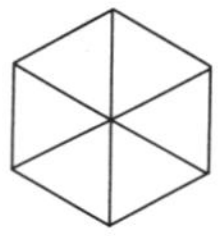
10. 101 cm

Day 173

1. 70
2. 84%
3. 3
4. 4 R7
5. one thousand, eight hundred forty-six
6. 2
7. The clocks should read 1:35.
8. 6
9. 3 acute angles
10. $7.50

Day 174

1. 19
2. 72
3. 6
4. 10 R1
5. 3,047
6. 3
7. grams
8. 3
9. A perpendicular line should be drawn.
10. 4 boxes

Day 175

1. 67
2. 0.25
3. 4
4. 14
5. 1,905
6. 56
7. m^2
8. 3
9. A triangular front view should be drawn.
10. 42 race cars

Day 176

1. 15
2. 10¢
3. 8
4. 9 R5
5. no
6. 20/100
7. 5 liters
8. 6 months
9. 7 different sports are played
10. 12

Day 177

1. 32
2. yes
3. 8
4. 6 R8
5. 6,042
6. 10
7. December 24
8. km
9. false
10. $2.67

Day 178

1. 19
2. $\frac{47}{100}$
3. 7
4. 6
5. 2,536
6. 3
7. 20
8. $3\frac{3}{4}$ or 3.75 inches
9. yes
10. 68 tickets

Day 179

1. 42
2. no
3. 7 R4
4. 9
5. 2,400
6. 39
7. square feet
8. 1 cm^3
9. 1 obtuse angle
10. 50 minutes

Day 180

1. 17
2. 0.81
3. 18 fives
4. 7 R3
5. tens
6. $0.60, $0.90, $1.20, $1.50, $1.80; 6 pens cost $1.80
7. yes
8. 70°F
9. square pyramid
10. 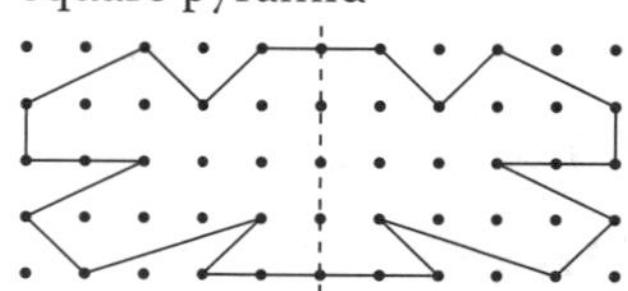

REFERENCES CITED

Kilpatrick, J., J. Swafford, and B. Findell, eds. 2001. *Adding it up: Helping children learn mathematics.* Washington, DC: National Academies Press.

Marzano, R. 2010. When practice makes perfect...sense. *Educational Leadership* 68 (3): 81–83.

McIntosh, M. E. 1997. Formative assessment in mathematics. *Clearing House* 71 (2): 92–96.

DIGITAL RESOURCES

Accessing the Digital Resources

The digital resources can be downloaded by following these steps:

1. Go to www.tcmpub.com/digital
2. Use the ISBN number to redeem the digital resources.
3. Respond to the question using the book.
4. Follow the prompts on the Content Cloud website to sign in or create a new account.
5. The content redeemed will now be on your My Content screen. Click on the product to look through the digital resources. All resources are available for download. Select files can be previewed, opened, and shared. For questions and assistance with your license key card, or to report a lost card, please contact Shell Education.

   mail: customerservice@tcmpub.com
   phone: 800-858-7339

CONTENTS OF THE DIGITAL RESOURCES

Teacher Resources

- Practice Page Item Analysis Chart
- Student Item Analysis Chart

Student Resources

- Practice Pages